John Robertson Henderson

A contribution to Indian carcinology

John Robertson Henderson

A contribution to Indian carcinology

ISBN/EAN: 9783337306274

Printed in Europe, USA, Canada, Australia, Japan

Cover: Foto ©Andreas Hilbeck / pixelio.de

More available books at **www.hansebooks.com**

THE

TRANSACTIONS

OF

LINNEAN SOCIETY OF LOND

A CONTRIBUTION TO INDIAN CARCINOLOGY,

BY

J. R. HENDERSON, M.B., F.L.S.,

FELLOW OF THE UNIVERSITY OF MADRAS, PROFESSOR OF BIOLOGY IN THE MADRAS CHRISTIAN COLLEGE

LONDON:

PRINTED FOR THE LINNEAN SOCIETY

BY TAYLOR AND FRANCIS, RED LION COURT, FLEET STREET.

SOLD AT THE SOCIETY'S APARTMENTS, BURLINGTON-HOUSE, PICCADILLY, W.,

AND BY LONGMANS, GREEN, AND CO., PATERNOSTER-ROW.

May 1893.

X. *A Contribution to Indian Carcinology. By* J. R. HENDERSON, *M.B., F.L.S., Fellow of the University of Madras, Professor of Biology in the Madras Christian College.*

(Plates XXXVI.–XL.)

Read 16th June, 1892.

INTRODUCTION.

THE Decapod and Stomatopod Crustacea referred to in this paper, though furnished by several distinct collections, are all from Indian localities, and it has therefore been found most convenient to incorporate the results of their examination in a single report. A large proportion of the species are contained in two collections, both of considerable size, the first formed by my friend Mr. Edgar Thurston, Superintendent of the Madras Government Museum, chiefly from stations in the Gulf of Manaar, the second by myself, from various localities in the Madras Presidency. Both collections were to some extent examined and the species identified in India, prior to my return to England on leave in 1891, and I fully anticipated that a short period of work at the British Museum would have enabled me to complete the identifications. But the time thus occupied proved much longer than I had calculated, a large portion of it being taken up with the examination of some of the commonest and longest known forms, which are certainly not so well known as they ought to be; and I may add that my later studies have convinced me that the working out of a large collection of shallow-water species cannot be satisfactorily accomplished in India.

While engaged in this work, Dr. Günther and Mr. Pocock, of the British Museum, kindly placed in my hands for examination a series of Indian Crustacea deposited in the National Collection, including a large number of specimens presented by the late Surgeon-General F. Day, C.I.E., and Mr. E. W. Oates, F.Z.S., which have enabled me considerably to enlarge the scope of this paper. Dr. Day's collection consists chiefly of the larger and better known Indian marine Decapods, from various localities, as well as a number of land and freshwater Crabs (Telphusidæ), and a large series of freshwater and marine Prawns, belonging to the genera *Palæmon* and *Penæus*, which have induced me to revise, to some extent, the characters of the Indian species belonging to the latter genus. Mr. Oates's collection, though not of large extent, includes a number of most interesting forms—principally Macrura—taken by dredging at depths of from ten to twenty fathoms, in the Gulf of Martaban, Burmah; and, as might be expected, it contains some of the species lately described by Dr. De Man, from the neighbouring Mergui Archipelago. In addition to these I have examined two small collections from Ceylon, the first consisting of between fifty and sixty species, which were sent me for identification before I left India, by Mr. Haly, of the Colombo Museum, the second a small series of littoral forms, presented to the British Museum by Mr. H. Nevill.

From all these sources I have been able to identify two hundred and eighty-nine species, of which thirty-three are described as new to science, including two which are regarded as the types of new genera. The number of new species is perhaps smaller than might be expected in a collection the size of that reported on, but I may state that want of time has compelled me to set aside a considerable number, either not yet identified or believed to be new. In certain of the larger genera, e. g. *Pilumnus*, *Leucosia*, and *Alpheus*, I have attempted to name only the better known forms; for, till someone with access to types provides us with a revision of these groups, the determination of many of the species must remain uncertain, if not impossible. The material at my disposal has enabled me to reduce several previously constituted species to the rank of synonyms, and work of this kind is perhaps quite as important as adding to the list of known forms. Space and other considerations have forced me to make my remarks concerning previously known species as brief as possible, and I have only attempted to record the publications in which these are originally or most fully described, or where their synonymy is discussed; while, in regard to distribution, I have merely indicated the chief localities in which they have been previously found, and in the case of the less perfectly known species have added the authorities for these.

The limited knowledge we possess in regard to most groups of the Invertebrate fauna of India has more than once been commented on, and is noteworthy considering the length of time that the country has been inhabited by Europeans; indeed, as regards Crustacea, up to a comparatively recent date, there was less definite knowledge of the Indian fauna than of the fauna of many other Asiatic and Australasian countries. The older writers are often extremely vague in the localization of their species, but there can be little doubt that a large proportion of the Crustacea recorded under such general terms as "Seas of Asia," "Eastern Seas," or "East Indies," came originally from India. Fabricius and Herbst, towards the end of last century, described a considerable number of Indian species, and at a later period collections, chiefly from Pondicherry, found their way to Paris, and some of the species are recorded by Milne-Edwards, in his well-known 'Histoire Naturelle des Crustacés.' Comparatively few English naturalists in India appear to have paid any attention to this group, but collections, both comparatively small, were made by General Hardwicke and Colonel Sykes, and the first of these collections is frequently referred to by White in his List of the Crustacea in the British Museum. In more recent times the late Sir Walter Elliot, of the Madras Civil Service, formed a collection on the Coromandel coast which passed into the hands of the late Mr. Spence Bate, who refers to a few of the species in his Report on the 'Challenger' Macrura. The work of Professor Wood-Mason, Superintendent of the Indian Museum, Calcutta, is well known; during the last twenty years he has published valuable papers, more especially on the Telphusidae, and during the past year a Report on the deep-sea Crustacea from the Bay of Bengal, taken by H.M.S. 'Investigator,' in which a number of new forms are described.

In 1857 the Austrian frigate 'Novara,' on a scientific voyage round the world, touched at Madras, Ceylon, and the Nicobars, and Prof. Camil Heller, in his Report on the Crustacea of the Expedition, enumerates over one hundred species of Decapods and Stomatopods taken in these localities. Recently the Crustacea collected by the brothers Sarasin at Trincomali in Ceylon, and amounting to ninety-two species, have been recorded, and some new species described by Dr. F. Müller*. But the most valuable contribution to the subject hitherto published is the Report by Dr. De Man, of Middelburg, on the Crustacea collected in the Mergui Archipelago by Dr. Anderson, late Superintendent of the Indian Museum, Calcutta. This Report, which was published in 1887-88, and forms vol. xxii. of the Linnean Society's Journal in Zoology, is valuable, not merely on account of its dealing with the first collection of any extent made in the Bay of Bengal, one which naturally comprised a considerable proportion of new species, but also on account of the careful manner in which the author has redescribed a number of common species, which had been imperfectly characterized by their first describers.

All naturalists who have worked at this group have felt the impossibility, in many cases, of determining the actual species which furnished the crude figures, or brief diagnoses, by means of which most of the commoner and more widely distributed forms have been handed down to us in the works of Herbst and Fabricius. Milne-Edwards appears to have interpreted the species of last-century writers, without an actual examination of their types, and any errors he may have made in consequence have been followed by most subsequent writers. It is therefore highly desirable, as De Man has suggested and partly done, to re-examine the earlier types, which were described in a manner that ampler material and increased knowledge have shown to be quite inadequate. In most cases where the original specimens are sufficiently well preserved to render their identity certain, and where there can be no doubt as to correctness of labelling, it is probably advisable to adopt the original designation, though whether a long-established and universally-adopted name should be displaced by the discovery of some forgotten specimen seems to me very questionable.

The greater part of my own collecting has been done at three differently-situated localities, some account of which, along with the chief features in their Crustacean fauna, I have ventured to draw up, such information being usually scanty in systematic works, where very often the writer has not been at the same time the collector of the specimens on which he reports.

The harbour of Madras, which may be taken as typical of the entire Coromandel coast, does not at first sight appear to offer much promise to the carcinologist, but more extended observation will show that it is far richer in species than could have been expected from the nature of the locality. On this coast the sea breaks at some distance from the shore in an almost constant surf, and the waves finally roll in on a low sandy beach, where the average range of the tide is not more than two or three feet. On the sandy shore species of *Ocypoda* (*O. platytarsis, O. macrocera*) are met with, running about towards the water's edge in countless numbers, chiefly in the

* "Zur Crustaceenfauna von Trincomali," Verhandl. d. naturf. Gesellsch. Basel. Theil viii. 1887.

18*

morning and evening, when the sun's rays are less powerful, and on the slightest sign of alarm they at once seek their burrows. One species of this genus (*O. cordimana*) is, however, a strictly terrestrial crab, and occurs at some distance from the sea, often living among the matted branches of a trailing convolvulus, which is frequently also the shelter of a sand-lizard (*Mabuia Bibronii*, Gray), and it may be seen even further inland, inhabiting the sandy soil of casuarina plantations. Hiding in the sand at low water, the curious anomurous forms *Hippa asiatica* and *Albunea symnista* are found, the former in particular being very abundant. On the stonework of the harbour, and in those few localities where rocks appear, species of *Grapsus* and *Plagusia* are seen clinging tenaciously to the surface by means of their sharp dactyli, which enable them effectually to withstand the force of the breakers among which they live. Outside the surf-zone is a belt of shallow water, with the bottom composed chiefly of broken shells and sand, in which the Crustacean fauna is undoubtedly rich. I have obtained considerably over one hundred species from it, and there are certainly many more yet to be discovered. All my gleanings from this belt come from the heaps of material thrown up on the beach by fishermen, who practise fishing by means of very long nets, taken out through the surf in catamarans, and afterwards drawn in on the shore. Here are found species of *Doclea*, *Egeria*, *Neptunus*, *Goniosoma*, *Matuta*, *Calappa*, *Philyra*, *Dorippe*, *Diogenes*, *Thenus*, and *Squilla*, along with representatives of other genera in smaller numbers. Indeed, it is scarcely possible to examine the shore-heaps without finding the following species :—*Doclea hybrida*, *Goniosoma cariegatum*, *Matuta cictrix*, *Philyra scabriuscula*, *Dorippe facchino*, *Diogenes custos*, and *Squilla nepa*, which are certainly those found in greatest abundance. Grey and sombre hues prevail among these species, which, doubtless, effectually protect them on a more or less sand-tinted bottom, while the comparative absence of fragile forms—the fossorial ones excepted—and the relative abundance of swimming species, *e. g.* Portunids, *Matuta*, and the curious hermit-crab, *Spiropagurus spiriger*, indicate an exposed and turbulent habitat. In the Madras fish bazaars numerous species of *Penaeus*, *Palaemon*, *Panulirus*, *Neptunus*, &c. are exposed for sale, for among the lower orders of the community size is apparently the sole criterion of edibility as regards Crustacea. The two edible species *par excellence* among Europeans are the large swimming crab (*Scylla serrata*) and the prawn (*Penaeus monodon*), although some of the specimens sold under the latter designation belong to the genus *Palaemon*, and come from fresh water. The so-called "river" Cooum, the water of which is brackish only towards its temporary outlet, and everywhere much contaminated by town sewage, affords shelter to species of *Palaemon*, *Penaeus*, and other Macrura. On its banks are seen the burrows of a large species of *Sesarma* (*S. tetragona*), and the crab itself may frequently be observed near the openings of drains, while the sand and mud-flats are honeycombed by species of *Gelasimus*. The tanks or freshwater ponds, and even the wells, are inhabited by species of *Palaemon*, *Telphusa*, and *Caridina*, the most conspicuous being the freshwater prawn *Palaemon carcinus*, which attains a considerable size, and the freshwater crab, *Telphusa Leschenaulti*. The burrows of *Telphusae* may be seen almost everywhere, except in the most arid situations. Though the Madras coast is, by its physical conditions, peculiarly unsuited for dredging,

I have taken by this method, in the sheltered water of Madras harbour, several species which I have not met with elsewhere.

Stretching along the Coromandel coast, for a very considerable distance both north and south of Madras, is a system of shallow backwaters or lagoons running parallel to the sea-line, though often separated from the sea itself by an interval of a mile or more, and joined by means of canals into a continuous waterway. In certain places the back-water widens out to form large lake-like expanses, one of which, the so-called Pulicat Lake, is thirty-seven miles in length. For the greater part of the year this system is practically shut off from the sea, but during the rainy season the intervening sandy bar, at intervals, is either artificially cut, or forced by the surplus accumulation of water, the result being that the sea is allowed to enter and a certain admixture takes place. Porpoises and sharks find their way in at this time, while sea-snakes (Hydrophidæ) are often extremely plentiful, and indeed may be found throughout the year. The fauna is extremely rich, more especially in free-swimming organisms, and is decidedly marine in character, though the water, as already stated, is more or less fresh. I have taken with the tow-net large numbers of Schizopods, *Lucifer*, and other marine forms, in places where the water was freely used for drinking purposes by my boatmen. At night the surface often teems with brilliantly phosphorescent organisms, which on examination prove to be mainly the smaller Crustacea. One of the best hunting-grounds on the backwater is the village of Ennore, about nine miles to the north of Madras, which formerly, before the hill ranges became so readily accessible by rail, was a favourite resort. Here is a considerable expanse of water, bounded on the landward side by low, flat, grass-grown plains, intersected by canals and creeks. In the lake, as it may be termed, *Scylla serrata* is very abundant, and large numbers are sent to the Madras market, while species of *Penæus*, and the swimming Grapsoid crab, *Varuna litterata*, are no less characteristic. The sandy or muddy shores, close to the water's edge, are everywhere pierced by the narrow cylindrical holes of two species of *Gelasimus* (*G. annulipes* and *G. triangularis*). The curious habit peculiar to the males, of waving the larger claw as if beckoning, which has earned for them the title of "calling crabs," is by no means general in the two above-mentioned species; at least I have observed it on comparatively few occasions. What the object of this move-ment is I am unable to say, but when I noticed it a large number of individuals were simultaneously engaged in the act; the claw which is so enormously developed on one side of the body in the male sex is, in all probability, used as a hole-boring organ. Locally the Gelasimi are known as "dhobi crabs," doubtless from the resemblance of their beckoning movement to the manner in which the native washerman swings the clothes over his head in the act of pounding them against a flat stone. One of the commonest backwater Decapods is the hermit-crab, *Clibanarius padavensis*, lately described from the Mergui Archipelago, the young of which are found in great numbers near the water's edge, and almost invariably inhabiting the shells of Cerithiids. Two other hermits, both species of *Cœnobita* (*C. rugosa* and *C. compressa*), also frequently occur, but they freely leave the water, and are often to be met with wandering some distance inland. In certain localities *Alpheus malabaricus* is found in muddy creeks

where it probably burrows in the soft bottom, and thus differs strikingly in habit from
its marine congeners. Four terrestrial species are characteristic of the marshy grass-
grown flats which skirt the backwater, all of them belonging to the group Catometopa
of the Brachyura. The most abundant of these are *Sesarma quadrata*, seen running in
and out of its burrows at all times, and the larger *Cardisoma carnifex*, which lives in
colonies, and is apparently very common, though the animal itself is rarely seen, as it
emerges from its hiding-places only by night. The latter species is occasionally met
with at some distance from the water, and its underground dwellings, unlike those of
most land-crabs, do not pass vertically downwards for the first part of their course; they
also lack the neat and finished appearance of the external opening, seen in the burrows
of most Telphusæ. The two remaining species, *Metasesarma Rousseauxii* and *Metaplax
distinctus*, are less frequent; the former is by no means uncommon at Ennore, while
the latter is more sparingly met with, and I am unable to state whether it, like the
others, seeks protection from its enemies by hiding underground. The backwater
fauna is one that will amply repay investigation, and in Crustacea much has still to be
done before the commoner species are even approximately known.

No collecting-ground in the Indian Seas can show a greater profusion of animal
life than the Gulf of Manaar, between India and Ceylon, famous for its pearl
fisheries. At various times many interesting zoological discoveries have been recorded
from this area, and within recent years valuable collections in most of the Invertebrate
groups have been formed by Mr. Thurston, of the Madras Museum. The Crustacea
which he has entrusted to me for examination were collected chiefly at Rameswaram
Island, Tuticorin, and the Pearl Banks on the Ceylon side of the Gulf (Muttuwartu Par,
Silavaturai Par, and Cheval Par), including many of the most interesting species referred
to in this paper. In the summer of 1889 I spent about three weeks in the first of these
localities, and for the opportunity which I thus enjoyed of collecting there I am largely
indebted to my friend the Setupathi, the Rajah of Ramnad, who not only placed at my
disposal his bungalow at the village of Pamban, but also provided me with boats and
efficient native divers. The island of Rameswaram, famed for its venerable temple—
the resort of large numbers of Hindu pilgrims—forms the first link in the chain of
islands and sandbanks which, known as Adam's Bridge, stretches from the mainland to
Ceylon. To the naturalist it presents special interest from the fact that a fringing coral
reef appears at intervals along the coast, and the marine fauna is consequently both
rich and varied, while a few miles to the south there is a series of smaller but more
completely reef-bound islands. As a rule, even outside the reef, there is complete
absence of the swell or surf so characteristic of the Coromandel coast, and during either
monsoon one side of the island at least is sheltered and the sea smooth. Remarkably
shallow water is met with on all sides, and within a mile or so of the shore the depth
probably nowhere exceeds five or six fathoms; on the outer portion of the reef, where
the living coral is most abundant, there is usually not more than from ten to fifteen feet
of water. The tidal zone varies considerably, both in character and extent. Within the
reef it forms a belt, perhaps averaging fifty yards or so in width, exposed at low water,
and then bounded by the still submerged growing coral, while elsewhere it consists of a

flat expanse of sand or mud, which frequently extends seawards for some considerable distance. In the tidal belt blocks of dead and water-worn coral are strewed about, and in places these enclose artificial rock pools, in which Crustacea, Molluscs, Sponges, Holothurians, &c. are very abundant. The Crustacea most commonly met with at low water are:—*Atergatis floridus, Leptodius exaratus, Pilumnus vespertilio, Eriphia laevimana, Thalamita prymna, Metopograpsus messor, Leiolophus planissimus, Petrolisthes dentatus*, and *Gonodactylus glaber*. Of these it may be mentioned that the *Pilumnus* is remarkably sluggish and apathetic; the *Thalamita* is extremely active, while the *Petrolisthes* conceals itself under stones or pieces of coral, and when captured usually throws off its claws. On walking over the coral blocks a peculiar clicking noise is heard on all sides, which is found to proceed from species of *Alpheus*, very common in the tidal pools. This noise is produced by the crustacean rapidly flexing the dactylus of its larger chela against the corresponding immobile finger, probably under the stimulus of fear, for the movement is very freely indulged in when the animal is handled. Near high-water mark, in places where slight pools are left by the tide, a minute hermit-crab (*Diogenes*, sp.), scarcely a quarter of an inch in length, is very common, and here and there on the sandy shore colonies of *Conobita rugosa* have established themselves, in company with the ubiquitous Ocypods. In a tidal backwater, which forms shallow lagoons at intervals round the island, the burrowing *Gelasimus annulipes* is seen in great numbers, and, on sand- or mud-banks, *Scopimera myctiroides*, a species of similar habits.

The great wealth of animal life on the reef is very apparent, for on a calm day, with no breeze to ruffle the surface, and with merely a few feet of clear water intervening, the growing coral can be readily examined from a boat, when it is seen to be arranged in irregular patches of varying size, often brightly coloured, and separated by spots of coral sand. Under favourable conditions objects even of moderate size can be readily discerned, the most conspicuous being Actiniæ, Asterids, Echini, large Molluscs, such as *Pterocera, Cypræa*, &c., and gaudily-hued fishes. The most satisfactory mode of collecting is by means of diving; practised divers have no difficulty in loosening large blocks of coral, and in bringing these to the surface, whence they are drawn into the boat. In this way large numbers of crustaceans are taken, either hiding in the crevices or clinging to the coral branches. The genera most numerously represented are:— *Chlorodius, Leptodius, Etisus, Pilumnus, Trapezia, Polyonyx, Alpheus*, and *Gonodactylus*, but a list of even the commoner species would occupy more space than can be allotted to it here. Very interesting and varied are the modes by which most of these are protected in this densely populated area, where the struggle for existence must necessarily be severe. The slow inactive Maioid forms are frequently rendered inconspicuous by heterogeneous collections of foreign objects, such as sponges, corallines, hydroids, &c. attached to the carapace or legs, the retention of which is, in some cases, facilitated by the presence of short hooked hairs. Some specimens of *Micippa* appear, however, to content themselves with a simple coating of sand-grains which are entangled in or held by the short hairs on the upper surface. The well-known habit possessed by many Dromiids, of seeking protection under an enveloping sponge or ascidian, which is deeply hollowed out by the body of the crab, is exemplified in most of the reef-dwelling species, and the canals of larger fixed Sponges afford a shelter to species of *Polyonyx*, *Alpheus*, and *Gebiopsis*. The larger species of *Alpheus*, and *Gonodactylus glaber*, are often found ensconced in short tunnels, bored through the coral probably by Lithodomi or other molluscs, and when captured the Stomatopod has the habit of alternately flexing and extending its tail with considerable rapidity and force. Certain representatives of widely separate families, e. g. *Œthra scruposa* and *Ebalia fallax*, have the carapace very irregularly elevated or even pitted, so that they bear an undoubted resemblance to pieces of eroded coral, and, as they move but slowly, this adaptation to their environment must often aid in their protection. But specially interesting in many of the species are the colour-markings, which probably, in most cases, are protective in their nature; and it may be added that an examination of dry or spirit specimens gives one but a meagre idea of the vivid tints which characterize many of the reef-dwellers during life. The colours which occur most frequently are purple, brown, and red, either uniformly diffused over the surface of the crab, or restricted so as to form spots or bands. A modification of the latter type is seen in such diverse forms as *Zebrida Adamsii*, *Cycloxanthus lineatus*, *Eupagurus zebra*, and *Galathea elegans*, in which there is an arrangement of dark, radiating, or subparallel lines, on the carapace and legs. A hint as to the possible use of these bands was afforded by a small semitransparent Lamellibranch (*Avicula zebra*, Reeve), with black radiating lines on its shell, which is met with adhering by its byssus to a hydroid (*Aglaophenia urens*, Kirchenpauer)[*] ; in this case the lines so exactly simulate the short lateral ramuli of the hydroid that the shell is with difficulty recognized, even by a practised eye. In all probability the above-mentioned crustaceans live on the stems of Gorgoniæ, Hydroids, or similar organisms. The Cancroid genera are more often brightly coloured than are those of other groups, and they include the species which are found in greatest numbers on the reef. It may be stated generally that the inactive forms are those most commonly disguised, either by the presence of foreign objects or by colour adaptations, while their more active neighbours, such as the Portunidæ and many Macrura, are, as a rule, of more sombre hue, but are more frequently armed with sharp spines, probably for defensive purposes, while those which seek safety in tunnels or burrows are often pale in colour, with their outer shell of thin texture. Before leaving this subject I may refer to a structural feature which is very noticeable in many species, more especially among the Cyclometopa, viz. the strong spoon-like excavation of the claws, which possibly enables these crabs to obtain a firmer hold of, and break off, the smaller coral branches when in search of food.

On the subject of geographical distribution there is little to be said, apart from the notes which appear in the body of this paper. The Indian Crustacean fauna is apparently very similar to that of a great portion of the Indo-Pacific area, and it is doubtful whether there is a single genus confined to or specially characteristic of India. The distribution

---

[*] I am indebted to Mr. Edgar Smith and Mr. Kirkpatrick, of the British Museum, for the identification of the mollusc and hydroid respectively.

of a large number of the marine species—which from time to time are discovered
in widely separate localities—is apparently to a great extent determined by the distribution of coral reefs, and as regards the higher Crustacea, at least, any attempt to
subdivide the large central or coral-reef region of the Indo-Pacific area seems of doubtful
value, and we can scarcely seek for natural subdivisions till we pass into the temperate
and colder waters, north and south of the coral region. Nearly two thirds of the total
number of species recorded in this paper are known to occur in the seas of the Malay
Archipelago; about one third occur at Mauritius or the neighbouring islands; the same
proportion in the seas of North Australia, and a slightly greater number in the islands
of the Pacific (New Caledonia, Fijis, Samoa, Sandwich Is., &c.). Nearly one fourth of
the number occur at Japan; while one fifth are found in the Red Sea, the same proportion on the east coast of Africa, and about the same in Australian localities excluding
those on the north coast. Not less than twenty-seven of our species occur on the
coast of Natal, and at least thirteen in the seas of New Zealand; while eight extend
their range into the Atlantic area. The same amount of attention has not been paid by
collectors to each of these regions, some having been more specially favoured; but, in
spite of this, there can be no doubt of the great affinity between the Indian and Malayan
Crustacean faunas.

The distribution of the freshwater species offers certain points of interest. The genus
Telphusa has representatives in South-Eastern Asia (Malay Archipelago, Malay Peninsula,
and China) or what may be termed a granulated group of species; in Burmah and Upper
India similar forms are met with, e. g. *T. Atkinsoniana*, Wood-Mason, and *T. Pealiana*,
Wood-Mason, which so far as is known do not extend their range into the Indian
Peninsula *; while further west, in Beloochistan and Persia, the allied *T. fluviatilis*
makes its appearance, and finally spreads along both sides of the Mediterranean. The
genus *Paratelphusa* has a somewhat similar range, extending from the Malay Archipelago along the Malay Peninsula into Burmah and Northern India, but no species
have yet been recorded from South India or Ceylon. Very little is as yet known
of the Indian species of *Palæmon*, but there can be no doubt that they are very
numerous. *P. scabriculus*, a very well-marked species, described originally from Ceylon,
occurs in Upper India and in the Malay Archipelago; it, however, remains to be seen
whether it does not also occur in Burmah and the Malay Peninsula. The marked
prevalence of freshwater prawns in the streams of South-eastern Asia and the Malay
Archipelago, with the apparently complete absence of crayfish from the same region,
seems to strengthen Professor Huxley's suggestion that the latter have been displaced
by better fitted competitors. The genus *Caridina* is represented at Madras, and
probably elsewhere in India, by a species which I am unable to separate from
C. Wyckii, described by Hickson from Celebes, and which itself is perhaps not distinct
from a longer-known species, found in North and East Africa, a remarkably extended
range for a fresh-water species.

* In the British Museum there is a specimen of *T. Atkinsoniana* from Ceylon.

In conclusion I would express my indebtedness to those gentlemen who have assisted me during the preparation of this paper. To Dr. Günther and Mr. Pocock, of the British Museum, my thanks are specially due for their having granted me ready access to the collections under their charge and facilitating my work in various ways, to the latter especially for having spent much time on my behalf and for kindly undertaking to supervise the figuring of the new species during my absence in India. I am indebted to Professor Alphonse Milne-Edwards, of Paris, for kindly examining and naming some specimens I sent him, which were referable either to species described by himself or to species of which the types are preserved in the Paris Natural History Museum. To Mr. E. Thurston my thanks are also due for assistance rendered in many ways.

List of Species, with the localities at which they were taken.

DECAPODA.

BRACHYURA.

Achœus lacertosus, Stm.—Gulf of Martaban.
—— *affinis,* Miers.—Gulf of Martaban.
Oncinopus aranea, De Haan.—Muttuwartu Par; Gulf of Martaban.
Huenia Proteus, De Haan.—Tuticorin; Rameswaram.
Simocarcinus simplex (Dana).—Tuticorin.
Menœthius monoceros (Latr.).—Tuticorin; Silavaturai Par; Muttuwartu Par; Rameswaram; Gulf of Martaban.
Doclea hybrida (Fabr.).—Ceylon; Madras.
—— *muricata* (Fabr.).—Madras; Gulf of Martaban.
Stenocionops cervicornis (Herbst).—Tuticorin.
Egeria arachnoides (Rumph.).—Madras; Gulf of Martaban.
Hyastenus Pleione (Herbst.—Silavaturai Par.
—— *convexus,* Miers.—Gulf of Martaban.
—— *Hilgendorfi,* De Man.—Tuticorin; Cheval Par; Rameswaram.
—— *Brockii,* De Man.—Gulf of Martaban.
Chlorinoides aculeatus (Milne-Edw.).—Gulf of Martaban.
—— *Coppingeri,* Haswell.—Muttuwartu Par; Gulf of Martaban.
Naxia hirta (A. Milne-Edw.).—Tuticorin.
—— *taurus,* Pocock.—Gulf of Martaban.
Schizophrys aspera (Milne-Edw.).—Ceylon; Tuticorin; Rameswaram; Madras.
Hoplophrys Oatesii, gen. et sp. n.—Gulf of Martaban.
Micippa Philyra (Herbst).—Tuticorin; Rameswaram.
—— *Thalia* (Herbst).—Tuticorin; Muttuwartu Par; Rameswaram.
—— *mascarenica,* Kossmann.—Gulf of Martaban.
—— *margaritifera,* n. sp.—Gulf of Martaban.
Tylocarcinus Styx (Herbst).—Tuticorin; Muttuwartu Par; Rameswaram.
Lambrus longimanus (Linn.).—Ceylon; Madras; Gulf of Martaban.
—— *contrarius* (Herbst).—Tuticorin.

Lambrus affinis, A. Milne-Edw.—Tuticorin ; Ceylon ; Rameswaram ; Gulf of Martaban.

—— *longispinus*, Miers.—Tuticorin.

—— *Holdsworthi*, Miers.—Tuticorin.

—— *sculptus*, A. Milne-Edw.—Gulf of Martaban.

—— *hoplonotus*, Ad. & White.—Muttuwartu Par.

Cryptopodia fornicata (Fabr.).—Gulf of Martaban.

Œthra scruposa (Linn.).—Ceylon.

Zebrida Adamsii, White.—Tuticorin.

Paralymolus sexspinosus, Miers.—Tuticorin.

Atergatis integerrimus (Lam.).—Tuticorin ; Ceylon ; Rameswaram.

—— *floridus* (Rumph.).—Tuticorin ; Ceylon ; Rameswaram.

—— *lævigatus*, A. Milne-Edw.—Tuticorin.

—— *dilutatus*, De Haan.– Ceylon.

Carpilius maculatus (Linn.).—Ceylon.

Carpilodes tristeis, Dana.—Muttuwartu Par.

—— *margaritatus*, A. Milne-Edw.—Tuticorin ; Rameswaram.

—— *rensus* (Milne-Edw.).– Ceylon.

—— *cinctimanus* (White).—Ceylon.

Liomera punctata (Milne-Edw.).—Tuticorin ; Muttuwartu Par; Ceylon.

—— *Rodgersii* (Stm.).—Ceylon.

Lophactæa granulosa (Rüpp.).—Tuticorin ; Rameswaram.

—— *semigranosa* (Heller).—Muttuwartu Par ; Rameswaram.

—— *fissa*, n. sp.—Tuticorin.

Actæa granulata (Aud.).—Tuticorin; Cheval Par ; Rameswaram.

—— *calculosa* (Milne-Edw.).—Tuticorin ; Muttuwartu Par.

—— *nodulosa* (White).—Tuticorin.

—— *Peronii* (Milne-Edw.), var. *squamosa*, n.—Muttuwartu Par.

—— *rufopunctata* (Milne-Edw.).—Tuticorin ; Cheval Par.

—— *Rüppellii* (Krauss).—Tuticorin; Rameswaram.

Hypocœlus rugosus, n. sp.—Tuticorin.

Xantho impressus (Lam.). Ceylon.

Medæus distinguendus (De Haan).—Gulf of Martaban.

Euxanthus Melissa (Herbst).—Tuticorin ; Ceylon.

Zozymus Æneus (Linn.).—Ceylon.

Polycremnus ochlodes (Herbst).—Muttuwartu Par ; Madras.

Halimede Thurstoni, n. sp.—Tuticorin.

Cyclaxanthus lineatus, A. Milne-Edw.—Tuticorin.

Lophozozymus Dodone (Herbst).—Tuticorin ; Muttuwartu Par ; Rameswaram

—— *cristatus*, A. Milne-Edw.—Muttuwartu Par.

Chlorodius niger (Forsk.).—Tuticorin ; Muttuwartu Par; Rameswaram.

Chlorodopsis spinipes (Heller). Muttuwartu Par; Ceylon.

Leptodius exaratus (Milne-Edw.). – Sind ; Tuticorin ; Silavaturai Par; Ceylon ; Rameswaram.

Etisus lævimanus, Randall.—Tuticorin ; Ceylon ; Rameswaram.

Etisodes Electra (Herbst . Tuticorin ; Rameswaram.

Phymodius angulatus (Milne-Edw.).—Ceylon.

—— *monticulosus* (Dana).—Tuticorin.

Cymo Andreossyi (Aud.).—Tuticorin ; Muttuwartu Par ; Rameswaram.

19*

Menippe Rumphii (Fabr.).—Tuticorin; Ceylon; Rameswaram; Madras.

Ozius tuberculosus, Milne-Edw.—Ceylon.

Epixanthus frontalis (Milne-Edw.).—Ceylon; Nicobars.

—— *dentatus* (White).—Nicobars.

Actumnus setifer (De Haan).—Muttuwartu Par; Gulf of Martaban.

—— *verrucosus*, n. sp.—Tuticorin; Muttuwartu Par.

Pilumnus vespertilio (Fabr.).—Tuticorin; Ceylon; Rameswaram.

—— *labyrinthicus*, Miers.—Rameswaram.

Trapezia Cymodoce (Herbst).—Tuticorin; Muttuwartu Par; Rameswaram.

—— *rufopunctata* (Herbst).—Tuticorin; Ceylon.

—— *maculata* (Macleay).--Ceylon.

—— *areolata*, Dana.—Ceylon.

Tetralia glaberrima (Herbst).—Tuticorin; Muttuwartu Par; Rameswaram.

Eriphia lævimana, Latr.—Tuticorin; Ceylon; Rameswaram.

Neptunus pelagicus (Linn.).—Sind; Bombay; Malabar; Tuticorin; Ceylon; Madras &c.; Akyab.

—— *gladiator* (Fabr.).—Ceylon; Rameswaram; Madras; Gulf of Martaban.

—— *sanguinolentus* (Herbst).—Sind; Bombay; Ceylon; Rameswaram; Madras.

—— *argentatus*, White.—Gulf of Martaban.

—— *hastatoides* (Fabr.).—Madras; Gulf of Martaban.

—— *Andersoni*, De Man.—Gulf of Martaban.

—— *tuberculosus*, A. Milne-Edw.—Gulf of Martaban.

—— *armatus*, A. Milne-Edw.—Rameswaram.

—— *Sieboldi*, A. Milne-Edw.— Muttuwartu Par.

Xiphonectes longispinosus (Dana).—Gulf of Martaban.

Achelous granulatus (Milne-Edw.).—Gulf of Martaban.

—— *Whitei*, A. Milne-Edw.—Madras; Gulf of Martaban.

—— *orbicularis*, Richters.—Gulf of Martaban.

Scylla serrata (Forsk.).—Ceylon; Madras, &c.; Calcutta.

Thalamita prymna (Herbst).—Tuticorin; Rameswaram; Madras.

—— *Admete* (Herbst).—Rameswaram; Gulf of Martaban.

—— *Sarignyi*, A. Milne-Edw.—Tuticorin; Rameswaram.

—— *sima*, Milne-Edw.—Tuticorin.

—— *integra*, Dana.—Tuticorin; Rameswaram; Gulf of Martaban.

—— *sexlobata*, Miers.—Tuticorin.

Goniosoma cruciferum (Fabr.).—Tuticorin; Ceylon; Madras; Akyab.

—— *affine* (Dana).—Madras.

—— *natator* (Herbst).—Ceylon; Rameswaram; Madras.

—— *luciferum* (Fabr.).—Ceylon.

—— *annulatum* (Fabr.).—Tuticorin; Rameswaram; Madras.

—— *Hellerii*, A. Milne-Edw.—Tuticorin; Ceylon; Rameswaram.

—— *erythrodactylum* (Lam.).--Ceylon.

—— *orientale* (Dana).—Tuticorin; Ceylon.

—— *ornatum*, A. Milne-Edw.—Madras.

—— *variegatum* (Fabr.).—Kurachi; Bombay; Madras.

—— *rostratum*, A. Milne-Edw.—Calcutta; Sunderbunds; Gulf of Martaban.

Lupocyclus inæqualis (Walker).—Gulf of Martaban.

Lissocarcinus polybioides, Ad. & White.—Gulf of Martaban.

Lissocarcinus lævis, Miers.—Tuticorin ; Gulf of Martaban.
Kraussia nitida, Stm.—Tuticorin ; Madras.

Heteroplax nitidus, Miers.—Madras ; Gulf of Martaban.
Scalopidia spinosipes, Stm.—Gulf of Martaban.
Cardisoma carnifex (Herbst).—Tuticorin ; Ceylon ; Madras, &c.
Telphusa indica, Latr.—Nilgiri hills.
—— *lugubris*, Wood-Mason.—Nepal.
—— *Masoniana*, n. sp.—North-West Provinces ; River Jumna.
—— *Leschenaudti*, Milne-Edw.—Ceylon ; Madras ; Ganjam.
—— *rugosa*, Kingsley.—Ceylon.
—— *enodis*, Kingsley.—Ceylon ; Madras
—— *Porockiana*, n. sp.—Jubbulpore.
—— *fluviatilis*, Latr.—Quetta.
—— *Atkinsoniana*, Wood-Mason.—Kangra ; Simla ; Burmah.
Paratelphusa sinensis, Milne-Edw.—Burmah.
—— *spinigera*, Wood-Mason.—Sind ; North-West Provinces ; Roorkee ; Calcutta ; Ganjam.
—— *Dayana*, Wood-Mason.—Burmah.
—— *Martensi*, Wood-Mason.—North-West Provinces ; Roorkee.
Ocypoda ceratophthalma (Pallas).—Tuticorin ; Rameswaram ; Madras, &c.
—— *macrocera*, Milne-Edw.—Tuticorin ; Rameswaram ; Madras.
—— *platytarsis*, Milne-Edw.—Ceylon ; Rameswaram ; Madras.
—— *cordimana*, Latr.—Tuticorin ; Madras.
Gelasimus annulipes, Latr.—Tuticorin ; Rameswaram ; Madras, &c.
—— *triangularis*, A. Milne-Edw.—Madras ; Ennore.
Macrophthalmus depressus, Rüpp.—Rameswaram.
—— *pectinipes*, Guérin.—Sind.
—— *Latreillei* (Desm.).—Ceylon (fossil).
Scopimera myctiroides (Milne-Edw.).—Tuticorin ; Rameswaram ; Ennore.
Myctiris longicarpus, Latr.—Akyab.
Metopograpsus messor (Forsk.).—Tuticorin ; Rameswaram ; Madras.
Grapsus strigosus (Herbst).—Tuticorin ; Rameswaram ; Madras, &c.
—— *maculatus* (Catesby).—Tuticorin.
Plagusia immaculata, Lam.—Madras.
Leiolophus planissimus (Herbst).—Rameswaram ; Madras.
Varuna litterata (Fabr.).—Ceylon ; Ennore ; Ganjam ; Calcutta ; Burmah.
Metaplax distinctus, Milne-Edw.—Ennore.
Sesarma tetragona (Fabr.).—Madras ; Ennore.
—— *quadrata* (Fabr.).—Tuticorin ; Madras ; Ennore.
Sarmatium indicum (A. Milne-Edw.), var. *malabaricum*, n.—Cochin.
Metasesarma Rousseauxii, Milne-Edw.—Ennore.
Xenophthalmus pinnotheroides, White.—Rameswaram.
—— *obscurus*, n. sp.—Gulf of Martaban.
Elamena unguiformis, De Haan.—Gulf of Martaban.
—— *truncata*, A. Milne-Edw.—Silavaturai Par.

Calappa hepatica (Linn.).—Tuticorin ; Ceylon ; Rameswaram ; Gulf of Martaban.
—— *gallus* (Herbst).—Tuticorin ; Ceylon ; Rameswaram ; Gulf of Martaban.

Calappa lophos (Herbst).—Ceylon ; Madras ; Gulf of Martaban.
—— *philargius* (Linn.).—Ceylon ; Gulf of Martaban.
Matuta victrix, Fabr.—Sind ; Tuticorin ; Ceylon ; Madras ; Ganjam ; Akyab.
—— *lunaris* (Herbst).—Madras ; Ganjam.
—— *Miersii*, Henderson.—Tuticorin ; Ceylon ; Madras.
Leucosia cranioluris (Linn.).—Ceylon ; Muttuwartu Par ; Rameswaram ; Madras ; Gulf of Martaban.
—— *Whitmeei*, Miers.—Gulf of Martaban.
Pseudophilyra Melita, De Man.—Muttuwartu Par ; Gulf of Martaban.
—— *pusilla*, n. sp.—Gulf of Martaban.
Philyra scabriuscula (Fabr.).—Tuticorin ; Rameswaram ; Madras, &c.
—— *verrucosa*, n. sp.—Madras.
—— *Adamsii*, Bell.—Silavaturai Par ; Rameswaram ; Gulf of Martaban.
—— *platycheira*, De Haan.—Silavaturai Par.
—— *globosa* (Fabr.).—Tuticorin ; Rameswaram ; Madras, &c.
—— *polita*, n. sp.—Madras.
Myra fugax (Fabr.).—Ceylon ; Rameswaram ; Gulf of Martaban.
—— *australis*, Haswell.—Gulf of Martaban.
Ebalia Pfefferi, De Man.—Muttuwartu Par.
—— *fallax*, n. sp.—Muttuwartu Par ; Gulf of Martaban.
Arcania septemspinosa (Fabr.).—Madras ; Gulf of Martaban.
—— *underimspinosa*, De Haan.—Gulf of Martaban.
Nursia plicata (Herbst).—Rameswaram ; Gulf of Martaban.
—— *abbreviata*, Bell.—Silavaturai Par ; Rameswaram ; Gulf of Martaban.
Dorippe dorsipes (Linn.).—Ceylon ; Silavaturai Par ; Rameswaram ; Madras.
—— *facchino* (Herbst).—Tuticorin ; Rameswaram ; Madras, &c.
—— *astuta*, Fabr.—Madras.
Cymopolia Jukesii, White.—Gulf of Martaban.

ANOMURA.

Dromidia unidentata (Rüpp.).—Tuticorin ; Ceylon.
—— *australiensis*, Haswell.—Silavaturai Par.
Cryptodromia pentagonalis, Hilg.—Muttuwartu Par ; Silavaturai Par.
Dromia Rumphii, Fabr.—Ceylon.
Pseudodromia integrifrons, Henderson.—Tuticorin.
Conchœcetes artificiosus (Fabr.).—Madras.

Raninoides serratifrons, n. sp.—Cheval Par.

Hippa asiatica, Milne-Edw.—Rameswaram ; Madras, &c.
Albunea symmista (Linn.).—Rameswaram ; Madras, &c.
—— *Thurstoni*, n. sp.—Cheval Par.

Cœnobita rugosa, Milne-Edw.—Tuticorin ; Silavaturai Par ; Rameswaram, &c.
—— *compressa*, Milne-Edw.—Madras, &c.
Diogenes Diogenes (Herbst).—Tuticorin ; Rameswaram ; Madras, &c.
—— *merguiensis*, De Man.—Muttuwartu Par ; Madras.
—— *miles* (Herbst).—Silavaturai Par ; Rameswaram ; Madras.

Diogenes custos (Fabr.).—Rameswaram : Madras, &c.
—— *affinis*, n. sp.—Madras.
—— *violareus*, n. sp.—Madras.
—— *planimanus*, n. sp.—Rameswaram ; Madras.
—— *ararus*, Heller.—Tuticorin ; Rameswaram ; Madras ; Ennore.
—— *costatus*, n. sp.—Tuticorin ; Rameswaram ; Madras.
—— *rectimanus*, Miers.—Madras.
Pagurus punctulatus, Oliv.—Tuticorin ; Rameswaram.
—— *Hessii*, Miers.—Madras ; Gulf of Martaban.
—— *deformis*, Milne-Edw.—Tuticorin ; Rameswaram.
—— *varipes*, Heller.—Tuticorin ; Muttuwartu Par.
—— *setifer*, Milne-Edw.—Tuticorin ; Madras ; Gulf of Martaban.
Troglopagurus manaarensis, gen. et sp. n.—Tuticorin ; Muttuwartu Par.
Aniculus aniculus (Fabr.).—Tuticorin ; Muttuwartu Par.
—— *strigatus* (Herbst).—Tuticorin.
Clibanarius clibanarius (Herbst).—Madras.
—— *infraspinatus*, Hilg.—Madras.
—— *padavensis*, De Man.—Tuticorin ; Rameswaram ; Madras, &c.
—— *Arethusa*, De Man.—Muttuwartu Par ; Rameswaram ; Madras.
Calapagurus ensifer, n. sp.—Gulf of Martaban.
Spiropagurus spiriger (De Haan).—Madras ; Gulf of Martaban.
Eupagurus zebra, n. sp.—Muttuwartu Par.

Petrolisthes dentatus (Milne-Edw.).—Tuticorin ; Muttuwartu Par ; Rameswaram.
—— *Boscii* (Aud.).—Muttuwartu Par ; Rameswaram.
—— *militaris* (Heller).—Muttuwartu Par ; Cheval Par ; Rameswaram.
Raphidopus indicus, n. sp.—Madras.
Pachycheles tomentosus, n. sp.—Kurachi.
Porcellanella triloba, White.—Rameswaram.
Polyonyx obesulus, Miers.—Tuticorin ; Rameswaram.
—— *tuberculosus*, De Man.—Cheval Par ; Rameswaram.
Galathea elegans, White.—Tuticorin ; Gulf of Martaban.
—— *spinosirostris*, Dana.—Muttuwartu Par ; Gulf of Martaban.
Munida spinulifera, Miers.—Muttuwartu Par ; Gulf of Martaban.

MACRURA.

Gebiopsis Darwinii, Miers.—Tuticorin ; Cheval Par ; Rameswaram.

Thenus orientalis (Fabr.).—Madras, &c.
Panulirus ornatus (Fabr.).—Ceylon.
—— *penicillatus* (Oliv.).—Ceylon.
—— *dasypus* (Latr.).—Silavaturai Par ; Madras.

Cacidina Wyckii (Hickson).—Madras.
Alpheus malabaricus, Fabr.—Pulicat.
—— *Edwardsii* (Aud.).—Kurachi ; Tuticorin ; Muttuwartu Par ; Rameswaram ; Gulf of Martaban.

Alpheus Hippothoë, De Man.—Rameswaram.
—— *frontalis*, Say.—Tuticorin.
—— *lævis*, Randall.—Tuticorin ; Rameswaram.
—— *Neptunus*, Dana.—Kurachi ; Rameswaram.
Dorodotes levicarina, Bate.—Gulf of Martaban.
Angasia Stimpsonii, n. sp.—Gulf of Martaban.
Rhynchocinetes rugulosus, Stm.—Tuticorin.
Pontonia tridacnæ, Dana.—Tuticorin ; Rameswaram
Leander longirostris (Say).—Kurachi ; Sunderbunds ; Gulf of Martaban ; Mergui.
—— *tenuipes*, n. sp.—Bombay ; Madras ; Gulf of Martaban.
—— *modestus*, Heller.—Madras.
Palæmon carcinus (Fabr.).—Bombay ; Ganjam ; Calcutta ; Sunderbunds ; Tavoy ; Burmah.
—— *dispar*, v. Mart.—Calcutta.
—— *scabriculus*, Heller.—River Indus.
—— *Dayanus*, n. sp.—Orissa ; Jubbulpore ; Calcutta ; Beerbhoom ; Delhi ; Roorkee ; Loodiana ; Hurdwar ; Debroo ; River Jumna ; Lahore.
—— *altifrons*, n. sp.—Delhi ; River Jumna ; Lahore.
Nika processa, Bate.—Gulf of Martaban.
Ægeon orientalis, n. sp.—Gulf of Martaban.

Penæus monodon, Fabr.—Bombay ; Madras, &c. ; Ganjam.
—— *indicus*, Milne-Edw.—Kurachi ; Madras ; Gaujam ; Calcutta ; Akyab.
—— *affinis*, Milne-Edw.—Kurachi ; Bombay ; Canara ; Madras.
—— *sculptilis*, Heller.—Kurachi ; Malabar ; Madras ; Sunderbunds ; Gulf of Martaban
—— *Dobsoni*, Miers.—Madras.
—— *velutinus*, Dana.—Gulf of Martaban.
—— *brevicornis*, Milne-Edw.—Kurachi ; Calcutta.
—— *canaliculatus*, Oliv.—Gulf of Martaban.
—— *compressipes*, n. sp.—Gulf of Martaban.
Solenocera crassicornis (Milne-Edw.).—Madras ; Gulf of Martaban.
Acetes indicus, Milne-Edw.—Gulf of Martaban.

STOMATOPODA.

Lysiosquilla maculata (Fabr.).—Tuticorin ; Madras.
Squilla nepa, Latr.—Tuticorin ; Ceylon ; Madras.
—— *affinis*, Berthold.—Rameswaram ; Madras ; Sunderbunds.
—— *scorpio*, Latr.—Madras.
—— *raphidea*, Fabr.—Madras ; Sunderbunds.
Pseudosquilla ciliata (Fabr.).—Madras.
Gonodactylus chiragra (Fabr.).—Ceylon ; Andamans.
—— *glaber*, Brooks.—Tuticorin ; Ceylon ; Silavaturai Par ; Rameswaram.
—— *Demanii*, n. sp.—Rameswaram.
Protosquilla trispinosa (Dana).—Ceylon ; Rameswaram ; Gulf of Martaban.

Order DECAPODA.

Suborder BRACHYURA.

Group OXYRHYNCHA.

Genus ACHÆUS, Leach.

1. ACHÆUS LACERTOSUS, Stimpson.

A. lacertosus, Stimpson, Proc. Acad. Nat. Sci. Philad. p. 218 (1857); Miers, ' Alert ' Crust. p. 188 (1884).

(= *A. breviceps*, Haswell).

Gulf of Martaban, two females with ova, and a male (*Oates*).

These specimens are not in a very good state of preservation, but there can be little doubt that they belong to this species.

Distribution. E. & N. Australia.

2. ACHÆUS AFFINIS, Miers.

A. affinis, Miers, ' Alert ' Crust. p. 188 (1884); De Man, Brock's Crust. p. 218 (1888).

Gulf of Martaban, a female (*Oates*).

This species is distinguished from the last chiefly by the presence of a prominent bilobed tubercle on the cardiac area, and by its tuberculated ocular peduncles.

Distribution. E., N., and W. Australia, Malay Archipelago.

Genus ONCINOPUS, De Haan.

3. ONCINOPUS ARANEA, De Haan.

O. aranea, De Haan, Crust. Japon. p. 100, pl. xxix. fig. 2 (1850).

(= *O. Neptunus*, Adams & White, *O. subpellucidus*, Stm., *O. angulatus*, Hasw.).

Muttuwartu Par, a female with ova, and a male carrying a *Sacculina* (*Thurston*). Gulf of Martaban, several specimens (*Oates*).

All the described species of this genus are referred by Miers to *O. aranea*, and he has shown that there is considerable variation in the length and robustness of the legs, characters on which the so-called species had been founded. The carapace and legs are much more attenuated in the male than in the female.

Distribution. Japan, Mindoro Sea, Singapore, N. & N.E. Australia, New Hebrides

Genus HUENIA, De Haan.

4. HUENIA PROTEUS, De Haan.

H. Proteus, De Haan, Crust. Japon. p. 95, pl. xxiii. figs. 4, 5 ♂, fig. 6 ♀ (1850).

(= *H. Dehaani*, White; *H. Proteus*, vars. *tenuipes*, *elongata*, and *heraldica*, Adams & White.

Tuticorin, several specimens, overgrown with sponges and polyzoa (*Thurston*).   Common on the reef at Rameswaram (*J. R. H.*).

Distribution. Japan, China, Malay Archipelago, N. & N.E. Australia.

Genus SIMOCARCINUS, Miers.

5. SIMOCARCINUS SIMPLEX (Dana).

Huenia simplex, Dana, Crust. U.S. Explor. Exped. vol. i. p. 133, pl. vi. fig. 3, ♂ (1852).
H. brevirostrata, Dana, l. c. p. 134, pl. vi. fig. 4, ♀ (1852).

Tuticorin, a male and a female (*Thurston*).

The male is of small size and has the rostrum much more elongated than is represented in Dana's figure, with the apex somewhat trigonal. In the female the rostrum has been broken off, and, as noted by Miers, the anterior pair of lateral lobes on the carapace are larger than figured by Dana, and their apices are subtruncated. In this species, as in the last, there is great sexual dimorphism.

Distribution. Sandwich Is. (*Dana, Miers*).

Genus MENÆTHIUS, Milne-Edwards.

6. MENÆTHIUS MONOCEROS (Latreille).

M. monoceros (Latr.), A. Milne-Edwards, Nouv. Arch. Mus. Hist. Nat. t. viii. p. 252 (1872), *ubi synon.*

Rameswaram, Tuticorin, Muttuwartu Par, Silavaturai Par (*Thurston*) ; Gulf of Martaban (*Oates*). Very common on the reef at Rameswaram, and usually overgrown with sponges and hydroids (*J. R. H.*).

No less than eleven so-called species have been referred by A. Milne-Edwards to this very variable and widely distributed form.

Distribution. From the Red Sea and East Coast of Africa to Japan, New Caledonia, and the Fiji Is.

Genus DOCLEA, Leach.

7. DOCLEA HYBRIDA (Fabr.).

D. hybrida (Fabr.), De Man, Mergui Crust. p. 9 (1887).
(=? *D. hybridoida*, Bleeker).

Ceylon (*Haly*). Very common at Madras, and elsewhere on the Coromandel coast (*J. R. H.*).

Distribution. Malay Archipelago, Mergui.

8. DOCLEA MURICATA (Fabr.).

D. muricata (Fabr.), Milne-Edwards, Hist. Nat. Crust. t. i. p. 295 (1834).

Gulf of Martaban (*Oates*). Madras, not uncommon (*J. R. H.*).

The spines on the carapace of this species are strongly developed, more especially in young individuals; the fourth lateral spine is nearly twice the length of the third. The carapace and legs are densely pubescent.

A male of average size (from Madras) gives the following measurements:—carapace (omitting spines) 31 mm. long, 27 mm. broad, third lateral spine 3 mm., fourth spine 5·5 mm., posterior median spine 4·5 mm., first ambulatory leg 60 mm. long.

Distribution. South India, Singapore.

Genus STENOCIONOPS, Latreille.

9. STENOCIONOPS CERVICORNIS (Herbst).

S. cervicornis (Herbst), Milne-Edwards, Hist. Nat. Crust. t. i. p. 338 (1834).

Tuticorin, four females (one with ova). three males (*Thurston*).

The carapace, rostral spines, ambulatory legs, and in males also the abdominal segments carry numerous tufts of strong curved hairs (each hair is about 3 mm. long) which help to form an attachment for the numerous sponges, hydroids, ascidians, &c., with which the specimens are beset. In the male the rostral spines are scarcely more marked than in the female, but the posterior prolongation of the carapace is narrower and more upturned, and the chelipedes are stronger, with a wider hiatus between the fingers.

The largest male has the carapace (not including rostral spines) 42 mm. long and 29 mm. broad, the rostral spines 25 mm. long. The largest female is somewhat larger.

Distribution. Mauritius (*Milne-Edwards*).

Genus EGERIA, Latreille.

10. EGERIA ARACHNOIDES (Rumph.).

E. arachnoides (Rumph.), Miers, ' Alert ' Crust. p. 191 (1884).
　　　　(= *E. indica*, Leach, *E. Herbstii*, Milne-Edwards).

Madras, common (*J. R. H.*); Gulf of Martaban (*Oates*).

There is great variation in the relative size and acuteness of the spines or tubercles on the carapace of this species. In all the specimens a small spine is present at the distal end of the meropodites of the chelipedes and ambulatory legs. In a single large specimen (a female with the carapace 30 mm. long and 23 mm. broad) the two most posterior tubercles on the middle line of the carapace are prolonged into rather prominent spines, as well as the last branchial tubercle.

The carapace of an average specimen (female) is 19 mm. long and 16 mm. broad, the second ambulatory leg 95 mm. long.

Distribution. N. & N.E. Australia, Malay Archipelago, China.

Genus HYASTENUS, White.

11. HYASTENUS PLEIONE (Herbst).

H. Pleione (Herbst), De Man, Brock's Crust. p. 225, taf. vii. fig. 3 (1888).

Silavaturai Par, a female with ova (*Thurston*).

In this specimen the carapace is yellowish in colour, mottled with red on the gastric area and at the sides of the cardiac area. The carapace, which is overgrown with sponges and ascidians, measures 35 mm. in length and 20 mm. in breadth ; the rostral spines are 11 mm. long, and measured between their apices 5·5 mm.

Distribution. Mergui, Malay Archipelago.

12. HYASTENUS CONVEXUS, Miers.

H. convexus, Miers, ' Alert' Crust. p. 196, pl. xviii. fig. B (1884).

Gulf of Martaban, a female with ova (*Oates*).

I refer this with some doubt to the present species. It agrees in having the gastric area of the carapace smooth and very convex, the cardiac area also smooth and but slightly less convex. But the rostral spines are somewhat less divergent, and a small epibranchial spine is present, while according to Miers there is none. In other respects it agrees with the description, and it is apparently identical with dried specimens from Penang, in the British Museum, labelled by Miers " *Hyastenus convexus*, Miers, var." The carapace measures 13 mm. long (not including the rostral spines), and the rostral spines 6 mm. long.

Distribution. N.E. Australia (*Miers*) ; Penang (*Brit. Mus.*).

13. HYASTENUS HILGENDORFI, De Man.

H. Hilgendorfi, De Man, Mergui Crust. p. 14, pl. i. figs. 3, 4 (1887).

Rameswaram, Tuticorin, Cheval Par (*Thurston*). Not uncommon on the reef at Rameswaram (*J. R. H.*).

Allied to *H. Pleione* (Herbst), from which it may be distinguished by the absence of median spines from the dorsal surface of the carapace, and the presence of only two tubercles on the anterior gastric region. The rostral spines are much longer in adult males than in females and young males. Most of the specimens are overgrown with hydroids and sponges.

The largest specimen (an adult male) has the carapace 34 mm. in total length (including rostral spines), and the rostral spines measured from the level of the anterior orbital margin 15 mm. long.

Distribution. Mergui (*De Man*).

14. HYASTENUS BROCKII, De Man.

H. Brockii, De Man, Brock's Crust. p. 221, taf. vii. fig. 1 (1888).

Gulf of Martaban (*Oates*).

In a single male specimen which I refer to this species (carapace 8·5 mm. long, 6 mm. broad, length of rostrum 10 mm.) the cardiac area of the carapace is more elevated than is represented in De Man's figure. It is chiefly characterized by its very long and slender rostral spines, which are longer even than the carapace.

Distribution. Amboina.

Genus CHLORINOIDES, Haswell.

15. CHLORINOIDES ACULEATUS (Milne-Edwards).

Chorinus aculeatus, Milne-Edwards, Hist. Nat. Crust. t. i. p. 316 (1834).
Paramithrax (*Chlorinoides*) *aculeatus*, var. *armatus*, Miers, 'Alert' Crust. p. 193, pl. xviii. fig. A (1884).

Gulf of Martaban, two males (*Oates*).

The var. *armatus* is distinguished, according to Miers, only by the form of the postocular spine ; but he has apparently overlooked De Haan's figure of *Maja* (*Chorinus*) *aculeata*, M.-Edw. (Crust. Japon. tab. xxiii. fig. 2), in which the postocular spine is represented of the same form as in this variety. Miers mentions the existence of spines at the distal end of the meropodites of the ambulatory legs, which are also represented in De Haan's figure, so perhaps the so-called var. *armatus* is really the typical form.

The carapace of the larger specimen is 20 mm. long and 14 mm. broad, the rostral spines 14 mm. long.

Distribution. Japan, N. Australia.

16. CHLORINOIDES COPPINGERI, Haswell.

Paramithrax Coppingeri, Haswell, Catal. Austral. Crust. p. 15 (1882).
Chlorinoides coppingeri (Hasw.), Miers, 'Challenger' Brachyura, p. 53, pl. vii. fig. 3 (1886).

Muttuwartu Par (*Thurston*); Gulf of Martaban, two young specimens (*Oates*).

These agree completely with dried specimens in the British Museum named by Miers, except that the cardiac spines are scarcely united basally. They are probably not full-grown, as the carapace of the largest measures only 12 mm. long. According to Miers it is perhaps a variety of *C. longispinus*, De Haan.

Distribution. N.E., N., and W. Australia (*Haswell, Miers*); Bass Strait (*Miers*).

Genus NAXIA, Milne-Edwards.

17. NAXIA HIRTA (A. Milne-Edwards).

Naxioides hirta, A. Milne-Edwards, Ann. Soc. Entom. France, ser. 4, t. v. p. 143, pl. iv. fig. 1 (1865).
Podopisa Petersii, Hilgendorf, Monatsb. Acad. Wissensch. Berlin, Nov. 1878, p. 785, taf. 1. fig. 1-5.
Naxia (*Naxioides*) *Petersii* (Hilg.), Miers, 'Alert' Crust. p. 523 (1884); De Man, Mergui Crust. p. 19 (1887).

Tuticorin, a female with ova (*Thurston*).

This specimen has more numerous tubercles on the carapace than are represented in Hilgendorf's figure (a male), and the spine on the posterior margin of the carapace is less acute; the last feature is also noticed by De Man, owing probably to the fact that his specimen, like the one which I have examined, was a female. The rostral spines are entire in the Tuticorin specimen and measure only about 6 mm. in length, while the carapace (including rostral spines) measures 31 mm. in length.

Distribution. East Africa, Amirante Is., Andaman Is., Philippines.

18. Naxia taurus, Pocock.

N. taurus, Pocock, Ann. Mag. Nat. Hist. ser. 6, vol. v. p. 77 (1890).

Gulf of Martaban, two males (*Oates*).

I have compared these with the type-specimen and can find no difference except that in the latter the rostral spines are much longer, being more than half the length of the carapace, whereas in the only Martaban specimen which is perfect as regard the spines they are less than half the length of the carapace. This difference cannot be regarded as one of any importance. The accessory rostral spinules are placed nearer the apices of the rostral spines than in the type, but this is perhaps only what might be expected in a variety with the rostrum shortened.

In the larger specimen the carapace (omitting rostral spines) is 15 mm. long; the type is similarly 20 mm. long.

Distribution. China Sea (*Pocock*).

Genus Schizophrys, White.

19. Schizophrys aspera (Milne-Edw.).

S. aspera (M.-Edw.), A. Milne-Edwards, Nouv. Arch. Mus. Hist. Nat. t. viii. p. 231, pl. x. fig. 1 (1872), *ubi synon.*

Tuticorin (*Thurston*); Ceylon (*Haly, Necill*); Rameswaram and Madras (*J. R. H.*).

Strongly marked sexual differences are noticeable in this very common and variable species. In the female the carapace is more uniformly granulated, the lateral spines of the carapace are shorter, and the accessory rostral spinules are rudimentary.

Distribution. From the Red Sea and East Africa, to Japan, New Caledonia, and the Navigator Is.

Genus Hoplophrys, n.

Carapace subovate, with the regions moderately defined, the surface spinose. Rostrum composed of two short, flattened, acute, and slightly divergent spines. A well-developed preocular or supraocular spine, and a closed fissure on the upper orbital margin. Orbit moderately circumscribed, only deficient below near the postorbital angle. Basal antennal joint rather narrow, its distal external angle prolonged into a flattened acute spine, which is distinctly seen when the carapace is viewed from above; the two succeeding joints of the peduncle slender. External maxillipeds with the ischium longitudinally sulcate in the middle line externally; the outer distal angle of the merus produced into a rounded projecting lobe, and the inner angle slightly emarginate for the carpus; the exognath tapers rather abruptly from about its middle to the narrow distal end. Chelipedes and ambulatory legs rather short, and spinose; the chelipedes not enlarged in the male, with the fingers excavate at the tips and a slight basal hiatus between the two. All the segments of the male abdomen distinct.

Possibly some of the above characters, *e. g.* the spiny nature of the carapace and limbs, may be specific and not generic. In some respects this genus is intermediate between the Subfamilies Schizophrysinae and Pericerinae of Miers; it at least illustrates the difficulty of assigning a place in either of these groups to some forms. The genera to which it appears most closely related are *Schizophrys*, White, and *Microphrys*, Milne-Edw. In the first of these the rostral spines carry secondary lateral spinules, there is no distinct supraorbital spine, the upper orbital margin shows two fissures, and the merus of the external maxillipedes is not produced externally and distally. In the second, to which it is perhaps more nearly related, the basal antennal joint is considerably broader, with a longer terminal spine, the rostral spines are longer, the orbits more complete below, and the chelipedes are enlarged in the male, with acute fingers. It also bears considerable resemblance to the American genus *Nemausa*, A. Milne-Edw., belonging to the Mithracinae, but in this the orbits are well-defined, the basal antennal joint broad and with two external spines, and the merus of the external maxillipedes is not specially produced at its distal external angle.

20. HOPLOPHRYS OATESII, n. sp. (Pl. XXXVI. figs. 1–4.)

Gulf of Martaban, a male (*Oates*).

The gastric region of the carapace is prominent, with two rows of spines arranged in curved lines, the anterior row (convex anteriorly) consisting of seven spines—three small spines on each side of a central slightly larger one, the posterior row (convex posteriorly) of three spines, the middle one of which is larger than any other on the gastric area and is somewhat broadly compressed laterally. The cardiac area with two spines, slightly less prominent than the posterior gastric one, arranged in transverse line, and two still smaller and obtuse spines on the genital area. The branchial area with three spines—an anterior one near the branchiogastric groove, which is the largest of all the spines on the carapace, a small posterior one placed in a line which passes between the cardiac and genital spines, and a large lateral one which is distinctly bifurcate, on the side margin of the carapace. There is a single short spine on the hepatic area a slight distance behind the external orbital angle, and a spine on the carapace internal to and smaller than the supraocular spine. Groups of short curved hairs occur on the frontal, gastric, and branchial regions, but otherwise the surface is perfectly smooth between the spines.

The chelipedes present a few spines on the upper surface of the merus, especially towards its distal end; the carpus has about half a dozen short obtuse spines on its upper surface; the hand has well-developed superior and inferior basal articular tubercles at the carpal articulation, and a single tubercle about the middle of the upper surface, while elsewhere it is smooth and glabrous; the fingers are finely toothed, with a more prominent tooth near the base of the dactylus, and the distal halves of the fingers are in contact. The ambulatory legs are spinose superiorly, the spines being most prominent at the distal ends of the meri and on the carpi; the dactyli with a few minute teeth on the proximal half of the posterior margin. The male abdomen is furnished with a single rounded elevation on each segment except the third, which has three. All the spines on this species are stout in proportion to their length, but with their apices more or less acute.

Very fine red lines are visible on the carapace, usually arranged in pairs, running up some of the spines and on the supraocular spine and rostrum; they are also seen crossing transversely the upper surface of the chelipedes and ambulatory legs.

The carapace is 9·3 mm. long, 7·3 mm. broad, chelipede 10 mm. long, first ambulatory leg 12 mm., second ambulatory leg 11 mm.

I have named the species after Mr. E. W. Oates, who discovered it and a number of other interesting forms referred to in this paper.

Genus MICIPPA, Leach.

21. MICIPPA PHILYRA (Herbst).

M. Philyra (Herbst), Miers, Ann. Mag. Nat. Hist. ser. 5, vol. xv. p. 6 (1885).

(= *M. platipes*, Rüpp., *M. bicarinata*, Ad. & Wh., *M. hirtipes*, Dana, *M. spatulifrons*, A. Milne-Edw.).

Rameswaram and Tuticorin (*Thurston*). Not uncommon on the reef at Rameswaram (*J. R. H.*).

Distribution. Red Sea, Cape of Good Hope, and Mauritius, to New Caledonia and Fiji.

22. MICIPPA THALIA (Herbst).

M. Thalia (Herbst), Miers, Ann. Mag. Nat. Hist. ser. 5, vol. xv. p. 10 (1885).

(= *M. inermis*, Hasw., *M. pusilla*, Bianconi).

Tuticorin and Muttuwartu Par (*Thurston*); Rameswaram (*J. R. H.*).

Like the other species of the genus, nearly always overgrown with sponges.

Distribution. Red Sea and Natal coast to New Caledonia.

23. MICIPPA MASCARENICA, Kossmann.

M. Philyra, var. *mascarenica*, Kossmann, Malacostraca in Zool. Ergebn. Reise Rothen Meeres, p. 7, pl. iii. fig. 2 (1877).

M. mascarenica, Miers, Ann. Mag. Nat. Hist. ser. 5, vol. xv. p. 7 (1885).

(= *M. superciliosa*, Hasw., *Paramicippa asperimanus*, Miers).

Gulf of Martaban, three females, one with ova and one bearing a *Succulina* (*Oates*).

Distribution. Red Sea, Mauritius, Singapore, N. Australia.

24. MICIPPA MARGARITIFERA, n. sp.   (Pl. XXXVI. figs. 5–7.)

Gulf of Martaban, a male and two females with ova (*Oates*).

The carapace is but little convex, with the hepatic regions deeply excavate, and the surface everywhere strongly granulated, though fewer granules are present in the hollows. Two short blunt spines occur on the margin of the posterior branchial area, and a third less marked is placed internal to these and on the surface of this region. The cardiac area is somewhat circumscribed, and behind it, nearly at the posterior margin of the carapace, there is a small strongly granulated elevation, with a similar but slighter elevation on each side. The anterior half of the lateral margin has a few irregular spines, the largest placed opposite the posterior part of the hepatic depression. The front is vertically deflexed, with the surface granulated and the apex retroflexed, terminating in two obtusely rounded equal lobes separated by a median notch, and on the outer margin of each lobe is a short curved spine directed forwards (an imaginary line joining these two spines marks the junction of the vertical rostrum with the horizontal apex). The anterior orbital fissure is linear and twice as deep as the wider posterior fissure. On the posterior margin of the carapace are three perfectly hemispherical smooth tubercles exactly resembling pearls set in the margin, and slightly smaller than the ocular corneæ; a finely crenulated line separates the median from the lateral pearl on each side. The basal antennal joint has two or three short spines in front of the orbit, and the second peduncular joint is not specially dilated; the flagellum carries a few short hairs.

The chelipedes in the male are finely granulated on the upper and lower surfaces of the merus, the whole of the carpus, and the inner surface of the hand and fingers; on the inner surface of the hand the granules become subspinulose, while the outer surface of the hand and fingers is smooth. The opposing edges of the fingers are finely crenulated, and there is a slight basal hiatus between them; the finger-tips are dark in colour. The ambulatory legs are very hairy, with the meral joints enlarged and flattened distally, and a slight lobe occurs on the posterior distal margin of these joints.

The male carapace is 15 mm. long and 12 mm. broad, the chelipedes 20 mm. long, and the second ambulatory leg 17 mm. long; the carapace of the larger female is only 9 mm. long.

This small species is distinguished by its three pearl-like tubercles, the form of the front and of the ambulatory legs, &c. *M. curtispina*, Haswell, has a similarly deflexed rostrum, but it terminates in four rounded lobes, and there are other points of difference.

Genus TYLOCARCINUS, Miers.

25. TYLOCARCINUS STYX (Herbst).

Microphrys Styx (Herbst), A. Milne-Edwards. Nouv. Arch. Mus. Hist. Nat. t. viii. p. 247, pl. xi fig. 1 (1872), *ubi synon.*

Rameswaram, Tuticorin, and Muttuwartu Par (*Thurston*). Common on the reef at Rameswaram (*J. R. H.*).

The general colour of this species is yellowish, with red mottlings on the gastric and branchial regions of the carapace, and along the upper surface of the legs; smaller red spots and lines are found on the chelipedes.

Distribution. From the Red Sea to the Pacific.

Genus LAMBRUS, Leach.

26. LAMBRUS LONGIMANUS (Linn.).

L. longimanus (Linn.), Milne-Edwards. Hist. Nat. Crust. t. i. p. 351 (1834); Miers, Ann. Mag. Nat. Hist. ser. 5, vol. iv. p. 20 (1879).

Ceylon (*Haly*); Gulf of Martaban (*Oates*); Madras (*J. R. H.*).

A male from Madras has the carapace 25·5 mm. long and 27·5 mm. broad, the right chelipede 102 mm. long.

Distribution. Mauritius. Mergui. Malay Archipelago, N. and N.E. Australia.

27. LAMBRUS CONTRARIUS (Herbst).

L. contrarius (Herbst), Milne-Edwards, Hist. Nat. Crust. t. i. p. 354 (1834) : Miers, 'Challenger' Brachyura, p. 94 (1886).

(= *L. spinimanus*, Desmarest).

Tuticorin, an adult male (*Thurston*).

The carapace of this specimen is 38 mm. long, 36 mm. broad, and the chelipedes 93 mm. long.

Distribution. Mauritius, Malay Archipelago.

28. LAMBRUS AFFINIS, A. Milne-Edw.

L. affinis, A. Milne-Edwards, Nouv. Arch. Mus. Hist. Nat. t. viii. p. 261, pl. xiv. fig. 1 (1872).

Tuticorin (*Thurston*); Rameswaram (*J. R. H.*); Gulf of Martaban (*Oates*); Ceylon (*Nevill*).

The chelipedes are stouter and proportionately shorter in the female than in the male, and in the latter the ambulatory legs are also more slender. The carapace of a male is 18 mm. long and 18·5 mm. broad.   It is a common and widely-distributed species, and, as suggested by Miers, may perhaps prove identical with the longer known *L. pelagicus*, Rüppell.

Distribution. Zanzibar, Seychelles, Singapore, Cochin China, Philippines, N. Australia, New Caledonia.

29. LAMBRUS LONGISPINUS, Miers.

L. longispinus, Miers, Ann. Mag. Nat. Hist. ser. 5, vol. iv. p. 18 (1879).

(= *L. spinifer*, Haswell).

Tuticorin, an adult male (*Thurston*).

This species may be recognized by the median row of large spines on its carapace, and by the presence of large rounded granulated tubercles on the under surface of the chelipedes.   The ambulatory legs are strongly compressed.

Distribution. Shanghai, Malay Archipelago, N. and N.E. Australia.

30. LAMBRUS HOLDSWORTHI, Miers.

L. Holdsworthi, Miers, Ann. Mag. Nat. Hist. ser. 5, vol. iv. p. 19, pl. v. fig. 3 (1879).

Tuticorin, a male (*Thurston*).

The specimens described by Miers were all females.   The male has more slender chelipedes and the inequalities of the carapace are more marked ; there is also a row of minute tubercles passing forwards on each side from the gastric spine towards the orbital margin, which is not represented in Miers's figure.   The carapace is 13 mm. long and 14·5 mm. broad, the chelipedes 36 mm. long.

Distribution. Ceylon (*Miers*).

31. LAMBRUS SCULPTUS, A. Milne-Edw.

L. (Aulacolambrus) sculptus, A. Milne-Edwards, Nouv. Arch. Mus. Hist. Nat. t. viii. p. 258, pl. xiv. fig. 3 (1872).

Gulf of Martaban, four specimens (*Oates*).

The largest specimen (a female) has the carapace 8 mm. long and 7·5 mm. broad.   In this small species there is a well-marked channel on each pterygostomial area leading to the branchial opening.   The *L. pisoides*, Adams & White, is a closely allied species, and the two are perhaps not distinct.

Distribution. New Caledonia (*A. Milne-Edwards*); " Eastern Seas," and Fiji (*Brit. Mus.*).

32. LAMBRUS HOPLONOTUS, Adams & White.

L. hoplonotus, Adams & White, ' Samarang ' Crust., p. 35, pl. vii. fig. 3 (1848).

Muttuwartu Par, a male (*Thurston*).

The single specimen belongs to the var. *planifrons* of Miers (Ann. Mag. Nat. Hist. ser. 5, vol. iv. p. 24, pl. v. fig. 7) founded on specimens collected by Holdsworth in Ceylon.   The carapace is 12 mm. long, and 17·5 mm. in breadth including the lateral epibranchial spines.

Distribution. Ceylon, Malay Archipelago, N.E. Australia, New Caledonia.

Genus CRYPTOPODIA, Milne-Edwards.

33. CRYPTOPODIA FORNICATA (Fabr.).

C. fornicata (Fabr.), Adams & White, ' Samarang ' Crust., p. 32, pl. vi. fig. 4 (1848).

Gulf of Martaban (*Oates*).   A single very young specimen apparently referable to this species.

Distribution. N., N.E., and E. Australia, Malay Archipelago, Singapore, China, Japan.

Genus ŒTHRA, Leach.

34. ŒTHRA SCRUPOSA (Linn.).

Œthra scruposa (Linn.), Milne-Edwards, Hist. Nat. Crust. t. i. p. 371 (1834).

Ceylon (*Haly*).

Distribution. Mauritius, Malay Archipelago, Strait of Gaspar.

Genus ZEBRIDA, White.

35. ZEBRIDA ADAMSII, White.

Zebrida Adamsii, White, Proc. Zool. Soc. 1847, p. 121 ; Adams & White, ' Samarang ' Crust., p. 24, pl. vii. fig. 1 (1848).

Tuticorin, two females (one with ova) and a male (*Thurston*).

These specimens completely agree as regards colour-markings with the original description and figure of this very beautiful species; the markings are doubtless protective. The single male has the carapace flatter and slightly narrower than in the females, and in the former the propodus of the right chelipede is more strongly developed than that of the other side.   The largest specimen (a female with ova) has the carapace 11 mm. long, and 10·5 mm. broad between the apices of the lateral spines ; the male is 9 mm. long and 8 mm. broad.   *Z. longispina*, Haswell, from Torres Strait, is distinguished only by its longer and more acute spines, and is perhaps merely a local variety.

Distribution. Sooloo Sea and coast of Borneo, 6–12 fathoms (*Adams & White*).

Genus PARATYMOLUS, Miers.

36. PARATYMOLUS SEXSPINOSUS, Miers.

P. sexspinosus, Miers, 'Alert' Crust. p. 261, pl. xxvii. fig. B (1884).

Tuticorin, a male specimen (*Thurston*).

Three spines are present on each antero-lateral margin of the carapace, the first (preocular) and second obtuse, the third at the antero-lateral angle subacute and directed forwards. The terminal joint of the antennal peduncle is greatly flattened and its margin ciliated. The carapace is finely pubescent. Length of carapace 8 mm., breadth 7 mm.

Distribution. Torres Strait (*Miers*).

Group CYCLOMETOPA.

Genus ATERGATIS, De Haan.

37. ATERGATIS INTEGERRIMUS (Lamarck).

A. integerrimus (Lam.), A. Milne-Edwards, Nouv. Arch. Mus. Hist. Nat. t. i. p. 235 (1865).
(= *A. subdivisus*, Adams & White).

Tuticorin, a series (*Thurston*); Ceylon (*Haly, Nevill*); Rameswaram, not uncommon at low water under blocks of dead coral (*J. R. H.*).

The carapace of a Tuticorin specimen measures 68 mm. in length and 104 mm. in breadth.

Distribution. From E. Africa to China and Japan.

38. ATERGATIS FLORIDUS (Rumph.).

A. floridus (Rumph.), A. Milne-Edwards, Nouv. Arch. Mus. Hist. Nat. t. i. p. 243 (1865).

Rameswaram and Tuticorin (*Thurston*); Ceylon (*Haly, Nevill*); Rameswaram, common on the reef and at low water (*J. R. H.*).

The carapace of a specimen from Rameswaram measures 41 mm. in length and 58 mm. in breadth.

Distribution. From the Red Sea and E. Africa to Japan, N. Australia, New Caledonia, and Tahiti.

39. ATERGATIS LÆVIGATUS, A. Milne-Edw.

A. lævigatus, A. Milne-Edwards, Nouv. Arch. Mus. Hist. Nat. t. i. p. 24, pl. xv. fig. 4 (1865).

Tuticorin, an adult female (*Thurston*).

In this species the carapace is very convex both from side to side and from before backwards. The antero-lateral margin terminates simply at its posterior end and is not continued into a transverse ridge; four closed and indistinct marginal fissures can be made out, three of them situated rather close together on the posterior half of the margin. The hand is not carinated superiorly and the finger-tips are excavated; the ambulatory legs are strongly carinated. It is regarded by Kossmann as a variety of *A. roseus* (Rüppell), but in the latter species, as described by A. Milne-Edwards, and in specimens from the Red Sea, in the British Museum, which I have examined, the carapace and chelipedes are covered with numerous small depressions or pits, giving them a rugose appearance, and this character is wanting in the present species; otherwise the two are nearly related.

Distribution. Malabar (*A. Milne-Edwards*).

40. ATERGATIS DILATATUS, De Haan.

A. dilatatus, De Haan, Crust Japon. p. 16, tab. xiv. fig. 2 (1850).

Ceylon (*Haly*).

I refer some young specimens doubtfully to this species. Müller has had similar doubt in regard to specimens from Trincomali.

Distribution. China (*De Haan*); New Caledonia (*A. Milne-Edwards*).

Genus CARPILIUS, Leach.

41. CARPILIUS MACULATUS (Linn.).

C. maculatus (Linn.), A. Milne-Edwards, Nouv. Arch. Mus. Hist. Nat. t. i. p. 214 (1865).

Ceylon (*Haly, Neeill*).

Distribution. From Mauritius to the Malay Archipelago, New Caledonia, and the Pacific.

Genus CARPILODES, Dana.

42. CARPILODES TRISTRIS, Dana.

C. tristris, Dana, Crust. U.S. Explor. Exped. vol. i. p. 193, pl. ix. fig. 7 (1852).

Muttuwartu Par, a male (*Thurston*).

Distribution. Paumotu Archipelago (*Dana*); N. and N.E. Australia (*Miers*); "Eastern Seas" (*Brit. Mus.*).

43. CARPILODES MARGARITATUS, A. Milne-Edw.

C. margaritatus, A. Milne-Edwards, Nouv. Arch. Mus. Hist. Nat. t. ix. p. 182, pl. v. fig. 2 (1873).

Rameswaram, two males; Tuticorin, two young males (*Thurston*).

These agree with A. Milne-Edwards's figure and brief description, though they have lost the vivid colour shown in the former. The pearly granulations show a tendency to linear arrangement on the hands. A wide hiatus exists between the fingers, and their margins are toothed. The inner border of the carpus carries two strong granulated and blunt teeth. The largest specimen has the carapace 17 mm. long and 27·5 mm. broad.

Distribution. New Caledonia (*A. Milne-Edwards*).

44. CARPILODES VENOSUS (Milne-Edw.).

Carpilius venosus, Milne-Edwards, Hist. Nat. Crust. t. i. p. 383 (1834).

Xantho obtusus, De Haan, Crust. Japon. p. 17, pl. xiii. fig. 5 (1850).

Liomera obtusa, Stimpson, Proc. Acad. Nat. Sci. Philad. March 1858, p. 32.

Carpilodes venosus, A. Milne-Edwards, Nouv. Arch. Mus. Hist. Nat. t. i. p. 227, pl. xii. fig. 2 (1865).

Ceylon (*Haly*).

Distribution. From Mauritius to Japan, New Caledonia, and N. Australia.

45. CARPILODES CINCTIMANUS (White).

Carpilius cinctimanus, White, Append. Jukes's Voy. ' Fly,' p. 336, pl. ii. fig. 3 (1817).

Liomera cinctimana, A. Milne-Edwards, Nouv. Arch. Mus. Hist. Nat. t. ix. p. 176, pl. v. fig. 4 (1873).

Carpilodes cinctimanus, Miers, Ann. Mag. Nat. Hist. ser. 5, vol. v. p. 234 (1880).

(= ? *Liomera lata,* Dana).

Ceylon (*Haly, Nevill*).

The general ground-colour of this species is bright red. The fingers are black, and a black band encircles the hand, though in young individuals it is sometimes absent. The dactyli of the ambulatory legs have a white band encircling their middle portion, while the narrow apical part is black.

Distribution. From Mauritius and the Seychelles, to the Pacific and west coast of North America.

Genus LIOMERA, Dana.

46. LIOMERA PUNCTATA (Milne-Edw.).

Xantho punctatus, Milne-Edwards, Hist. Nat. Crust. t. i. p. 396 (1834); A. Milne-Edwards, Nouv. Arch. Mus. Hist. Nat. t. ix. p. 199, pl. vii. fig. 6 (1873).

Liomera punctata, Miers, ' Alert ' Crust. p. 528 (1884).

(= *L. maculata,* Haswell).

Tuticorin, an adult male; Muttuwartu Par, a young male (*Thurston*); Ceylon (*Nevill*).

The carapace of the larger specimen is 18 mm. long and 30 mm. broad. The red spots on the carapace soon fade in spirit. There is a characteristic light-coloured band at the base of the mobile finger of each chelipede.

Distribution. Madagascar, Seychelles, Amirante Is., Red Sea, Malay Archipelago, N. Australia, New Caledonia.

47. LIOMERA RODGERSII (Stimpson).

Lachnopodus Rodgersii, Stimpson, Proc. Acad. Nat. Sci. Philad. March 1858, p. 32.

Liomera Rodgersii, Miers, Ann. Mag. Nat. Hist. ser. 5, vol. v. p. 231, pl. xiii. fig. 3 (1880); De Man, Brock's Crust. p. 237 (1888).

Ceylon (*Haly*).

Distribution. Malay Archipelago.

Genus LOPHACTÆA, A. Milne-Edwards.

48. LOPHACTÆA GRANULOSA (Rüppell).

L. granulosa (Rüpp.), A. Milne-Edwards, Nouv. Arch. Mus. Hist. Nat. t. i. p. 217 (1865).

(= *Cancer limbatus,* Milne-Edw.).

Rameswaram, a male; Tuticorin, three males and three females (*Thurston*). Not uncommon on the reef at Rameswaram (*J. R. H.*).

In most of these there is an ill-defined granular ridge on the upper surface of the hand, and in one female it is sharp and prominent; this ridge is one of the chief distinguishing features of the closely-allied *L. cristata,* A. Milne-Edw. In the same female the granulations are more pronounced on the carapace, and they occur even on the mesogastric lobe and towards the lateral and posterior margins of the carapace, whereas in the other specimens they are deficient in these localities. In a third species, *L. Eydouxii*, A. Milne-Edw., the only difference of importance is that the gastric region is less distinctly lobulated, and the lobes separated merely by shallow grooves. It is perhaps possible that all three are varieties of a single variable species. The largest specimen, a male, has the carapace 35 mm. long and 49 mm. broad.

Distribution. From the Red Sea and E. Africa to the Pacific.

49. LOPHACTÆA SEMIGRANOSA (Heller).

Atergatis semigranosus, Heller, Sitzungsb. kais. Akad. Wiss. Wien, p. 313 (1861).
Lophactæa semigranosa, A. Milne-Edwards, Nouv. Arch. Mus. Hist. Nat. t. i. p. 248 (1865) ; De Man, Brock's Crust. p. 246, taf. viii. fig. 1 (1888).

Muttuwartu Par, two males and a female with ova (*Thurston*); Rameswaram (*J. R. H.*).

These agree well with a specimen in the British Museum from Suakim, though in the Indian specimens the crest on the upper margin of the hand is more strongly marked. The antero-lateral margin of the carapace somewhat resembles that of a *Lophozozymus*. The carapace is granulated anteriorly and towards the sides, smooth posteriorly ; but De Man has recently pointed out that the entire surface may be granulated. The carpus and propodus of the cheke are granular externally, with the granules arranged in lines, and a large tooth is present on the inner surface of the immobile finger. The ambulatory legs are carinated, but not granulated, and have ciliated margins. The largest specimen, a female with ova, is 9 mm. long and 13 mm. broad.

Distribution. Red Sea, Amirante Is., Malay Archipelago.

50. LOPHACTÆA FISSA, n. sp. (Plate XXXVI. figs. 8, 8 *a*).

Tuticorin, a male (*Thurston*).

The areolation and armature of the carapace are similar to those of *L. granulosa*, except that the granules are somewhat fewer in number, and towards the sides of the carapace they tend to become spinulose ; a smooth transverse area also exists near the posterior margin. The lateral margins are scarcely so produced as is usual in the genus, and the spiniform granules extend on to them : three wide open fissures are met with, two close together anteriorly, and the posterior one near the hinder termination of the antero-lateral margin. The portion of the antero-lateral margin contiguous to the orbit, i. e. between the latter and the first fissure, is straight, thickened, and separated from both the upper and the lower orbital margin by a very narrow fissure; a second narrow fissure is present as usual in the upper orbital margin. The frontal lobes are regularly rounded. The antennal peduncles and external maxillipedes are similar to those of *L. granulosa*.

The chelipedes are like those of *L. granulosa*, i. e. strongly tuberculated externally ; the fingers are black, compressed, and ridged externally, with a well-marked internal lobe on the immobile finger. The ambulatory legs have the carpal and propodal joints rather less carinated than usual, and their posterior surfaces (especially of the propodi) strongly granulated ; well-marked articular facets are present between these joints on each leg.

The male abdomen has merely a few granules on the first two segments; but the sternal region of the thorax is granulated.

The whole upper surface of the carapace, and outer surface of the chelipedes and legs, carry long yellowish green hairs, which are specially elongated on the margins of the legs.

The carapace is 17·5 mm. long and 25·5 mm. broad; the distance between the outer orbital angles 14 mm., lower margin of hand and immobile finger 14·5 mm., height of hand 7·7 mm., length of dactylus 8 mm.

This species is distinguished by the form of the lateral margin of its carapace, and especially by the wide fissures, but also by the peculiar hairs with which it is clothed.

Genus ACTÆA, De Haan.

51. ACTÆA GRANULATA (Aud.).

A. granulata (Aud.), A. Milne-Edwards, Nouv. Arch. Mus. Hist. Nat. t. i. p. 275 (1865).
(= *A. pura*, Stimpson).

Tuticorin, three specimens, one carrying a *Sacculina*; Cheval Par (*Thurston*); reef at Rameswaram (*J. R. H.*).

I have examined the type of *A. carcharias*, White, in the British Museum, and agree with Miers that it is probably only a variety of *A. granulata*.

Distribution. From the Red Sea and East Africa to China and Australia.

52. ACTÆA CALCULOSA (Milne-Edw.).

A. calculosa (Milne-Edw.), A. Milne-Edwards, Nouv. Arch. Mus. Hist. Nat. t. i. p. 276, pl. xviii. fig. 3 (1865).

Tuticorin, thirteen specimens, including four females with ova; Muttuwartu Par (*Thurston*).

This species is allied to *A. granulata*, but is smaller; the carapace is flatter and less contracted posteriorly, with the granules on its surface smoother; the posterior margin is granulated and there is a smooth transverse groove immediately in front of it, which is not seen in *A. granulata*. In the present species also, the tubercles on the hand are more rounded, the abdominal and sternal regions are smooth or only faintly granulated, and the whole aspect is more glabrous.

The largest specimen (a male) has the carapace 11·3 mm. long and 15·5 mm. broad, while the smallest female with ova is only 8·5 mm. long and 12 mm. broad.

Distribution. Australia (*A. Milne-Edwards*).

53. ACTÆA NODULOSA (White).

A. nodulosa (White), Adams & White, 'Samarang' Crust. p. 39, tab. viii. fig. 1 (1848); Miers, 'Challenger' Brachyura, p. 120 (1886).

Tuticorin, three females (one with ova) and two males (*Thurston*).

The types in the British Museum are obviously young and only about half the size of the largest Tuticorin examples, but there can be no doubt, I think, as to the identity of the latter. The carapace is only moderately convex, with the anterior regions well-defined, and separated by somewhat deep smooth grooves; smooth rounded tubercles are everywhere present, as well as a few scattered tufts of hair, which are not seen in the types. On the antero-lateral margin are four elevations, each composed of a collection of tubercles; on the posterior margin is a continuous row of tubercles, and immediately in front of it a second row, which, however, is interrupted in the middle. The chelipedes and ambulatory legs are tuberculate externally, and the latter are fringed with hairs. The digits are black and both are granulated proximally; the black colour occasionally extends back for some distance on both the inner and outer surface of the hand. The sternal region is granulated.

The largest male is 16 mm. long and 23·5 mm. broad; a female with ova is 11·5 mm. long and 17 mm. broad.

A specimen in the British Museum, taken by H.M.S. 'Challenger' at Honolulu, has the carapace slightly broader in proportion to its length, and the tubercles on its surface both smaller and more numerous; the ambulatory legs without hairs. It may perhaps rank as a variety.

Distribution. Mauritius (*White*): Honolulu (*Miers*).

54. ACTÆA PERONII (Milne-Edw.), var. SQUAMOSA, n.

A. peronii (Milne-Edw.). Miers, 'Challenger' Brachyura, p. 122 (1886).
(= *Xantho spinosus*, Hess).

Muttuwartu Par, a female (*Thurston*).

This specimen differs from the typical form in having the tubercles of the carapace replaced by flattened, polished, scale-like elevations; each scale is raised higher from the carapace anteriorly than it is posteriorly, and the whole series presents a filed or ground appearance, as if the filing had been performed from behind forwards. The scales are also present, though of smaller size, on the posterior part of the carapace, whereas in the typical form this part is almost smooth. In the variety the ambulatory legs are hairy and the merus of the last leg is strongly tuberculate (smooth in the typical form); the tubercles of the carpus and propodus of the chelipedes are more conical, and the tubercles present on the eye-stalks and immediately below the suborbital margin are more strongly developed. I cannot regard this specimen as belonging to a distinct species, for I have observed a tendency towards the above characters in undoubted specimens of *A. Peronii*; still it may be useful to distinguish it by a special name.

The carapace measures 9·5 mm. in length and 12 mm. in breadth.

Distribution. Australia (*Milne-Edwards, Hess*); Bass Strait (*Miers*).

55. ACTÆA RUFOPUNCTATA (Milne-Edw.).

A. rufopunctata (Milne-Edw.), A. Milne-Edwards, Nouv. Arch. Mus. Hist. Nat. t. i. p. 268, pl. xviii fig. 1 (1865).
(= *A. pilosa*, Stimpson).

Tuticorin; Cheval Par (*Thurston*).

In this species the fingers are almost excavated at the tips, so it might with equal justice be placed in the genus *Actæodes*.

Distribution. From the Red Sea, Seychelles, and Mauritius, to China and the Fijis. It has also been recorded from the Mediterranean, the Canaries, Madeira, and the S. Atlantic.

56. ACTÆA RUPPELLII (Krauss).

A. Ruppellii (Krauss), Miers, Ann. Mag. Nat. Hist. ser. 5, vol. v. p. 232 (1880), *ubi synon.*

Tuticorin, many specimens (*Thurston*). Common on the reef at Rameswaram (*J. R. H.*). The amount of pubescence varies greatly in different individuals. After examination of the type of *Ægle rugata*, Adams & White, I have come to the same conclusion as Hilgendorf and Miers, viz. that it is merely a variety of the present species. *A. hirsutissima*, Rüpp., is also closely allied and perhaps not distinct.

Distribution. Natal, Zanzibar, Mauritius, Malay Archipelago, N. and N.E. Australia.

Genus HYPOCŒLUS, Heller.

57. HYPOCŒLUS RUGOSUS, n. sp. (Pl. XXXVI. figs. 9–11.)

Tuticorin, two females (*Thurston*).

This species is closely allied to *H. granulatus* (De Haan), which has been well described and figured by both De Haan and A. Milne-Edwards, so that only the characters wherein it differs from the latter need be pointed out. The areolation of the carapace is very like that of *H. granulatus*, but the granules are much smaller. The posterior half of the lateral margin of the carapace is irregular and three-toothed, the most anterior tooth being well-defined, and marking the hinder limit of the pterygostomial cavity; whereas in *H. granulatus* this margin is slightly irregular, but not dentate. The pterygostomial cavity has the upper and lower margins straight, and gradually converging to a rather broad truncated hinder end, which is fully half the width of the anterior end; while in *H. granulatus* the lower margin of the cavity is strongly curved and the hinder end narrow and pointed (see Pl. XXXVI. fig. 12); in our new species the cavity also approaches nearer to the orbit.

In both species the chelipedes are somewhat similar in general appearance. In *H. rugosus* the carpus is more strongly tuberculate, and the granules on the outer surface of the hand are arranged in reticulating lines, while the upper surface is convex and covered with prominent granular tubercles; whereas in the longer known form the granules on the outer surface of the hand are arranged in more or less parallel lines along the joint, and the upper surface is flattened or almost concave, with a median and two lateral granulated lines on this area. The ambulatory legs are also more strongly tuberculated in the new species.

The gastric and branchial regions of the carapace are reddish (in spirit specimens), while the carpal joints of the chelipedes, and the legs, show traces of the same colour.

All the comparisons have been made with a single dried specimen of *H. granulatus* (locality unknown) in the collection of the British Museum.

In the larger specimen the carapace is 12·3 mm. long and 17·5 mm. broad; the front is 5·3 mm. broad.

Genus XANTHO, Leach.

58. XANTHO IMPRESSUS (Lamarck).

X. impressus (Lam.), A. Milne-Edwards, Nouv. Arch. Mus. Hist. Nat. t. ix. p. 198, pl. vi. fig. 2 (1873).

Ceylon, five specimens (*Nevill*).

Distribution. Mauritius. Mergui, New Caledonia.

Genus MEDÆUS, Dana.

59. MEDÆUS DISTINGUENDUS (De Haan).

Cancer (Xantho) distinguendus, De Haan, Crust. Japon. p. 18, tab. xiii. fig. 7 (1850).
Medæus distinguendus (De Haan), De Man, Mergui Crust. p. 31 (1887).
Xantho Macgillivrayi, Miers, 'Alert' Crust. p. 211, pl. xx. fig. C (1884).

Gulf of Martaban, two young specimens (*Oates*).

I have compared these and found them identical with specimens of similar size from Mergui, in the British Museum, which were referred by De Man—and as I think correctly—to De Haan's species. *Xantho Macgillivrayi*, Miers, from Australia, of which both dry and spirit specimens exist in the British Museum collection, is also in my opinion referable to the same species, the differences being unimportant; indeed De Haan's figure is a better representation of *X. Macgillivrayi* than is the one given in the Report on the 'Alert' Crustacea. Miers ('Alert' Crust. p. 530) appears to have regarded De Haan's species as a variety of *Leptodius exaratus* (Milne-Edw.). In old specimens the granules on the hands appear to be lost, and simply a rugose appearance is left.

Distribution. Red Sea, Mergui, China, Japan, N. and N.E. Australia.

Genus EUXANTHUS, Dana.

60. EUXANTHUS MELISSA (Herbst).

E. Melissa (Herbst), A. Milne-Edwards, Nouv. Arch. Mus. Hist. Nat. t. i. p. 293 (1865).

Tuticorin (*Thurston*); Ceylon (*Haly, Nevill*).

Distribution. From India to Australia and the Pacific (Fijis, Tongatabu, &c.).

Genus ZOZYMUS, Milne-Edwards.

61. ZOZYMUS ÆNEUS (Linn.).

Z. Æneus (Linn.), Milne-Edwards, Hist. Nat. Crust. t. i. p. 385 (1834).

Ceylon (*Haly, Nevill*).

Distribution. Red Sea, Mascarenes, Malay Archipelago, Loo Choo Is., Australia, South Pacific.

Genus POLYCREMNUS, Gerstaecker.

62. POLYCREMNUS OCHTODES (Herbst).

Galene ochtodes (Herbst), Adams & White, 'Samarang' Crust. p. 43, tab. x. fig. 2 (1848).

Muttuwartu Par (*Thurston*); Madras (*J. R. H.*).

The carapace of a specimen from Madras is 23 mm. long and 29 mm. broad.
Distribution. Indian Ocean (*Herbst, White*); Malay Archipelago (*Adams & White*).

Genus HALIMEDE, De Haan.

63. HALIMEDE THURSTONI, n. sp.   (Pl. XXXVI. figs. 13, 14.)

Tuticorin, a male (*Thurston*).

This species is closely allied to *H. fragifer*, De Haan, from Japan, but is, I think, distinct, though possibly it may afterwards be shown to be a variety of that species, which in general form it much resembles. The carapace is covered with short tufts of hair, which spring from the different elevations, and these last are much less marked than in De Haan's species; they consist simply of minute clustered granules on the gastric, cardiac, and branchial regions. The short antero-lateral margin has two strongly marked teeth, one at the posterior limit of the margin, the other between this and the orbit; opposite the latter tooth there is a strongly-marked flattened tubercle on the hepatic region, and between the tooth and the orbit a third small antero-lateral tooth. External to the postorbital angle is a flattened lobe, and the lower orbital margin is similarly flattened. The frontal lobes are strongly produced, with a deep intervening median fissure; each lobe is regularly convex anteriorly and the margin is finely crenulated. The inferior and internal angle of the orbit is produced, and along with a considerable portion of the lower orbital wall can be distinctly seen from above. The basal antennal joint is joined to the subfrontal process, but does not extend into the inner orbital hiatus as in *Halimede Coppingeri*, Miers (so this latter species is, as surmised by Miers, probably referable to another genus). The merus of the external maxillipedes is faintly emarginate at its distal end, the outer distal angle is slightly produced, and there is a distinct notch for the carpus.

The chelipedes are similar to those of De Haan's species, but the carpus and hand are much less strongly tuberculate, the tubercles being almost obsolete on the outer and lower surface of the hand, while those on the upper surface are regularly flattened. The ambulatory legs and male abdomen resemble those of De Haan's species.

The most important difference between the two species is seen in the frontal lobes, which in that just described have a convex crenulated margin, while in *H. fragifer* they are concave and entire; in the new species also, the carapace and outer surface of the hand are much less tuberculated. The *Medaeus nodosus*, A. Milne-Edwards, from New Caledonia, bears a general resemblance to our species, but the antero-lateral margin of the carapace has four teeth, the front is less produced, and the lobes are not rounded; it is perhaps congeneric with the present species.

The carapace is 9 mm. long and 10 mm. broad.

Genus CYCLOXANTHUS, A. Milne-Edwards.

64. CYCLOXANTHUS LINEATUS, A. Milne-Edw.

C. *lineatus*, A. Milne-Edwards, Ann. Soc. Entom. France, t. vii. p. 269 (1867); id. Nouv. Arch. Mus. Hist. Nat. t. ix. p. 209, pl. vi. fig. 5 (1873).

Tuticorin, a male (*Thurston*).

The colour is at first very vivid, but the lines on the carapace soon fade in spirit. The carapace is 11·5 mm. long and 15·5 mm. broad. Milne-Edwards's type-specimen was slightly larger.

Distribution. New Caledonia, Lifu, Torres Strait, Arafura Sea.

Genus LOPHOZOZYMUS, A. Milne-Edwards.

65. LOPHOZOZYMUS DODONE (Herbst).

L. Dodone (Herbst), De Man, Brock's Crust. p. 270, Taf. x. fig. 2 (1888), *ubi synon.*
(= *Xantho radiatus*, Milne-Edwards, *Atergatis lateralis*, White, *Atergatis elegans*, Heller).

Tuticorin, a series ; Muttuwartu Par (*Thurston*); Rameswaram (*J. R. H.*).

I have examined the types of *Atergatis lateralis*, White, from Mauritius, and find that they are identical with this species, as more than one writer had already suspected.

Distribution. East Africa, Mauritius, Malay Archipelago, New Caledonia.

66. LOPHOZOZYMUS CRISTATUS, A. Milne-Edw.

L. cristatus, A. Milne-Edwards, Nouv. Arch. Mus. Hist. Nat. t. ix. p. 203, pl. vi. fig. 4 (1873).

Muttuwartu Par, three specimens (*Thurston*).

These are probably young, the largest measuring only 13·5 mm. in length and 22 mm. in breadth. Immersion in spirit has completely removed all trace of the vivid colour shown in Milne-Edwards's figure.

Distribution. New Caledonia (*A. Milne-Edwards*).

Genus CHLORODIUS, Rüppell.

67. CHLORODIUS NIGER (Forskål).

C. niger (Forsk.), De Man, Mergui Crust. p. 32 (1887).

Tuticorin, many specimens ; Muttuwartu Par (*Thurston*); Rameswaram, one of the commonest species on the reef (*J. R. H.*).

Distribution. From the Red Sea and East Africa to Australia and the Pacific.

Genus CHLORODOPSIS, A. Milne-Edwards.

68. CHLORODOPSIS SPINIPES (Heller).

C. spinipes (Heller), A. Milne-Edwards, Nouv. Arch. Mus. Hist. Nat. t. ix. p. 230, pl. viii. fig. 6 (1873).

Ceylon (*Haly*); Muttuwartu Par, a male (*Thurston*).

The Muttuwartu specimen measures 8 mm. in length and 10·5 mm. in breadth. It is more hirsute than is represented in Milne-Edwards's figure, the carapace, legs, and chelipedes carrying many reddish brown hairs ; the under surface is without hairs, and the sternal region is finely granulated. The male abdomen is very narrow, and the penultimate segment is slightly wider at its distal than at its proximal end.

Distribution. Red Sea, Malay Archipelago, New Caledonia.

Genus LEPTODIUS. A. Milne-Edwards.

69. LEPTODIUS EXARATUS (Milne-Edw.).

L. *exaratus* (Milne-Edw.), A. Milne-Edwards, Nouv. Arch. Mus. Hist. Nat. t. ix. p. 222 (1873) ; Kossmann, Malacostraca in Zool. Ergebn. Reise Rothen Meeres, p. 32, taf. ii. (1877).

Tuticorin, many specimens ; Silavaturai Par (*Thurston*) : Ceylon (*Haly, Nevill*); Sind, several specimens (*Day*); very common on the reef at Rameswaram (*J. R. H.*).

A very common and very variable species. A male from Silavaturai has the carapace flatter and less distinctly areolated than usual; the colour in spirit light grey, with a large brownish spot on the gastric area of the carapace, and the distal joints of the ambulatory legs darkly banded. Similar specimens from West Australia are in the British Museum collection, and this variety is figured by Kossmann. An old male from Sind (22·5 mm. long and 35 mm. broad) has the postero-lateral surface of the carapace excavated on each side for the last pair of legs, while its front and chelipedes are twisted and deformed.

Distribution. From the Red Sea and E. Africa to Japan and the Pacific.

Genus ETISUS. Milne-Edwards.

70. ETISUS LÆVIMANUS, Randall.

E. *lævimanus* (Rand.), Dana, Crust. U.S. Explor. Exped. vol. i. p. 185, pl. x. fig. 1 (1852) ; A. Milne-Edwards, Nouv. Arch. Mus. Hist. Nat. t. ix. p. 231 (1873).

Rameswaram and Tuticorin, many specimens (*Thurston*); Ceylon (*Haly*); common on the reef at Rameswaram (*J. R. H.*).

Distribution. From the Red Sea and E. Africa to Japan, the Sandwich Is., and Fijis.

Genus ETISODES, Dana.

71. ETISODES ELECTRA (Herbst).

E. *Electra* (Herbst), Miers, ' Alert ' Crust. p. 217 (1884), *ubi synon.*
    (=E. *frontalis*, Dana, E. *rugosa*, Lucas, E. *sculptilis*, Heller, *Chlorodius dentifrons*, Stm., *Chlorodius samoensis*, Miers).

Tuticorin (*Thurston*); Rameswaram, not uncommon (*J. R. H.*).

Distribution. Red Sea, Seychelles, Malay Archipelago, N. Australia, Samoa, Sandwich Is.

Genus PHYMODIUS, A. Milne-Edwards.

72. PHYMODIUS UNGULATUS (Milne-Edw.).

P. *ungulatus* (Milne-Edw.), A. Milne-Edwards, Nouv. Arch. Mus. Hist. Nat. t. ix. p. 218 (1873).
    (=*Chlorodius ureolatus*, Adams & White).

Ceylon (*Haly*).

Distribution. From India to New Caledonia and the Pacific.

73. PHYMODIUS MONTICULOSUS (Dana).

P. monticulosus (Dana), Miers, 'Challenger' Brachyura, p. 139 (1886), *ubi synon.*

Tuticorin, four females and one male (*Thurston*).

The largest specimen—a female—is 16 mm. long and 22 mm. broad.

Distribution. From the Indian Ocean to the Pacific.

Genus CYMO, De Haan.

74. CYMO ANDREOSSYI (And.).

C. Andreossyi (And.), Miers, 'Alert' Crust. p. 532 (1884).

(= *C. melanodactylus*, De Haan).

Tuticorin, a female with ova; Muttuwartu Par, a male (*Thurston*); Rameswaram, not uncommon (*J. R. H.*).

The carapace has a few granules arranged transversely on the gastric region and towards the lateral margins, while two conspicuous denticles are present towards the centre of the lateral margin. The front is denticulated, the two submedian denticles being largest. The fingers, with the exception of their tips, are black as in the variety *melanodactylus*, De Haan, but at the same time the lower and outer surface of the larger hand is often granulated, whereas according to Miers it is usually smooth in this variety.

Distribution. Red Sea, Rodriguez, Malay Archipelago, Samoa, New Caledonia, Tahiti, Fijis.

Genus MENIPPE, De Haan.

75. MENIPPE RUMPHII (Fabr.).

M. Rumphii (Fabr.), De Man, Mergui Crust. p. 36 (1887), *ubi synon.*

(= *Pseudocarcinus Belangeri*, Milne-Edw.).

Rameswaram, an adult male; Tuticorin, two males (*Thurston*); Ceylon (*Haly*); Madras, an adult male (*Day*). Not uncommon at Madras and elsewhere on the Coromandel coast (*J. R. H.*).

In the Rameswaram specimen the carapace is 51 mm. long and 73 mm. broad, while the larger hand is 66 mm. long, measured along the lower border and including the immobile finger. The Madras specimen collected by Day has the curved line with a forward convexity, which runs across the branchial region of the carapace to the middle of the gastro-branchial groove, bounded in front by a series of six flattened pustular elevations.

Distribution. Bay of Bengal (Tranquebar, Nicobars, and Mergui), Malay Archipelago.

Genus OZIUS, Milne-Edwards.

76. OZIUS TUBERCULOSUS, Milne-Edw.

O. tuberculosus (Milne-Edw.), A. Milne-Edwards, Nouv. Arch. Mus. Hist. Nat. t. ix. p. 238, pl. xi fig. 2 (1873).

Ceylon (*Italy*).

Distribution. Mauritius, Nicobars, Mergui, New Caledonia.

Genus EPIXANTHUS, Heller.

77. EPIXANTHUS FRONTALIS (Milne-Edw.).

E. frontalis (Milne-Edw.), A. Milne-Edwards, Nouv. Arch. Mus. Hist. Nat. t. ix. p. 241 (1873).

Ceylon, an adult male (*Nevill*); Nicobars, three specimens (*Day*).

The Ceylon male is 22·5 mm. long and 38 mm. broad; a female with ova from the Nicobars is 13 mm. long and 21 mm. broad. The right chelipede is greatly enlarged in the male, and a wide hiatus appears between the fingers; the fingers of the left chelipede are slender, incurved, and in contact throughout their length.

Distribution. From the Red Sea and E. Africa to Japan and New Caledonia.

78. EPIXANTHUS DENTATUS (White).

Panopæus dentatus (White), Adams & White, ' Samarang ' Crust. p. 41, pl. xi. fig. 1 (1848).

Epixanthus dentatus (White), Miers, Ann. Mag. Nat. Hist. ser. 5, vol. v. p. 233 (1880).

(= *E. dilatatus*, De Man, *Panopæus acutidens*, Hasw.).

Nicobars, an adult female (*Day*).

The carapace is 27 mm. long and 17 mm. broad, slightly broader proportionately than in either of White's types, but this is perhaps a sexual characteristic. The chelipedes, legs, and marginal parts of the carapace are slightly hirsute, while the hairs appear to have been rubbed off in the types. Purplish reticulating lines are present on the surface of the carapace.

Distribution. Mergui, Philippines, Java, N. Australia.

Genus ACTUMNUS, Dana.

79. ACTUMNUS SETIFER (De Haan).

A. setifer (De Haan), A. Milne-Edwards, Nouv. Arch. Mus. Hist. Nat. t. i. p. 287, pl. xviii. fig. 5 (1865); Miers, ' Alert ' Crust. p. 225 (1884).

(= *A. tomentosus*, Dana).

Muttuwartu Par, a young male (*Thurston*); Gulf of Martaban, three young specimens (*Oates*).

Distribution. Mauritius, Malay Archipelago, Japan, N., N.E., and W. Australia, New Caledonia, New Hebrides, Tahiti, Fijis.

**80. ACTUMNUS VERRUCOSUS, n. sp.	(Pl. XXXVI. figs. 15, 16.)**

Tuticorin, a series of both sexes; Muttuwartu Par (*Thurston*).

The carapace is very convex, covered with a short brown pubescence, and provided with a series of remarkable granulated lobes. The frontal margin is granulated and four-lobed, the rounded prominent submedian lobes separated by a narrow median fissure, the outer lobes of small size. The antero-lateral margin has four prominent, subequal, granulated or subspinose lobes, while the postero-lateral margin is smooth and deeply excavated; the upper orbital margin is granulated and has two well-marked fissures. The granulated lobes on the carapace are arranged as follows :—on the anterior gastric region, behind the front, two pairs, of which the posterior is much larger; on the posterior gastric region three lobules, one median and anterior, two posterior; on each protogastric or lateral gastric region a peculiar W-shaped lobule; on the cardiac region two lobules which are slightly excavated in the centre; on the branchial region three lobules, anterior, postero-external (which is the largest of the three), and a postero-internal one placed external to and between the posterior gastric and cardiac lobules.

The right chelipede is slightly larger than the left in both sexes; both are clothed with a short pubescence on the outer surface of the carpus and hand, except towards the base of the immobile finger. The carpus is sparingly tuberculate externally, with a sulcus running parallel to the articulation with the hand, and separated from the latter by a tuberculated strip; the outer surface of the hand is strongly tuberculate, the tubercles with more or less acute apices, rather closely crowded and without any definite arrangement. The fingers are short, with white and obtuse tips, and the immobile one is placed in a straight line with the lower border of the hand; the dactylus is tuberculated superiorly on its proximal half, and a prominent tooth is present on either finger. The ambulatory legs are simply pubescent. The abdomen is smooth and seven-jointed in both sexes. The external maxillipedes are smooth, with a faint impressed line in the middle of the proximal two-thirds of the ischium. The basal joint of the antennal peduncle is joined to the subfrontal process, and the terminal joints lie in the orbital hiatus.

The largest specimen (a male) has the carapace 18·5 mm. long and 25·3 mm. broad, the lower margin of the hand and immobile finger 18 mm., mobile finger 9·7 mm., height of hand 11·5 mm. There is great disparity shown in the size of adult females (carrying ova) from the same locality—the largest is 18 mm. long and 25 mm. broad, while the smallest is 9 mm. long and 11·5 mm. broad.

This well-marked species in general appearance comes nearest to *A. globulus*, Heller, from the Red Sea and Zanzibar, but the latter has the carapace differently lobulated and the antero-lateral margin with only three projections.

Genus PILUMNUS, Leach.

81. PILUMNUS VESPERTILIO (Fabr.).

P. vespertilio (Fabr.), Miers, Ann. Mag. Nat. Hist. ser. 5, vol. v. p. 234 (1880), *ubi synon.*
(= *P. ursulus*, Adams & White, *P. mus*, Dana).

Rameswaram and Tuticorin, many specimens (*Thurston*); Ceylon (*Haly*); Rameswaram, very common on the reef and between tide-marks (*J. R. H.*).

Distribution. From the Red Sea and E. Africa to Japan, Australia, and the Pacific.

82. PILUMNUS LABYRINTHICUS, Miers.

P. labyrinthicus, Miers, ' Alert ' Crust. p. 224, pl. xxii. fig. C (1884).

Rameswaram, a single specimen (*J. R. H.*).

This specimen, though probably young (carapace 4 mm. long and 5 mm. broad), shows the very characteristic markings or lines on its dorsal surface, which bear some resemblance to a face.

Distribution. N. Australia, Singapore.

Genus TRAPEZIA, Latr.

83. TRAPEZIA CYMODOCE (Herbst).

T. Cymodoce (Herbst), Miers, Ann. Mag. Nat. Hist. ser. 5, vol. ii. p. 409 (1878), *ubi synon.*
(= *T. dentifrons*, Latr., *T. hirtipes*, Jacq. & Lucas, *T. cærulea*, Heller, *T. dentata*, A. Milne-Edw.).

Rameswaram, Tuticorin, and Muttuwartu Par; many specimens (*Thurston*). Very common on the reef at Rameswaram (*J. R. H.*).

Distribution. Red Sea, Mascarenes, Malay Archipelago, N. Australia, Pacific.

84. TRAPEZIA RUFOPUNCTATA (Herbst).

T. rufopunctata (Herbst), De Man, Brock's Crust. p. 318, Taf. xiii. fig. 1 (1888).

Tuticorin, a female with ova (*Thurston*); Ceylon (*Haly*).
Distribution. Malay Archipelago, Pacific.

85. TRAPEZIA MACULATA (MacLeay).

T. maculata (MacLeay), Dana, Crust. U.S. Explor. Exped. vol. i. p. 256, pl. xv. fig. 4 (1852); De Man, Brock's Crust. p. 319, Taf. xiii. fig. 2 (1888).
             (= ? *T. guttata*, Rüppell).

Ceylon (*Haly*).

This species is closely allied to the last, but their distinctive features have been recently pointed out by Dr. De Man, in his Report on the Crustacea collected by Dr. Brock in the Malay Archipelago. Both species are probably widely distributed, but it is impossible, owing to the confusion that formerly existed, to determine which form is referred to in connexion with many of the recorded localities.

Distribution. Red Sea, E. Africa, Amirantes, Mauritius, Rodriguez.

86. TRAPEZIA AREOLATA, Dana.

T. areolata, Dana, Crust. U.S. Explor. Exped. vol. i. p. 259, pl. xv. fig. 8 (1852); De Man, Brock's Crust. p. 317 (1888).

Ceylon (*Haly*).
Distribution. Malay Archipelago, New Caledonia, Tahiti.

Genus TETRALIA, Dana.

87. TETRALIA GLABERRIMA (Herbst).

T. glaberrima (Herbst), De Man, Brock's Crust. p. 321 (1888).
(= *T. armata*, Dana, *T. cavimana*, Heller, ? *T. heterodactyla*, Heller, *T. nigrifrons*, Dana).

Tuticorin, a female; Muttuwartu Par, two males (*Thurston*); Rameswaram, several specimens (*J. R. II.*).

It is very doubtful whether all the described species of this genus should not be referred to a single variable species. Most of the specimens I have observed had the front and anterior half of the lateral margin of the carapace edged with brown, as in *T. nigrifrons*, Dana, and in some the merus of the chelipedes carries the same colour anteriorly and distally, while brown spots are apparent at the distal end of the meri and propodi of the ambulatory legs. The pit or hollow, characteristic of *T. carimana*, Heller, and which occurs on the outer proximal surface of the hand, is usually present, but of varying extent. An adult measured 7·5 mm. long and 7 mm. broad.

Distribution. Red Sea. Natal. Mascarenes. Malay Archipelago. Australian seas, Pacific.

Genus ERIPHIA, Latr.

88. ERIPHIA LÆVIMANA, Latr.

E. lævimana (Latr.), De Man, Mergui Crust. p. 68 1887).

Rameswaram and Tuticorin, many specimens (*Thurston*); Ceylon (*Haly, Nevill*): Rameswaram, common on the reef and among blocks of dead coral between tide-marks (*J. R. II.*).

All the specimens I have examined belong to the typical form, none showing any trace of granulation or tuberculation on the outer surface of the larger chela, as in the variety *Smithii* of MacLeay. A female with ova from Rameswaram is noteworthy on account of its large size, the carapace measuring 58 mm. in length and 72 mm. in breadth ; the propodus of the right chela 62 mm., measured along its lower border.

Distribution. East Africa and Natal, Mauritius, Malay Archipelago, China, Japan. N. Australia, Pacific.

Genus NEPTUNUS, De Haan.

89. NEPTUNUS PELAGICUS (Linn.).

N. pelagicus (L.), A. Milne-Edwards, Nouv. Arch. Mus. Hist. Nat. t. x. p. 320 (1861 .

Tuticorin (*Thurston*); Ceylon (*Haly*) ; Bombay, Sind, Malabar, Akyab (*Day*). Very common on the S. Indian coast (*J. R. II.*).

Distribution. From the Red Sea and E. Africa to the Pacific.

90. NEPTUNUS GLADIATOR (Fabr.).

N. gladiator (Fabr.), A. Milne-Edwards, Nouv. Arch. Mus. Hist. Nat. t. x. p. 330 (1861).

Rameswaram (*Thurston*); Gulf of Martaban (*Oates*); Ceylon (*Haly*). Common at Madras (*J. R. II.*).

A male from Rameswaram measures 26 mm. long and 18 mm. broad (including the lateral spines).

Distribution. From India to Japan and N. Australia.

91. NEPTUNUS SANGUINOLENTUS (Herbst).

N. sanguinolentus (Herbst), A. Milne-Edwards, Nouv. Arch. Mus. Hist. Nat. t. x. p. 319 (1861).

Rameswaram (*Thurston*) ; Ceylon (*Haly*) ; Sind, Bombay, Madras (*Day*).   Very common on the S. Indian coast (*J. R. H.*).

Distribution. Mascarenes, Malay Archipelago, Japan, Australia, Sandwich Islands.

92. NEPTUNUS ARGENTATUS, White.

N. argentatus (White), A. Milne-Edwards, Nouv. Arch. Mus. Hist. Nat. t. x. p. 332, pl. xxi. fig. 4 (1861) ; Miers, ' Challenger ' Brachyura, p. 177 (1886).

Gulf of Martaban, four specimens (*Oates*).

The largest specimen (a female with ova) measures 15 mm. long and 27 mm. broad, including the lateral spines.   This species is characterized by the presence of a silvery metallic lustre on the ridges of the chelipedes, on the transverse ridges of the abdomen, and elsewhere, still visible both in the above recorded spirit specimens and in White's dried types.   It is very closely allied to *N. gladiator*, of which species Miers regarded it as constituting a variety, but I am inclined to consider the two as distinct.   It is a smaller species than *N. gladiator* ; the ridge on the outer surface of the hand is much more prominent, as also are the ridges on the second and third abdominal segments ; while a black spot is present towards the apex of the swimming dactylus as in *N. hastatoides*, but which is not seen in *N. gladiator*.   There are also differences in the form of the abdomen —more particularly of the female—in the two species.   The median frontal spines are scarcely less developed than in some young specimens of *N. gladiator*, and there is a rudimentary tooth on the supraorbital margin, as in young *N. gladiator*, but in older individuals of the latter this becomes a prominent spine.

Distribution. Borneo (*White*) ; Celebes Sea (*Miers*).

93. NEPTUNUS HASTATOIDES (Fabr.).

N. hastatoides (Fabr.), A. Milne-Edwards, Nouv. Arch. Mus. Hist. Nat. t. x. p. 332 (1861).

Gulf of Martaban, a series including two with *Sacculina* (*Oates*).   Common at Madras (*J. R. H.*).

A female is 20 mm. long and 31 mm. broad, not including the lateral spines.   In this species the posterior angles of the carapace are acute and terminate in spinules—the character on which Prof. A. Milne-Edwards has founded his subgenus *Hellenus*.   The lateral spines are longer than in *N. gladiator* ; the posterior gastric granulated elevations are more pronounced, so as to become almost tubercular ; and the distal half of the swimming dactylus is dark in colour.

Distribution. From India to Japan and N. Australia.

94. NEPTUNUS ANDERSONI, De Man.

N. Andersoni, De Man, Mergui Crust. p. 70, pl. iv. figs. 3, 4 (1887).

Gulf of Martaban, ten specimens (*Oates*).

I refer these with some doubt to *N. Andersoni*, as I have not had an opportunity of comparing them with De Man's type; but they agree on the whole with his description and figures. In all the specimens the distance between the external orbital angles is about equal to the length of the carapace, the character on which De Man lays most stress in distinguishing the species from *N. hastatoides.* The arms of the chelipedes are variable in length, but scarcely so short, even in females, as represented by De Man. The characters of the front are not stated in the original description, as the single type-specimen was injured in this respect; in the Martaban examples the two median frontal teeth are obtuse and of small size, being less prominent than the lateral teeth, whereas in *N. rugosus,* A. Milne-Edw., with which De Man also compares his species, there is but a single median tooth. The carapace carries seven antero-lateral teeth between the external orbital angle and the long lateral spine, and these teeth, especially the anterior ones, are usually shorter and more obtuse than represented in De Man's figure. The postero-lateral angles of the carapace terminate in a somewhat obtuse tooth, whereas De Man describes it as a spinule. I have some doubt whether the specimens are not referable to a stunted variety of *N. hastatoides,* for, on examining a large series of the latter, I find variation in the direction of the characters assigned to *N. Andersoni;* the characteristic black spot is, however, absent from the swimming dactylus.

The largest specimen—a female with ova—has the carapace only 9 mm. long and 14 mm. broad, not including the lateral spines.

Distribution. Mergui (*De Man*).

95. NEPTUNUS TUBERCULOSUS, A. Milne-Edw.

N. tuberculosus, A. Milne-Edwards, Nouv. Arch. Mus. Hist. Nat. t. x. p. 333, pl. xxxi. fig. 5 (1861).
N. Brockii, De Man, Brock's Crust. p. 328, Taf. xiii. fig. 4 (1888).

Gulf of Martaban, four specimens (*Oates*).

De Man, when describing *N. Brockii,* stated that it might possibly prove to be identical with *N. tuberculosus,* and the above specimens certainly tend to confirm this opinion. There can be no doubt, I think, that they are identical with the species so well described and figured by De Man. At the same time the median frontal projections are slightly larger than shown in his figure, and they project as far forwards as the contiguous pair, as in *N. tuberculosus;* while, as regards the lateral spines of the carapace, the second, fourth, and sixth are smaller than the others, an arrangement which is indicated in the figures of both writers. In the largest specimen the hand is almost as described by De Man, though a rudimentary spine can be made out over the base of the mobile finger; in a younger specimen, a second small spine is seen near the articulation with the carpus and on the outer surface, as described by A. Milne-Edwards, and his description was evidently taken from a young individual. I thus imagine the two species are identical. In all probability we have to deal with a species in which certain spines, present in the young, diminish in size or altogether disappear in the adult.

The carapace of the largest specimen (a female) is 12·5 mm. long and 22 mm. broad, including the lateral spines; it has a swelling on the left side, evidently due to the presence of a Bopyrid.

Distribution. Sandwich Is. (*A. Milne-Edwards*): Aru Is. (*Miers*): Amboina (*De Man*).

96. NEPTUNUS ARMATUS, A. Milne-Edw.

N. armatus, A. Milne-Edwards, Nouv. Arch. Mus. Hist. Nat. t. x. p. 322. pl. xxxiii. fig. 2 (1861).

Rameswaram, five specimens (*J. R. H.*).

The types of this species are preserved in the British Museum. The surface of the carapace is finely granulated, and the lateral spines are strongly developed, though somewhat shorter in my specimens than in the types. The outer surface of the carpus and propodus of the chelipedes carries a series of finely granulated ridges, with the intervening surface smooth; two fainter ridges are seen on the inner surface of the propodus. The fingers, with the exception of their tips, are dark in colour, and there is a well-defined black spot on the inner surface of the palm near the insertion of the dactylus; the first tooth of the dactylus, as in some other Portunids, is enormously developed.

The carapace of the largest specimen is 17 mm. long and 30·5 mm. broad, not including the lateral spines, which are each about 5 mm. long. A. Milne-Edwards gives the length as 13 mm. and the breadth as 50 mm., but reference to the types and to his figure shows that there is some mistake, probably in the length noted.

Distribution. West Australia (*A. Milne-Edwards*).

97. NEPTUNUS SIEBOLDI, A. Milne-Edw.

N. Sieboldi, A. Milne-Edwards, Nouv. Arch. Mus. Hist. Nat. t. x. p. 323. pl. xxxv. fig. 5 (1861).

Muttuwartu Par, a male (*Thurston*).

This species may be recognized by its four similar, subobtuse frontal projections, the short lateral spines of the carapace, the unarmed hinder margin of the merus of the chelipedes, and the strongly ridged hand, the ridges being seen even on the inner surface. In the Muttuwartu specimen, the median notch or fissure of the front is deeper and narrower than the one on either side, whereas in A. Milne-Edwards's figure they are equally deep and narrow.

The carapace is 12 mm. long and 18 mm. broad.

Distribution. Mauritius (*A. Milne-Edwards, Miers*).

Genus XIPHONECTES, A. Milne-Edw.

98. XIPHONECTES LONGISPINOSUS (Dana).

X. longispinosus (Dana), Miers, 'Challenger' Brachyura, p. 183 (1886), *ubi synon.*
(=*X. leptocheles*, A. Milne-Edw.; *Amphitrite vigilans*, Dana).

Gulf of Martaban, a male and a female (*Oates*).

The genus founded for the reception of this variable species comes very near to *Neptunus*, and perhaps the two should be united. The larger specimen (female) is 0·7 mm. long and 9·5 mm. broad.

Distribution. From the Seychelles to the Pacific (New Caledonia, Tongatabu, &c.).

99. ACHELOUS GRANULATUS (Milne-Edw.).

A. granulatus (Milne-Edw.), A. Milne-Edwards, Nouv. Arch. Mus. Hist. Nat. t. x. p. 344 (1861).

Gulf of Martaban, six specimens (*Oates*).

The largest male is 14 mm. long and 19·5 mm. broad, while a female with ova is somewhat smaller. The same silvery sheen is seen as in *Neptunus argentatus*, though much less strongly marked in the present species.

Distribution. From the Red Sea and E. Africa to Japan and the Pacific (New Caledonia. Sandwich Is., Fiji Is.).

100. ACHELOUS WHITEI, A. Milne-Edw.

A. Whitei, A. Milne-Edwards, Nouv. Arch. Mus. Hist. Nat. t. x. p. 343, pl. xxxi. fig. 6 (1861).
(=? *Neptunus gracilimanus*, Stm.).

Gulf of Martaban, seven specimens (*Oates*). Common at Madras (*J. R. H.*).

This species may be recognized at once by its remarkable chelipedes, the merus of which is long and very broad, while the more distal joints, and especially the fingers, are extremely slender; the fingers also are acute and slightly upturned. *Neptunus gracilimanus,* Stimpson, is probably identical with *A. Whitei*; the description of the former agrees with that of the present species, and the posterior lateral spine is distinctly longer than those in front of it, especially in young individuals, which gives the species almost the appearance of a *Neptunus*. Indeed, it shows that *Neptunus* and *Achelous* can scarcely be separated, though it is perhaps convenient to retain the latter term for those forms in which the lateral spines are greatly reduced.

The largest specimen (a female) is 19 mm. long and 30 mm. broad, not including the lateral spines; the merus of the left chelipede is 17·5 mm. long and 8 mm. broad; the carpus and propodus 30 mm. long, and the greatest breadth or height of the hand 4 mm.

Distribution. Borneo (*A. Milne-Edwards*); south of New Guinea (*Miers*).

101. ACHELOUS ORBICULARIS, Richters.

A. orbicularis, Richters, Beiträge zur Meeresfauna der Insel Mauritius und der Seychellen, p. 153, Taf. xvi. figs. 14, 15 (1880).

Gulf of Martaban, two males (*Oates*).

The carapace is narrow, smooth, and depressed, with the nine antero-lateral teeth subequal in size, or even diminishing slightly on passing backwards; the postero-lateral margin is almost straight and without any concavity. The front is six-toothed, and the median teeth minute. The merus of the chelipedes is enlarged, angulated externally, and with two spines on the posterior margin.

In the larger specimen the carapace is 8·5 mm. long and 10·5 mm. broad; the distance between the external orbital angles is 7·6 mm.

Distribution. Seychelles (*Richters*).

Genus SCYLLA, De Haan.

102. SCYLLA SERRATA (Forskål).

S. serrata (Forsk.), A. Milne-Edwards, Nouv. Arch. Mus. Hist. Nat. t. x. p. 349 (1861).

Calcutta (*Day*); Ceylon (*Haly*). Abundant in the S. Indian backwaters (*J. R. H.*). This is the chief edible crab of India.

Distribution. From the Red Sea, E. and S. Africa, to Japan, the Fiji Is., and New Zealand.

Genus THALAMITA, Latreille.

103. THALAMITA PRYMNA (Herbst).

T. prymna (Herbst), De Man, Mergui Crust. p. 75, pl. iv. figs. 5, 6 (1887).

Rameswaram and Tuticorin (*Thurston*). Rameswaram, common between tide-marks; Madras (*J. R. H.*).

These belong to the typical form of the species as characterized by De Man. The carapace is smooth, with the exception of the first transverse line, placed behind the orbital margin, which usually carries a fringe of hairs; the natatory legs are also provided with a short marginal fringe. The ridge on the basal joint of the antennal peduncle has two or more spinules, the first of which is well-developed, acute, and usually with traces of a compound origin.

A male from Rameswaram has the carapace 44 mm. long and 62 mm. broad, the right hand 52 mm. long. A female from Tuticorin is 32 mm. long and 45 mm. broad, the right hand 32 mm. long.

Distribution. Indian Ocean, Mergui, Malay Archipelago, Japan, Australia, New Caledonia.

104. THALAMITA ADMETE (Herbst).

T. Admete (Herbst), A. Milne-Edwards, Nouv. Arch. Mus. Hist. Nat. t. x. p. 356 (1861).

Rameswaram (*Thurston, J. R. H.*); Gulf of Martaban (*Oates*).

The carapace is only slightly pubescent, and the chelipedes are devoid of granules. The outer surface of the hand is glabrous, and only carries faint raised lines, the usual spines being present on the upper surface.

A female with ova is 10 mm. long and 15 mm. broad.

Distribution. From the Red Sea and Natal to Ousima Is., the Fijis, and the Sandwich Islands.

105. THALAMITA SAVIGNYI, A. Milne-Edw.

T. Savignyi, A. Milne-Edwards, Nouv. Arch. Mus. Hist. Nat. t. x. p. 357 (1861).

Tuticorin, many specimens (*Thurston*); Rameswaram (*J. R. H.*).

This species only differs from *T. Admete* in having the carapace more strongly granulated, as well as the chelipedes, the hand being provided with several longitudinal granulated lines on its outer surface, and granules are scattered over the intervening areas, especially on the upper surface. There is a good deal to be said in favour of Miers's view, that it is probably only a variety of *T. Admete*, to which species it was originally referred by Audouin ; the amount of granulation certainly varies considerably in a series of specimens.

The largest male is 12·5 mm. long and 19 mm. broad, and the largest female is nearly the same size; but some females with ova are of much smaller size, a disparity which has been noted by De Man.

Distribution. Red Sea (*Savigny, Miers*). Mergui (*De Man*), N.W. Australia (*Miers*), New Caledonia (*A. Milne-Edwards*).

106. THALAMITA SIMA, Milne-Edw.

T. sima (Milne-Edw.), A. Milne-Edwards, Nouv. Arch. Mus. Hist. Nat. t. x. p. 359 (1861).
  (= *T. arcuatus*, De Haan).

Tuticorin, two females with ova (*Thurston*).

I refer these specimens with some hesitation to *T. sima*, and possibly they belong to a distinct and undescribed species. The first three antero-lateral teeth are very broad basally, and merely separated by narrow fissures, with their apices subacute, whereas in the typical *T. sima*, as figured by De Haan, these teeth are more prominent and acute, with wider intervening fissures. The carapace is finely granulated and the elevated lines rather poorly marked ; the front is regularly arcuate, with the median notch scarcely represented. The outer surface of the hand is almost smooth. In *T. Chaptali*, Aud., which is recorded by Miers from Ceylon ('Alert' Crust. p. 231), and in which the antero-lateral teeth are also obtuse, the last tooth, unlike what is seen in our specimens and in the typical form, is slightly smaller than the preceding tooth.

The larger specimen is 10 mm. long and 14·5 mm. broad.

Distribution. Malay Archipelago, China, Japan, New Caledonia, Australia, and New Zealand.

107. THALAMITA INTEGRA, Dana.

T. integra, Dana, Crust. U.S. Explor. Exped. pt. 1, p. 281, pl. xvii. fig. 6 (1852) ; A. Milne-Edwards, Nouv. Arch. Mus. Hist. Nat. t. x. p. 358 (1861).

Tuticorin (*Thurston*) ; Rameswaram, not uncommon (*J. R. H.*) ; Gulf of Martaban (*Oates*).

In this species a characteristic dark band encircles the fingers near their apices, but the apices themselves are white.

Distribution. E. Africa, Malay Archipelago, and the Pacific (Fiji, Sandwich Is., &c.). The var. *africana* of Miers occurs in the Atlantic area (Senegambia and Canaries).

108. THALAMITA SEXLOBATA, Miers.

T. sexlobata, Miers, 'Challenger' Brachyura, p. 196, pl. xvi. fig. 2 (1886).

Tuticorin, a male (*Thurston*).

This species is distinguished by its six-lobed front and by its very minute fourth antero-lateral spine. The chelipedes are crossed by strigose lines, which are specially noticeable on the upper and distal surface of the merus, the under surface of the propodus, and which are even seen on the inner surface of the latter joint; similar pubescent lines are also met with running longitudinally on the ambulatory legs. The sternal region, anteriorly and at the sides, is seen with a lens to be very finely granulated. In Miers's figure the last antero-lateral spine is more prominent than in my specimen, the fingers are longer in relation to the palm, and of the two spines on the upper margin of the palm the posterior one is much larger than the anterior, while in the Tuticorin example it is only slightly larger. These differences are, however, probably not of much importance.

The carapace is 8 mm. long and 10·5 mm. broad.

Distribution. Tongatabu, 18 fathoms (*Miers*).

Genus GONIOSOMA, A. Milne-Edwards.

109. GONIOSOMA CRUCIFERUM (Fabr.).

G. *cruciferum* (Fabr.), De Man, Mergui Crust. p. 79, pl. v. fig. 1 (1887).

Tuticorin (*Thurston*) ; Ceylon (*Haly*) ; Akyab (*Day*) ; Madras. not uncommon (*J. R. H.*).

Distribution. Indian Ocean, Malay Archipelago, China, Japan, E. Australia.

110. GONIOSOMA AFFINE (Dana).

G. *affine* (Dana), De Man, Mergui Crust. p. 80, pl. v. fig. 2 (1887).

Madras, three adult males and one female (*J. R. H.*).

The carapace of a male is 33 mm. long and 47 mm. broad, not including the lateral spines.

Distribution. Singapore (*Dana*) ; Mergui (*De Man*).

111. GONIOSOMA NATATOR (Herbst).

G. *natator* (Herbst), De Man, Brock's Crust. p. 331, Taf. xiii. fig. 5 (1888).
(= *Charybdis granulatus*, De Haan).

Rameswaram, three males (*Thurston*); Ceylon (*Haly*); Madras (*J. R. H.*).

A Rameswaram specimen is 58 mm. long and 87 mm. broad ; the right hand measured along its lower border 76 mm.

Distribution. Natal, Mascarenes, Malay Archipelago, China, Japan.

112. GONIOSOMA LUCIFERUM (Fabr.).

G. *luciferum* (Fabr.), De Man, Mergui Crust. p. 83, footnote (1887).
(= G. *quadrimaculatum*, A. Milne-Edw.).

Ceylon (*Haly*).

Distribution. Malabar ; Java (*A. Milne-Edwards*).

113. GONIOSOMA ANNULATUM (Fabr.).

G. *annulatum* (Fabr.), A. Milne-Edwards, Nouv. Arch. Mus. Hist. Nat. t. x. p. 371 (1861)
(= *G. orientale*, Heller).

Rameswaram and Tuticorin (*Thurston*); Madras (*J. R. H.*).

In all the specimens violet rings are present on the legs. Miers regarded *G. sexdentatum* (Rüpp.) as scarcely distinct from this species, and, according to De Man, *G. annulatum* is itself perhaps merely a younger state of *G. luciferum*; but the size of a Rameswaram specimen scarcely confirms this, for the carapace is 54 mm. long and 77 mm. broad, the left hand 69 mm. along its lower border. There can be little doubt, however, that a revision of the genus *Goniosoma*, founded on the examination of a large series of specimens from different localities, would result in the union of several of the species as at present constituted.

Distribution. From Madagascar to the Malay Archipelago.

114. GONIOSOMA HELLERII, A. Milne-Edw.

G. *Hellerii*, A. Milne-Edwards, Bull. Soc. Entom. France, t. vii. p. 282 (1867).
G. *merguiense*, De Man, Mergui Crust. p. 82, pl. v. figs. 3, 4 (1887).

Tuticorin (*Thurston*); Ceylon (*Haly*); Rameswaram (*J. R. H.*).

These specimens are identical with *G. merguiense*, but De Man has recently pointed out, in his Report on the Decapoda collected in the Malay Archipelago by Dr. Brock, that this species is probably identical with *G. Hellerii*, and the descriptions of the two certainly agree. *G. spiniferum*, Miers, from Queensland, is closely allied, but differs in having the posterior margin of the penultimate joint of the swimming-feet not denticulated. *G. Hellerii* is distinguished from *G. luciferum* and *G. annulatum* by the form of the antero-lateral teeth, the last of which is always longer than the others; the carpal joints of the swimming-legs have an acute spine on the under surface, and in adults both the antero-lateral and the frontal teeth are very acute.

An adult male from Tuticorin is 38 mm. long and 52 mm. broad, the right hand 48 mm. long.

Distribution. New Caledonia (*A. Milne-Edwards*); Mergui, Amboina (*De Man*).

115. GONIOSOMA ERYTHRODACTYLUM (Lam.).

G. *erythrodactylum* (Lam.), A. Milne-Edwards, Nouv. Arch. Mus. Hist. Nat. t. x. p. 369 (1861).

Ceylon (*Haly*).

Distribution. Red Sea (*De Man*); Marquesas Islands and Moluccas (*A. Milne-Edwards*).

116. GONIOSOMA ORIENTALE (Dana).

Charybdis orientalis, Dana, Crust. U.S. Explor. Exped. pt. 1, p. 285, pl. xvii. fig. 10 (1852).
G. *orientale* (Dana), A. Milne-Edwards, Nouv. Arch. Mus. Hist. Nat. t. x. p. 383 (1861).
(= *G. dubium*, Hoffmann).

Tuticorin, six specimens (*Thurston*); Ceylon (*Haly*).

54*

This species does not appear to be common; in fact Prof. A. Milne-Edwards had not met with specimens when he wrote his Revision of the Portunidæ. It is distinguished by the rudimentary state of the second lateral spine of the carapace, which is very minute, and appears as if merely a portion of the first spine; the remaining antero-lateral spines are practically subequal. The median and submedian frontal teeth are obtusely rounded and subequal, while the two outermost teeth on each side are more or less triangular. The merus of the chelipedes carries two or three spines on its anterior margin, while the posterior margin is unarmed; the carpus has a large spine on its upper surface, and three spinules on the outer surface; the hand has three finely-granulated ridges on its outer surface, two spines on the upper margin, and two on the outer surface, one of the latter placed at the articulation with the carpus. The fingers are slightly ridged externally. The penultimate joint of the swimming-legs is spinulose along its posterior margin, and a prominent spine is placed on the posterior margin near the distal end of the merus.

The largest specimen, a female without eggs, is 11 mm. long and 17 mm. broad, while a second female, carrying eggs, is considerably smaller.

Distribution. Philippines (*Dana*); Timor (*De Man*); Réunion (*Hoffmann*).

117. GONIOSOMA ORNATUM, A. Milne-Edw.

G. *ornatum*, A. Milne-Edwards, Nouv. Arch. Mus. Hist. Nat. t. x. p. 376 (1861).

(= *Thalamita truncata*, De Haan).

Madras, not uncommon (*J. R. H.*).

The carapace of a male is 21 mm. long and 30 mm. broad, the right chelipede 35 mm. long; a female with ova is 15 mm. long and 22 mm. broad. Specimens in the British Museum are considerably larger.

Distribution. Malay Archipelago; Japan.

118. GONIOSOMA VARIEGATUM (Fabr.).

G. *variegatum* (Fabr.), Miers, ' Alert ' Crust. p. 232 (1881).

Madras, very common (*J. R. H.*); Bombay (*Day*); Kurachi (*Brit. Mus.*).

In this species, and in the form which I term var. *callianassa*, the frontal teeth are more or less obtusely rounded in the adult, the last lateral spine of the carapace is about twice the length of the preceding spines, the hands are somewhat swollen, and the carapace is pubescent. De Haan seems to have regarded the two forms as belonging to distinct species; on the other hand, A. Milne-Edwards probably united both in his G. *callianassa.* In what I regard as the typical form, the median frontal projections are very obtusely rounded, the surface of the carapace is finely punctate when the hairs are removed, and the transverse ridges are only moderately developed, there being none on the branchial area, and they are only faintly seen on the cardiac area. The merus of the chelipedes has usually two spines on its anterior margin, and there are also two spines on the upper surface of the hand; the ridges on the outer surface of the hand are smooth, while on the inner surface they are almost obsolete; the under surface of the hand is perfectly smooth and glabrous. The posterior surface of the three pairs of ambulatory legs is smooth. The penultimate segment of the male abdomen is not specially dilated. A *Sacculina* is frequently attached to the abdomen, and *Portunicepon Hendersonii*, Giard and Bonnier, occurs in the branchial chamber.

G. VARIEGATUM, var. CALLIANASSA (Herbst).

In the specimens which I refer to this variety, which also is common at Madras, the median frontal projections are less rounded, and the transverse ridges of the carapace are more strongly developed, especially two on the cardiac area, and there are two parallel lines on the branchial area. The merus of the chelipedes has usually three spines on the anterior margin; there are four spines on the upper surface of the hand, and strongly granulated ridges on both the inner and the outer surfaces of the hand. The whole surface of the chelipedes is more or less strigose, but more particularly the under surface of the hand. Longitudinal pubescent lines are met with on the posterior surface of the ambulatory legs. The penultimate joint of the male abdomen is so dilated as almost to form part of a circle in outline. The specimens are almost certainly identical with that figured by Herbst (Naturgesch. Krabben u. Krebse, pl. liv. fig. 7) as *Cancer callianassa*; at the same time they are probably the same as that figured by De Haan as *Portunus* (*Charybdis*) *variegatus*, Fabr. (Crust. Japon, tab. i. fig. 2).

I have examined a large series of both forms from Madras, and as a rule any specimen can be determined at once by the characters I have enumerated for each variety. I have met with a few specimens, however, in connexion with which some difficulty is experienced, and in which there appears to be an admixture of the two sets of characters.

The var. *bimaculatum*, Miers, taken by the 'Challenger' at Japan, is, I think, perhaps a distinct species; its frontal teeth are quite different in form and very obtuse; if it is really a variety of *G. variegatum*, there is an extraordinary range of variation in this species.

Distribution. Malay Archipelago, China, Japan, N. Australia. (It is impossible to say which variety is referred to in regard to the localities assigned to this species.)

119. GONIOSOMA ROSTRATUM, A. Milne-Edw.

G. rostratum, A. Milne-Edwards, Nouv. Arch. Mus. Hist. Nat. t. x. p. 379, pl. xxxv. fig. 2 (1861).

Sunderbunds and Calcutta, several specimens (*Day*); Gulf of Martaban, eight specimens (*Oates*).

This species is distinguished by the general form of its front, and especially by the great prominence of the median frontal teeth, which are obtusely rounded. In all the above-recorded specimens the last lateral spine of the carapace is considerably larger than those preceding it; but, judging from a larger and apparently full-grown specimen from the Hoogly, in the British Museum, this spine diminishes with age, for in this example it is scarcely larger than those in front of it.

The largest specimen is a female with a Bopyrid in its right branchial chamber; it measures 17 mm. in length and 20 mm. in breadth, including the lateral spines.

G. rostratum is also closely allied to *G. variegatum*, of which it may possibly prove to be a variety. The only important difference lies in the character of the front, and I have observed specimens of the latter species in which the median projections were more prominent than the others.

Distribution. Mouth of the Ganges (*A. Milne-Edwards*).

Genus LUPOCYCLUS, Adams & White.

120. LUPOCYCLUS INÆQUALIS (Walker).

Goniosoma inæquale, Walker, Journ. Linn. Soc., Zool. vol. xx. p. 116, pl. viii. fig. 1 (1887).

Gulf of Martaban, a male and a female (*Oates*).

The carapace is armed with nine lateral spines, of which the fourth, sixth, and eighth are rudimentary, especially the eighth, which is very minute, and the second is smaller than the third. *L. rotundatus*, Adams & White, has five lateral teeth, with a single minute one alternating in each interspace, but the carapace is more convex, proportionately narrower, and with a more prominent front. I am unable to say how *L. philippinensis*, Nauck, differs, as this species has only been very shortly and imperfectly characterized.

I think there can be little doubt that the above specimens are referable to Walker's species; at the same time, it ought to be placed in the genus *Lupocyclus*, on account of its general form, its peculiar front, and the basal antennal joint freely movable in the orbital hiatus.

The larger specimen, a female, is 12 mm. long and 15 mm. wide.

Distribution. Singapore (*Walker*).

Genus LISSOCARCINUS, Adams & White.

121. LISSOCARCINUS POLYBIOIDES, Adams & White.

L. polybioides, Adams & White, 'Samarang' Crust. p. 46, pl. xi. fig. 5 (1848).

Gulf of Martaban, a female (*Oates*).

This species is distinguished from *L. lævis*, Miers, by its flatter carapace, more prominent front, the lateral teeth, which gradually diminish in size on passing backwards, and a line runs in from the last lateral tooth on to the surface of the branchial region.

The carapace is 7·2 mm. long and 7 mm. broad.

Distribution. Borneo (*Adams & White*); Ceylon (*Miers*); Port Jackson (*Haswell*).

122. LISSOCARCINUS LÆVIS, Miers.

L. lævis, Miers, 'Challenger' Brachyura, p. 205, pl. xvii. fig. 3 (1886).

Tuticorin, a female with ova (*Thurston*); Gulf of Martaban, a single young specimen (*Oates*).

In this species the front is broad and not specially prominent. The first and fifth antero-lateral teeth are small, while the second, third, and fourth are larger and subequal. The hand is without spines.

The carapace of the Tuticorin example is 11 mm. long and 13·5 mm. broad.

Distribution. Celebes Sea. 10 fathoms (*Miers*).

Genus KRAUSSIA, Dana.

123. KRAUSSIA NITIDA, Stimpson. (Pl. XXXVII. fig. 9.)

K. nitida, Stimpson, Proc. Acad. Nat. Sci. Philad. Mar. 1858, p. 10; Miers, ' Alert ' Crust. p. 235 (1881).

Tuticorin, a female (*Thurston*); Madras coast (*J. R. H.*).

The front is quadrilobed, with the median slightly smaller than the outer lobes, and the margin of all finely crenulated and fringed with long brown hairs. A median and two lateral fissures on each side of the front are present, which, though obsolete, extend some distance back on the carapace, and the most external arises from the upper orbital margin. The carapace is minutely granulated anteriorly and towards the sides. The lateral margin is crenulated, with a slight tooth about one third of the distance back, and immediately in front of this the margin is slightly indented. The hands are finely granulated externally, and long hairs are present on the legs and on the meral joints of the chelipedes.

The Tuticorin specimen is 13·7 mm. long and 15 mm. broad.

Distribution. Chinese and Japanese Seas, on a sandy bottom at a depth of 20-24 fathoms (*Stimpson*); Torres Straits (*Miers*).

Group CATOMETOPA.

Genus HETEROPLAX, Stimpson.

124. HETEROPLAX NITIDUS, Miers.

H. nitidus, Miers, Proc. Zool. Soc. 1879, p. 39, pl. ii. fig. 2.

Gulf of Martaban, a male (*Oates*); Madras coast, several specimens, including females with ova (*J. R. H.*).

I have compared these with the type-specimen in the British Museum, and can find no difference except that the Indian specimens are somewhat smaller.

Distribution. Corean Straits. 10 fathoms (*Miers*).

Genus SCALOPIDIA, Stimpson.

125. SCALOPIDIA SPINOSIPES, Stimpson.

S. spinosipes, Stimpson, Proc. Acad. Nat. Sci. Philad., April 1858, p. 95.

Gulf of Martaban, an adult female (*Oates*).

I have compared this with typical specimens from Hong Kong, named by Stimpson, and presented to the British Museum by the Smithsonian Institution. The carapace is granulated and punctate, with an acute spinule at the posterior limit of the sharply defined antero-lateral margin. The hands are glabrous externally and sparingly punctate; curved spinules are present on the margins of the ambulatory legs.

The carapace is 11 mm. long and 15 mm. broad; the third ambulatory leg is 33 mm. long.

The genus *Hypophthalmus*, Richters (in Lenz and Richters' 'Beitrag zur Krustaceen-fauna von Madagascar '), is, as pointed out by Miers, synonymous with *Sealopidia*, and the *H. leucochirus*, Richters, apparently differs but little from Stimpson's species.

Distribution. Hong Kong. 5 fathoms (*Stimpson*).

Genus CARDISOMA, Latr.

126. CARDISOMA CARNIFEX (Herbst).

C. carnifex (Herbst), De Man, Max Weber's Crust. p. 285 (1891).
          (= *C. Urvillei*, Milne-Edw.).

Tuticorin (*Thurston*); Ceylon (*Haly*). A very common species found burrowing near the margins of the S. Indian backwaters (*J. R. H.*).

Distribution. From E. Africa to the Pacific (Samoa, Fijis. Sandwich Is.. &c.).

Genus TELPHUSA, Latr.

127. TELPHUSA INDICA. Latr.

T. indica (Latr.), Milne-Edwards, Crust. in Jacquemont's ' Voyage dans l'Inde,' p. 7, pl. ii. fig. 1 (1844); A. Milne-Edwards, Nouv. Arch. Mus. Hist. Nat. t. v. p. 181 (1869).

T. cunicularis, Westwood, Trans. Ent. Soc. vol. i. p. 183, pl. xix. fig. 1 (1836).

Very common in hill-streams at Kotagiri and elsewhere on the Nilgiri Hills, at an elevation of about 6000 feet (*J. R. H.*).

I sent a specimen to Prof. A. Milne-Edwards, who kindly informed me that it was referable to *T. indica*, the types of which are preserved in the Paris Natural History Museum; it is also identical with *T. cunicularis*, examples of which from Dukhan, Western Ghats, are in the collection of the British Museum.

The postfrontal ridge is strongly marked and continuous, being well marked even behind the inner canthus of the eye, and only interrupted by the mesogastric furrow; the cervical groove is also well defined. The carpal spine of the chelipedes is acute. The ischial line on the outer surface of the external maxillipedes is absent or faintly defined, and not prolonged to each end of the joint. The penultimate segment of the male abdomen has the lateral margins straight. The colour is a dark, almost black brown, paler in the young.

The carapace of a female is 35 mm. long and 50 mm. broad; of a male, 34 mm. long and 49·5 mm. broad.

Distribution. India : Western Ghats (Poona, &c.); South-east Berar : Chota Nagpur; Ranigunj : Parisnath Hill, at an elevation of 3000 feet ; Morar (*Wood-Mason*).

128. TELPHUSA LUGUBRIS, Wood-Mason.

T. lugubris, Wood-Mason, Journ. As. Soc. Bengal, vol. xl. p. 197, pl. xii. figs. 5–7 (1871).

"Environs of Calcutta." Coll. Schlagintweit, two specimens. (They are labelled *T. indica*, and more probably came from the Himalayas.) Nepal, an adult female (*Dr. J. Scully*).

These specimens completely agree with Wood-Mason's excellent description. The species is closely allied to *T. indica*, but may be distinguished as follows:—The post-frontal ridge is not placed so far back on the carapace as in *T. indica*, and is some-what wrinkled and ill-defined behind the inner canthus of the eye. The carpal spine is blunt. The ischial line on the outer surface of the external maxillipedes is well marked. The penultimate segment of the male abdomen has the lateral margins concave. The ridge connecting the epibranchial tooth with the external orbital angle is nearly straight, whereas in *T. indica* it is curved. The colour, as in the other species, is a very dark brown, and the epidermis readily peels off in *T. lugubris*.

The Nepal specimen has the carapace somewhat more convex than indicated by Wood-Mason, and seen in the other examples, but this is perhaps due to its being an adult female. It carries a large number of newly-hatched young attached to the swimmerets under the abdomen.

Distribution. North India: Sikkim, Nepal, and Khasi Hills (*Wood-Mason*).

129. TELPHUSA MASONIANA, n. sp. (Pl. XXXVII. figs. 1–4.)

River Jumna, a series; North-West Provinces, four males (*Day*); "India," two dried specimens (*Brit. Mus.*).

The carapace is scarcely depressed. The postfrontal ridge is well defined towards the sides, but the epigastric portions are wrinkled, and almost deficient behind the inner canthus of the eye; the mesogastric furrow is rather deep and slightly bifurcate posteriorly. The cervical groove is broad and well defined, not interrupting the post-frontal ridge; a very distinct anterior and posterior pair of puncta are present on the gastric region adjoining the cervical groove. Both the epibranchial tooth and the external orbital tooth are strongly developed. The branchial region of the carapace is swollen dorsally and laterally in its anterior portion, and numerous faint interrupted crenulated lines run transversely along the whole margin. The frontal margin is somewhat concave, and both it and the orbital margin are finely crenulated; the orbits are remarkably large and shallow.

The chelipedes are unequal, either the right or left being larger, and they are very similar to those of *T. lugubris*, with the exception that the carpal spine is prominent and acute. The external maxillipedes, and also the ambulatory legs, are similar to those of *T. lugubris*, but the ambulatory dactyli are rather more slender than in Wood-Mason's species, and the horny spinules with which they are armed are much less prominent. The penultimate segment of the male abdomen has the lateral margins concave, as in *T. lugubris*, but the concavity is not apparent in very young individuals.

T. Masoniana is allied to *T. lugubris*, but on comparing it with that species the following differences can be made out :—The carapace is less flat, and the frontal margin more concave; the epibranchial and external orbital teeth are much larger and more prominent, with the margin connecting them less oblique; the postfrontal ridge is separated by a wider interval from the orbital margin, the orbits are larger and more open, the carpal spine of the chelipedes is acute and more prominent, and the general colour is apparently not so dark as in *T. lugubris*. The carapace is also proportionately longer when compared with the breadth, as shown by the following table, in which individuals of both species, of the same sex, and as nearly equal in size as the series would permit, are compared :—

	T. lugubris.	*T. Masoniana.*
1. A young Female.	mm.	mm.
Breadth between epibranchial teeth	26	26
Length of carapace .	22	23·7
2. An adult Male.		
Breadth between epibranchial teeth .	39	37·7
Length of carapace	32·3	34

The largest specimen, a male, is 39·5 mm. long, and the greatest breadth of the carapace 52 mm.; the distance between the epibranchial teeth 45 mm., and between the external orbital angles 29 mm.; breadth of front 12 mm.

T. Masoniana is perhaps a representative on the plains of *T. indica*, as *T. lugubris* may be on the hills. I have associated it with the name of Prof. Wood-Mason of Calcutta.

130. TELPHUSA LESCHENAULTI (Milne-Edw.).

T. Leschenaulti (Milne-Edw.), A. Milne-Edwards, Nouv. Arch. Mus. Hist. Nat. t. v. p. 165, pl. viii. fig. 3 (1869).

Ganjam (*Day*); Madras, common in wells and ponds, also met with burrowing in rice-fields and in all the larger compounds (*J. R. H.*); Ceylon (*Brit. Mus.*).

The carapace and limbs are usually mottled with minute dark brown spots. An adult male from Madras has the carapace 28·5 mm. long, and 37 mm. in greatest breadth.

Distribution. Ceylon; Pondicherry; Madras; Malabar; Nicobars; also recorded from Mauritius and Tahiti.

131. TELPHUSA RUGOSA, Kingsley.

T. rugosa, Kingsley, Proc. Acad. Nat. Sci. Philad. p. 37 (1880).

Pundaloya, Ceylon (*E. E. Green*); Ceylon mountain streams, a series (*Holdsworth*).

As the specimens collected by Holdsworth were referred without hesitation by Miers to this species, I venture to supplement the very brief original description by the following account:—The carapace is subquadrate and depressed. The postfrontal ridge, though interrupted, is well-defined, and the edge crenulated; the median portion bounding the epigastric lobes is placed well in front of, and quite separate from the lateral portions, which are sinuous and curve slightly forwards to pass into the well-marked epibranchial tooth on each side. The mesogastric furrow is shallow and somewhat broad. The cervical groove is well defined, and passes as far as the postfrontal ridge, slightly internal to the epibranchial tooth, but it does not interrupt the ridge; it is most strongly marked between the anterior branchial and the protogastric lobes. The branchial regions carry many transverse finely crenulated lines, which posteriorly curve round to the under surface of the carapace. The epibranchial tooth is continued into a finely crenulated carina, which extends along the anterior half of the anterior branchial region, and finally curves inwards on the carapace. The border between the epibranchial tooth and the external orbital angle is sinuous and finely crenulated. The frontal margin is slightly concave towards the middle, and both it and the orbital margin are obscurely crenulated.

The chelipedes are unequal in both sexes, either right or left being larger ; the merus and carpus have short raised lines externally which almost impart a squamose appearance ; the carpal spine is well developed and acute, with a small obtuse tooth in front of its base ; the hand is smooth externally, but slightly rugose on the inferior proximal margin ; the fingers are strongly toothed, and in adults there is usually a single specially enlarged tooth on the immobile finger of the larger chelipede. The ischial line of the external maxillipedes is placed considerably nearer the inner or median margin of the joint. The ambulatory legs are carinated along the anterior margin, and the carpal joints of the first three pairs have in addition a carina on both the anterior and the posterior surfaces. The male abdomen is slightly constricted towards the middle, becoming wider towards the distal end of the penultimate segment.

The carapace of an adult female is 43 mm. long, and 52 mm. in greatest width.

Distribution. Ceylon (*Kingsley*).

132. TELPHUSA EXODUS. Kingsley.

T. exodis, Kingsley, Proc. Acad. Nat. Sci. Philad. p. 36 (1880).

Pundaloya, Ceylon, a male (*E. E. Green*); "Madras," a single specimen (*Brit. Mus.*). The latter specimen probably came from one of the South Indian hill-ranges, and not from the neighbourhood of Madras.

I refer these with some hesitation to this insufficiently described species. It is, as Kingsley remarks, closely allied to *T. lævis*, Wood-Mason, and the two may afterwards prove to be identical. The carapace is smooth and moderately convex, with no postfrontal ridge, and merely the rudiment of an epibranchial tooth. A faint depression between each anterior branchial and protogastric lobe indicates the cervical groove, and there is a shallow indication of the mesogastric furrow. The median portion of the frontal margin is inflected. The ischial line of the external maxillipedes is placed nearly in the centre of the joint. The ambulatory legs are very slender, and the three terminal joints are provided with many short setose hairs. In the above specimens the chelipedes are similar to those of *T. lævis*, as described and figured by Wood-Mason.

The Ceylon example is 12 mm. long, and 15·5 mm. broad.

In the British Museum there is a series of a closely allied and perhaps identical species from North India, which I refer to *T. lævis*, as the specimens agree well with Wood-

Mason's description and figures. The adult males, however, have a very wide gape between the fingers of the larger chelipede, as in *T. difformis*, Milne-Edw. ; and as the latter species appears to be closely allied to *T. lœvis* in other respects, perhaps the two are not distinct. The wide gape of the fingers is not specially referred to by Wood-Mason, and it is probably confined to old males; it is not seen in either of the specimens which I refer to *T. enodis*.

Distribution. Ceylon (*Kingsley*).

133. TELPHUSA POCOCKIANA, n. sp.   (Pl. XXXVII. figs. 5-8.)

Jubbulpore, three males and three females (*Day*).

The carapace is smooth and slightly convex anteriorly, with the branchial regions somewhat expanded laterally. Commencing at the mesogastric furrow, which is fairly well marked, and bifurcated posteriorly, the postfrontal ridge curves outwards and slightly backwards, but stops abruptly a short distance from the side of the carapace : in other words, it does not pass into the epibranchial tooth ; throughout its course it is sharply defined and nowhere interrupted, though near the middle line it is slightly wrinkled. It approaches rather nearer than usual to the orbital margin, and the surface of the carapace between the external orbital angle and the outer end of the ridge is considerably excavated. A shallow groove, not always seen in young individuals, passes from this excavation between the end of the ridge and the free margin of the carapace. The cervical groove is well marked at the posterior limit of the gastric area, but shallow and faint elsewhere, and scarcely reaches the postfrontal ridge, which it does not indent ; it is better marked in young individuals. The epibranchial tooth is very rudimentary, in fact indicated merely by the posterior limit of a slight notch, and placed a little in advance of the level of the postfrontal ridge, *i. e.* quite close to the external orbital angle, which is itself but little prominent. The antero-lateral margin, behind the epibranchial tooth and bounding the anterior branchial area, is regularly curved and obsoletely dentate; behind the posterior limit of this margin are the usual slight transverse ridges extending to the concave postero-lateral margin. A few very slight rugosities or lines are seen on the anterior branchial region, behind the outer limit of the postfrontal ridge. On the gastric region adjoining the cervical groove an anterior and posterior punctum are seen on each side. The frontal margin is almost straight and is scarcely crenulated. The orbits are remarkably large and subtriangulate in outline, the apex of the triangle being placed at the external orbital angle. The epistome is comparatively deep, and the lower margin gives rise to a broad obtuse tooth. The ischial line of the external maxillipedes is faint, and scarcely extends throughout the length of the joint ; it is placed nearer the inner margin.

The chelipedes are unequal in size, and very similar to those of *T. indica* ; the carpal spine is short but acute, the outer surface of the hand sparingly punctate, and the puncta are arranged in lines on the outer surface of the fingers. The ambulatory legs are also similar to those of *T. indica*. The meropodites have the anterior margin finely crenulated, and a few short horny spinules are met with, on the posterior margin of the propodi. The terminal segments of the male abdomen are wider than those of *T. indica*, and the lateral margins of the penultimate segment are almost straight.

This species bears some general resemblance to *T. indica*, but is distinguished from that species by the peculiar nature of the postfrontal ridge, which, though well marked, does not pass to the lateral margin of the carapace, stopping short abruptly before reaching it; the rudimentary epibranchial tooth is placed near the external orbital angle, and the contiguous part of the carapace is deeply hollowed out. In *T. celebensis*, De Man, a species also with a well-marked postfrontal ridge which does not pass into the epibranchial tooth, there is a second small tooth placed between the epibranchial one and the external orbital angle.

The largest specimen, a male, has the carapace 30·5 mm. long, and the greatest breadth 43·3 mm. ; the distance between the external orbital angles is 28·3 mm., and between the epibranchial teeth 34·5 mm. ; the front is 12 mm. in breadth.

I have named the species after Mr. R. I. Pocock, of the British Museum Staff.

134. TELPHUSA FLUVIATILIS, Latr.

T. fluviatilis (Latr.), A. Milne-Edwards, Nouv. Arch. Mus. Hist. Nat. t. v. p. 161 (1869).

Quetta, a series in the British Museum, collected by W. T. Blanford, and another series from the same locality presented by the Secretary of State for India. " Environs of Calcutta " (*Coll. Schlagintweit*). The latter locality is probably erroneous, and the specimen perhaps came from the Himalayas.

The occurrence of this species so far east is interesting. I have compared the specimens carefully with a large series in the British Museum from various localities on both the European and African sides of the Mediterranean, and can find no differences of any importance. There are specimens in the British Museum from Sustan, Persia.

Distribution. Italy, Greece, Turkey, Crimea, Syria, Egypt, Algeria, Cyprus (*A. Milne-Edwards*).

135. TELPHUSA ATKINSONIANA. Wood-Mason.

T. Atkinsoniana, Wood-Mason, Journ. As. Soc. Bengal, vol. xl. p. 205, pl. xiv. figs. 12–16 (1871).

Kangra, four females (*Day*) ; British Burmah, a male (*W. Theobald*) ; Simla, several young specimens (*Coll. Schlagintweit*).

The Kangra examples are not fully grown (the largest is only 21 mm. long and 27·5 mm. broad) and they have apparently not acquired all the typical characters. The granulations are scarcely represented on the epigastric and protogastric lobes of the carapace, and the outer surface of the hands is only sparingly tuberculate ; there can, I think, be no doubt, however, of their identity.

This species is closely allied to *T. fluviatilis*, but the two may be distinguished as follows :—In *T. fluviatilis*, the portion of the postfrontal ridge bounding the epigastric lobes is placed well in advance of, and is practically cut off from, the rest of the ridge, while in *T. Atkinsoniana* it is continuous with the rest. In *T. fluviatilis*, the ridge is somewhat ill defined and more or less interrupted laterally, where it passes into the epibranchial tooth, while in *T. Atkinsoniana* it is strongly defined and prominent at this point.

Specimens of the two allied species *T. denticulata*, Milne-Edw. (China), and *T. Larnaudii*, A. Milne-Edw. (Siam), are in the collection of the British Museum, and they were regarded by Miers as scarcely distinct from *T. fluviatilis.* In the present limited state of our knowledge as to what constitutes a species in this difficult genus, I think they must be held to be distinct. *T. denticulata* is distinguished, from both *T. fluviatilis* and *T. Atkinsoniana,* by its poorly marked postfrontal ridge, and the small size of the epibranchial tooth. *T. Larnaudii* is even more closely allied, but is distinguished from both by the greater convexity of the branchial regions, which are sparingly granulated; the protogastric and epigastric lobes are not granulated as in *T. Atkinsoniana*; the postfrontal ridge resembles that of *T. Atkinsoniana,* but towards the epibranchial tooth it becomes interrupted as in *T. fluviatilis.*

Distribution. North India: Darjeeling; Thancote Hills, Nepal; Khasi Hills (*Wood-Mason*); Ceylon (*Brit. Mus.*)

Genus PARATELPHUSA, Milne-Edwards.

136. PARATELPHUSA SINENSIS, Milne-Edw.

P. sinensis, Milne-Edwards, Arch. du Mus. vol. vii. p. 173, pl. xiii. fig. 2 (1854–55).

Burmah, an adult male (*Day*).

Distribution. China (*Milne-Edwards*); Siam (*Von Martens*); Moulmein, Burmah (*Wood-Mason*).

137. PARATELPHUSA SPINIGERA, Wood-Mason.

P. spinigera, Wood-Mason, Journ. As. Soc. Bengal, vol. xl. p. 191, pl. xii. figs. 1–4 (1871).

Calcutta, Roorkee, North-West Provinces, Sind, Ganjam (*Day*).

According to Wood-Mason this species is very common in the Calcutta tanks. The British Museum has a series from Bengal.

Distribution. North India (*Wood-Mason*). It is not known to occur further south than Ganjam.

138. PARATELPHUSA DAYANA, Wood-Mason.

P. Dayana, Wood-Mason, Journ. As. Soc. Bengal, vol. xl. p. 192, pl. xi. (1871).

Tounghoo, Burmah; ten specimens (*Oates*).

This species is characterized by the great convexity of its carapace, and the well-marked postfrontal ridge, with the epigastric portions almost nodose. The four epibranchial teeth (not counting the external orbital angle) very gradually diminish in size on passing backwards, and the greatest diminution is seen in the most posterior one.

The largest specimen, a female, is 30 mm. long, and 41 mm. broad.

Distribution. Burmah: Prome and Mandalay (*Wood-Mason*).

139. PARATELPHUSA MARTENSI, Wood-Mason.

P. Martensi, Wood-Mason, Ann. Mag. Nat. Hist. ser. 4, vol. xvii. p. 121 (1876).

Roorkee, two males; North-West Provinces, three males, two females (*Day*).

A comparatively small species with three epibranchial teeth as in *P. sinensis*, but the meropodites of the ambulatory legs unarmed. The largest specimen, a female, is 21·5 mm. long and 27 mm. broad.

Distribution. North India: Hurdwar, Purneah, Allahabad, Jessore district (*Wood-Mason*).

Genus OCYPODA, Fabr.

140. OCYPODA CERATOPHTHALMA (Pallas).

O. ceratophthalma (Pallas), Miers, Ann. Mag. Nat. Hist. ser. 5, vol. x. p. 379, pl. xvii. fig. 1 (1882).

Rameswaram and Tuticorin (*Thurston*). Common on the South Indian coast (*J. R. H.*).

The stridulating ridge on the inner surface of the hand is coarsely striated above, and very finely striated below.

Distribution. From the Red Sea, E. Africa and Natal, to Japan and the Pacific (Samoa. Fijis, Sandwich Is., &c.), also the coasts of Australia.

141. OCYPODA MACROCERA, Milne-Edw.

O. macrocera (Milne-Edw.), Miers, Ann. Mag. Nat. Hist. ser. 5, vol. x. p. 381, pl. xvii. fig. 2 (1882).

Rameswaram, many specimens; Tuticorin, two males (*Thurston*); Madras, not uncommon (*J. R. H.*).

This species does not appear to be common. It differs from *O. ceratophthalma* in having the finger-tips of both chelipedes, but especially of the smaller one, dilated and flattened. The outer surface of both hands is also more finely granulated. The colour is a reddish orange, most pronounced on the chelipedes. It occurs at Madras, above high-water mark, but is much less common than the next species.

A Rameswaram specimen (female) has the carapace 30 mm. long and 38 mm. broad.

Distribution. India (*Milne-Edwards, Miers*).

142. OCYPODA PLATYTARSIS, Milne-Edw.

O. platytarsis (Milne-Edw.), Miers, Ann. Mag. Nat. Hist. ser. 5, vol. x. p. 383, pl. xvii. fig. 5 (1882).

Rameswaram (*Thurston*); Ceylon (*Haly*); Madras, very abundant (*J. R. H.*).

The stridulating ridge is narrow and tuberculate in both sexes. The dactyli of the ambulatory legs are broad and flattened in adults. This is the commonest species of *Ocypoda* at Madras, where it occurs in great numbers, burrowing in the sand near high water mark, never at any great distance from the sea. It attains a large size, and a male obtained by Mr. Thurston in Ceylon has the carapace 56 mm. long and 66 mm. broad.

Distribution. India and Ceylon (*Milne-Edwards, Miers*).

143. OCYPODA CORDIMANA, Desmarest.

O. cordimana (Desm.), Miers, Ann. Mag. Nat. Hist. ser. 5, vol. x. p. 387, pl. xvii. fig. 9 (1882).

Tuticorin (*Thurston*). Common at Madras (*J. R. H.*).

This is a smaller species than the foregoing, and distinguished at once by the absence of a stridulating ridge from the chelipedes in both sexes. It is a terrestrial crab and lives in burrows at some distance from the sea.

Distribution. From Mauritius and the Seychelles to China, Australia, and the Pacific (New Caledonia, New Hebrides, Fijis, &c.).

Genus GELASIMUS, Latreille.

144. GELASIMUS ANNULIPES, Latr.

G. *annulipes* (Latr.), De Man, Mergui Crust., p. 118, pl. viii. figs. 5-7 (1887), *ubi synon.*
(= *G. perplexus,* Milne-Edw.; *G. pulchellus,* Stm.).

Rameswaram and Tuticorin (*Thurston*). Abundant on the margins of the South Indian backwaters, burrowing in sand or mud (*J. R. H.*).

A curious sexual difference has been pointed out by De Man, viz. the infra-orbital ridge is simple and finely crenulated in the male, whereas in the female the crenulations are larger, and in addition there is an accessory row of acute granules parallel to the ridge, but placed within the orbital cavity.

An adult male from Rameswaram has the carapace 12 mm. long and 21 mm. broad at the level of the external orbital angles; the hand of the larger chela 38 mm. long.

Distribution. From E. Africa to the Pacific (Tahiti and the Fijis).

145. GELASIMUS TRIANGULARIS. A. Milne-Edw.

G. *triangularis* (A. Milne-Edw.), De Man, Mergui Crust. p. 119, pl. viii. figs. 8-11 (1887).
(= *G. perplexus,* Heller).

Madras and Ennore (*J. R. H.*).

This species is found living with G. *annulipes* at the above localties, and the two are almost equally common. G. *triangularis* is, however, a slightly smaller species, and its colour-markings are different, but I omitted to note these in living specimens. The carapace is narrower posteriorly in the present species, and the larger hand has only two granulated ridges on the inner suface, while there are three in G. *annulipes*. The immobile finger of the larger chela is acute at its distal end, whereas in G. *annulipes* it is subtruncated, or almost bidentate, owing to the presence of an accessory tooth near the apex. In the two species there is considerable variation, and varieties of both are common in which the inner margin of both fingers is without any prominent teeth. The females of G. *triangularis* lack the accessory orbital row of granules met with in the females of the other species.

Distribution. New Caledonia (*A. Milne-Edwards*); Mergui (*De Man*); Ceylon and Madras (*Heller*).

Genus MACROPHTHALMUS, Latr.

146. MACROPHTHALMUS DEPRESSUS, Rüppell.

M. depressus, Rüppell, Beschreib. u. Abbild. Kurzschwänzigen Krabben, p. 19. tab. iv. fig. 6 (1830);
De Man, Notes Leyden Mus. vol. iii. p. 255 (1881); id. Brock's Crust. p. 356, taf. xv. fig. 3 (1888).
M. affinis, Guérin, Crust. 'Favorite,' p. 172, pl. 1. fig. 2 (1839).

Rameswaram, three specimens (*J. R. H.*).

The carapace is finely granulated, with the exception of the central part of the gastric area, and in young specimens it is only granulated towards the sides. The carpus and hand are smooth and glabrous externally, without spines and with merely a row of granules on the upper margin of the hand internally; the mobile finger has an obtuse crenulated lobe on its inner margin near the base. The ambulatory legs are pubescent, with a single tooth near the anterior distal end of the merus.

I have little doubt that my specimens are referable to Guérin's species, and at the same time they seem to be identical with *M. depressus*, as characterized by De Man, though in the figure of the latter writer the palm is shorter in proportion to the length of the fingers than in the Rameswaram examples. This difference is, however, unimportant. A male specimen is 11 mm. long and 17 mm. wide.

Distribution. Red Sea (*Rüppell, De Man*); Bombay, Pondicherry (*Guérin*); North Australia (*Haswell*).

147. MACROPHTHALMUS PECTINIPES, Guérin.

M. pectinipes, Guérin, Crust. 'Favorite,' p. 167, pl. xlix. (1839); Milne-Edwards, Ann. Sci. Nat. sér. 3, Zool. t. xviii. p. 158 (1852).

Sind, five specimens (*Day*).

This large species is characterized by its spiny-bordered ambulatory legs, and the presence of large scattered tubercular granules on the carapace.

The largest individual is 34 mm. long, and 57 mm. wide at the level of the external orbital angles.

Distribution. Bombay (*Guérin, Brit. Mus.*); Penang (*Brit. Mus.*).

148. MACROPHTHALMUS LATREILLEI (Desm.).

M. Latreillei (Desm.), A. Milne-Edwards, Nouv. Arch. Mus. Hist. Nat. t. ix. p. 278, pl. xiii. fig. 3 (1873).

Ceylon, in a fossil state; two specimens (*Haly*).

This species has been previously recorded in a fossil state from the recent deposits of Ceylon, the Philippines, Malacca, and New Caledonia, but it has not yet been found living in the Indian seas. One of Mr. Haly's examples was in an excellent state of preservation, and there could be no doubt as to its identity with the species figured by A. Milne-Edwards. According to De Man *M. Polleni*, Hoffmann, from Madagascar, is perhaps synonymous with the present species.

Distribution. Living in the seas of New Caledonia (*A. Milne-Edwards*).

Genus SCOPIMERA, De Haan.

149. SCOPIMERA MYCTIROIDES (Milne-Edw.).

Doto myctiroides, Milne-Edwards, Ann. Sci. Nat. sér. 3, Zool. t. xviii. p. 152, pl. iv. fig. 24 (1852).

Rameswaram and Tuticorin (*Thurston*). Common at Rameswaram, burrowing in sand and mud; Ennore (*J. R. H.*).

De Man, on what are apparently good grounds, unites *Dotilla*, Stm. (= *Doto*, De Haan, nom. præocc.), and *Scopimera*, De Haan, selecting the former name for the genus; but *Scopimera* is preferable as it is the older name, and *Dotilla* has more recently been used to designate a genus of Mollusca.

In a very large series of this species I have as yet only met with males. There is still much to be learned about the genus, especially as to the nature of the curious 'tympana' on the sterna and on the meral joints of the ambulatory legs.

Distribution. Malabar (*Milne-Edwards*); Strait of Gaspar (*Stimpson*); Java (*Brit. Mus.*); Singapore (*Walker*); Seychelles (*Miers*).

Genus MYCTIRIS, Latr.

150. MYCTIRIS LONGICARPUS, Latr.

M. longicarpus (Latr.), De Man, Brock's Crust. p. 358 (1888).

(= ? *M. brevidactylus*, Stm.).

Akyab, several specimens (*Day*).

Distribution. Malay Archipelago, China, Australia and Tasmania, New Caledonia.

Genus METOPOGRAPSUS, Milne-Edw.

151. METOPOGRAPSUS MESSOR (Forsk.).

M. messor (Forsk.), De Man, Mergui Crust. p. 144, pl. ix. fig. 11 (1888); id. Brock's Crust. p. 361, taf. xv. fig. 6 (1888).

(= *Pachygrapsus æthiopicus*, Hilg.).

Tuticorin (*Thurston*). Very common at Rameswaram between tide-marks; common at Madras (*J. R. H.*).

Distribution. From the Red Sea, E. Africa, and Natal to the Pacific (Samoa, Fijis, Sandwich Is., &c.).

Genus GRAPSUS, Lam.

152. GRAPSUS STRIGOSUS (Herbst).

G. strigosus (Herbst), A. Milne-Edwards, Nouv. Arch. Mus. Hist. Nat. t. ix. p. 286 (1873), *ubi synon.*

Rameswaram and Tuticorin (*Thurston*). Abundant on the harbour walls at Madras, and elsewhere on the Coromandel coast (*J. R. H.*).

Distribution. From the Red Sea and E. Africa to the Pacific as far as the coast of Chili.

153. GRAPSUS MACULATUS (Catesby).

G. maculatus (Catesby), A. Milne-Edwards, Nouv. Arch. Mus. Hist. Nat. t. ix. p. 285 (1873).

Tuticorin (*Thurston*).

Distribution. Atlantic Region (from Florida to the Cape of Good Hope). Throughout the Indo-Pacific Region.

Genus PLAGUSIA, Latr.

154. PLAGUSIA IMMACULATA, Lam.

P. immaculata (Lam.), Miers, Ann. Mag. Nat. Hist. ser. 5, vol. i. p. 150 (1878).

(= *P. depressa*. Latr., nec Fabr.).

Madras, common, associated with *Grapsus strigosus* (*J. R. H.*).

Distribution. Bay of Bengal, Malay Archipelago, Chinese Seas, N. Australia, and the Pacific as far as the Sandwich Is. and the W. coast of Central America.

Genus LEIOLOPHUS, Miers.

155. LEIOLOPHUS PLANISSIMUS (Herbst).

L. planissimus (Herbst), Miers, Ann. Mag. Nat. Hist. ser. 5, vol. i. p. 153 (1878), *ubi synon.*

Rameswaram, not uncommon between tide-marks (*Thurston, J. R. H.*); Madras (*J. R. H.*).

Distribution. Atlantic Region (Florida, West Indies, Madeira, &c.); Indo-Pacific Region, from the Mascarenes to Korea, the coasts of California, Chili, and New Zealand.

Genus VARUNA, Milne-Edw.

156. VARUNA LITTERATA (Fabr.).

V. litterata (Fabr.), Milne-Edwards, Ann. Sci. Nat. sér. 3, Zool. t. xviii. p. 176 (1852).

Ceylon (*Haly*); Calcutta, several specimens preserved in the same bottle with *Paratelphusa spinigera*, a fresh-water species; Sittoung; Ganjam (*Day*). Not uncommon in the backwater at Ennore (*J. R. H.*).

If there is no mistake in connection with the locality Sittoung, this species occurs about one hundred miles inland in the Sittoung River, Burmah; it has previously been recorded from fresh water by Miers and others.

Distribution. Mauritius, Bay of Bengal, Malay Archipelago, China, Japan, New Caledonia, Australia, New Zealand.

Genus METAPLAX, Milne-Edw.

157. METAPLAX DISTINCTUS, Milne-Edw.

M. distinctus, Milne-Edwards, Ann. Sci Nat. sér. 3, Zool. t. xviii. p. 162, pl. iv. fig. 27 (1852); De Man, Mergui Crust. p. 158, pl. x. figs. 7-9 (1888).

Ennore (*J. R. H.*).

This species is not uncommon in the above locality, found running about in grass, and living in company with *Metasesarma Rousseauxii*. The spinules on the meropodites of the ambulatory legs vary in number in different specimens, and sometimes even on the two sides of the same specimen. In the Ennore examples the ambulatory legs are without hairs, whereas in those from Mergui examined by De Man they were hairy on the terminal joints.

The largest specimen has the carapace 11 mm. long and 15 mm. wide.

Distribution. Bombay (*Milne-Edwards*) ; Mergui (*De Man*).

Genus SESARMA, Say.

158. SESARMA TETRAGONA (Fabr.).

S. tetragonum (Fabr.), A. Milne-Edwards, Nouv. Arch. Mus. Hist. Nat. t. ix. p. 304, pl. xvi. fig. 4 (1873).

Madras, very common on the banks of the Cooum ; Ennore (*J. R. H.*).

The carapace is densely pubescent, especially in front, and the hairs are arranged in tufts ; a single tooth is placed behind the antero-lateral angle. The upper margin of the hand carries a narrow longitudinal ridge which is finely striated transversely, and the outer surface of the same joint is finely granulated, with a short ill-defined line of granules about the middle of the surface ; the dactylus is armed above with ten or eleven horny-tipped tubercles.

An adult male has the carapace 36 mm. long and 40 mm. wide, the right hand and immobile finger 40 mm. long and 24 mm. in height.

Distribution. From the Red Sea, E. Africa, and Natal to China and the Pacific (New Caledonia, Fijis, &c.).

159. SESARMA QUADRATA (Fabr.).

S. quadratum (Fabr.), Miers, Phil. Trans. Roy. Soc. vol. clxviii. p. 490 (1879).

(= *S. affinis*, De Haan ; *S. angulata*, Milne-Edw. ; *S. aspera*, Heller).

Tuticorin (*Thurston*). Very common at Madras and Ennore (*J. R. H.*).

The Tuticorin examples belong to the typical form ; the carapace of a male is 17·5 mm. long and 21 mm. wide, and there are eleven tubercles on the upper margin of the immobile finger. The Madras and Ennore examples belong to the variety *aspera* of Heller, and the largest male that I have met with is only 15·8 mm. long and 19·5 mm. wide. On examining a large series of adult males I find from thirteen to eighteen tubercles on the immobile finger ; as a rule each tubercle is oval and symmetrical, but in one or two specimens they are each slightly curved. *S. Melissa*, De Man, founded on a single specimen from Mergui, with the tubercles horse-shoe shaped, may therefore be only a variety of *S. quadrata*. Tufts of hair are sometimes present on the postfrontal lobes.

Distribution. From E. Africa and Natal to Japan and the Pacific (New Caledonia, Fijis).

Genus SARMATIUM, Dana.

160. SARMATIUM INDICUM (A. Milne-Edw.), var. MALABARICUM, n. (Pl. XXXVI. fig. 17.)

Metagrapsus indicus, A. Milne-Edwards, Nouv. Arch. Mus. Hist. Nat. t. iv. p. 174, pl. xxvi. figs. 1–5 (1868).

Sarmatium indicum, Kingsley, Proc. Acad. Nat. Sci. Philad. p. 213 (1880).

Cochin, several specimens, collected by my former pupil A. G. Paul.

I at first felt disposed to refer these specimens to *S. punctatum* (A. Milne-Edw.), but Prof. A. Milne-Edwards, to whom I sent an example, informed me that it did not belong to that species, but was rather referable to *S. indicum* (A. Milne-Edw.). They differ from the description and figures of the latter species in having the carapace strongly punctate and the inner surface of the hand with a well-marked tubercular ridge (characters which A. Milne-Edwards assigned to *S. punctatum*); the fingers in the male have a much wider gape, and the male abdomen has the terminal segment narrower, and the basal segments relatively broader, than represented in Milne-Edwards's figure. On the other hand, I have compared them with specimens in the British Museum from the Indo-Malayan seas, referred by Miers to *S. punctatum*, and I find the following differences :—In Miers's specimens the fingers in the male have a much narrower gape, and there is a distinct ridge or carina on the outer surface of the immobile finger, running parallel to and near the toothed edge, which is entirely absent from the Cochin specimens. In our specimens the immobile finger is more compressed, and there is a very prominent tooth on its inner margin near the base, while there are also prominent teeth near the apices of both fingers at the posterior limit of the horny plate which is seen on each digit.

Neither *S. punctatum* nor the typical form of *S. indicum* are yet known to occur in India.

The carapace of a male is 21·3 mm. long and 26 mm. broad, the front is 14·3 mm. broad, the right hand (including the immobile finger) is 22 mm. long and 13·5 mm. in height ; the dactylus 14·5 mm. long.

Distribution. The typical form occurs in Celebes (*A. Milne-Edwards, De Man*).

Genus METASESARMA, Milne-Edwards.

161. METASESARMA ROUSSEAUXII, Milne-Edw.

M. Rousseauxii, Milne-Edwards, Ann. Sci. Nat. sér. 3, t. xx. p. 188 [1853] ; id. Arch. du Mus. t. vii. p. 158, pl. x. fig. 1 (1854).

Sesarma Aubryi, De Man, Mergui Crust. p. 168 (1888), nec *S. Aubryi*, A. Milne-Edw.

Ennore, not uncommon (*J. R. H.*).

I sent a specimen to Prof. A. Milne-Edwards, who referred it to the present species, which also includes examples from Mergui in the British Museum relegated to *Sesarma Aubryi* by De Man. The colour markings are very characteristic. The deflexed portion of the front is dark purplish brown, and immediately behind, a grey or yellow band crosses the carapace transversely and is continued on to each eye-stalk ; the remainder of the carapace shows purplish-brown mottlings. The chelipedes and legs are yellow.

A male is 16 mm. long and 19·5 mm. broad, the front 11·3 mm. broad.

Distribution. Zanzibar (*Milne-Edwards*) ; Mergui and Malay Archipelago (*De Man*).

Genus XENOPHTHALMUS, White.

162. XENOPHTHALMUS PINNOTHEROIDES, White.

X. pinnotheroides, White, Ann. Mag. Nat. Hist. vol. xviii. p. 178, pl. ii. fig. 2 (1846); Adams and White, ' Samarang ' Crust. p. 63, pl. xii. fig. 3 (1848).

Rameswaram, four males, one female (*Thurston*).

The carapace of the largest male is 6 mm. long and 9 mm. broad.

Distribution. Philippines (*White*); Hong Kong (*Stimpson*).

163. XENOPHTHALMUS OBSCURUS, n. sp.   (Pl. XXXVI. figs. 18, 19.)

Gulf of Martaban, a female (*Oates*).

The carapace is moderately convex, glabrous, and somewhat uneven, with a decided anterior declivity.   The gastro-branchial grooves are rather deep, and faint sulci pass forwards from them; two slight epigastric swellings are present.   The lateral margins are ill-defined anteriorly, while behind they are not represented by any distinct margin. The antero-lateral margin is a very slightly marked ridge, and below it on the pterygo-stomial area two similar and almost parallel ridges are seen.   The mid-branchial region is slightly better defined by the lateral margin, but the ridge here is not continuous with the antero-lateral ridge, and posteriorly it curves on to the surface of the carapace to form a prominent wrinkle, which extends to the posterior limit of the gastro-branchial groove.   The eyes are placed somewhat obliquely, and are distinctly visible in the orbital fissures.   The front when viewed from above appears obtusely bilobed, but when viewed from before it is seen to have the sides parallel and the free end truncated, with a median and two lateral slight projections.

In the single specimen—a female—the chelipedes are very minute and slender, being even shorter than the last pair of legs; superior and inferior marginal ciliated lines are seen on the hand.   The ambulatory legs are faintly pubescent towards their apices, and the meropodites of the first three pairs are armed on the anterior and posterior margins with short curved spinules, which are best marked on the posterior margins.   The ab-dominal segments are glabrous externally.

The carapace is 6·5 mm. long and 7 mm. wide; the first leg is 10 mm. long, the second leg 14 mm., the third leg 17 mm., the chelipede 7 mm., and the last leg 10 mm.

I have compared the specimen with the types of *X. pinnotheroides*.   In White's species the front is obtusely rounded and without distal projections, the orbital fissures are deeper and pass straight, not obliquely, back on the carapace; there is a granular line on the postero-lateral margin of the carapace, and a second line on the post-branchial region; lastly, there is only a single obscure ridge on the pterygostomial area.

Genus ELAMENE, Milne-Edw.

164. ELAMENE UNGUIFORMIS, De Haan.

E. unguiformis, De Haan, Crust. Japon. p. 75, tab. xxiv. fig. 1 (1850).

Gulf of Martaban, an adult male (*Oates*).

Distribution. Japan (*De Haan*).

165. ELAMENE TRUNCATA, A. Milne-Edw.

E. truncata, A. Milne-Edwards, Nouv. Arch. Mus. Hist. Nat. t. ix. p. 323 (1873).

Silavaturai Par; five females with ova, one male (*Thurston*).

The above specimens seem to be referable to this species, with the short description of which they entirely agree. The front is rounded and entire, with an inferior vertical prolongation which partially separates the antennules. The carapace is bounded by a slightly raised marginal line. The meral and carpal joints of the ambulatory legs each terminate in an anterior distal spine. The last abdominal segment in the female has its free margin broadly emarginate.

Distribution. New Caledonia (*A. Milne-Edwards*).

Group OXYSTOMATA.

Genus CALAPPA, Fabr.

166. CALAPPA HEPATICA (Linn.).

C. hepatica (Linn.), Miers, 'Challenger' Brachyura, p. 285 (1886), *ubi synon.*
(= *C. tuberculata*, Fabr.).

Rameswaram and Tuticorin (*Thurston*); Ceylon (*Haly, Nevill*); Gulf of Martaban (*Oates*).

In young individuals the postero-lateral lobes of the carapace are not nearly so strongly developed as in adults, but the margins are more strongly dentate.

Distribution. Throughout the Indo-Pacific Region, from the Red Sea, E. Africa, and Natal to China, the Sandwich Is., and New Zealand.

167. CALAPPA GALLUS (Herbst).

C. gallus (Herbst), Milne-Edwards, Hist. Nat. Crust. t. ii. p. 105 (1837).

Rameswaram and Tuticorin (*Thurston*); Ceylon (*Haly, Nevill*); Gulf of Martaban (*Oates*).

There is a remarkable difference between the eyes in this species and in the last ; in *C. hepatica* they are elongated and slender, in *C. gallus* short and stout.

Distribution. Red Sea, Mascarenes, Malay Archipelago, Pacific. If *C. galloides*, Stm., should prove identical, as Miers supposes, it occurs also in the West Indies.

168. CALAPPA LOPHOS (Herbst).

C. lophos (Herbst), De Haan, Crust. Japon. p. 72, tab. xx. fig. 1 (1850).

Ceylon (*Haly*); Gulf of Martaban (*Oates*); very common at Madras (*J. R. H.*).

In young individuals the anterior half of the carapace is provided with smooth rounded tubercles which are not seen in the adult. There is considerable variation in the size of the granulated teeth on the posterior margin, and in very young specimens they are represented by slender acute slightly curved spines.

Distribution. Indian Ocean, Malay Archipelago, Japan.

169. CALAPPA PHILARGIUS (Linn.).

C. philargius (Linn.), De Haan, Crust. Japon. p. 71, tab. xix. fig. 1 (1850).
    (= *C. cristata*, Fabr.).

Ceylon (*Haly*); Gulf of Martaban (*Oates*).
Distribution. Indian Ocean, Malay Archipelago, China, Japan.

Genus MATUTA, Fabr.

170. MATUTA VICTRIX, Fabr.

M. victrix (Fabr.), Miers, Trans. Linn. Soc. ser. 2, Zool. vol. i. p. 243, pl. xxxiv. figs. 1–3 (1877).

Tuticorin (*Thurston*); Ceylon (*Haly, Nevill*); Sind, Ganjam, Akyab (*Day*). Very common at Madras (*J. R. H.*).
Distribution. From the Red Sea, E. Africa, and Natal to Japan, Australia, and the Pacific (New Hebrides, Fijis, &c.).

171. MATUTA LUNARIS (Herbst).

M. rubro-lineata, Miers, Trans. Linn. Soc. ser. 2, Zool. vol. i. p. 244, pl. xxxix. figs. 5–6 (1877), nec *M. lunaris*, Miers.

Ganjam (*Day*); Madras, not uncommon (*J. R. H.*).
Distribution. Indian and Pacific Oceans; Chefoo (*Miers*).

172. MATUTA MIERSII, Henderson.

M. Miersii, Henderson, Madras Journ. Liter. & Science, session 1886–87, p. 66, pl. i, figs. 1–4 (1887).

Tuticorin (*Thurston*); Ceylon (*Haly, Nevill*); Madras, not uncommon (*J. R. H.*).

This species may be recognized by its colour markings and by the characters of the ridge on the outer surface of the hand, which in both sexes is composed of five short finely granulated teeth, all more or less blunt, except the second, which is subacute; the surface below the ridge is also finely granulated.

Since describing the species, I have had the advantage of examining a large series of this genus in the British Museum, and I am still of opinion that *M. Miersii* is a good species. Its nearest ally is *M. picta*, Hess (Miers), but in this the front is rounded or only very slightly emarginate, whereas in *M. Miersii* it is always distinctly bilobed. In *M. picta* there is a well-marked tubercle on the lateral margin of the carapace behind the lateral spine, which is not seen in our species. The markings are somewhat similar in the two, but in *M. picta* there is a greater tendency towards linear arrangement, and the spots are dark brown or almost black in colour; while in *M. Miersii* the maculæ consist of minute reddish or rust-coloured spots, which remain distinct and do not run into lines; indeed, they show a marked tendency to group themselves around circular or oval areas of the carapace in which there are no spots. One such oval or pear-shaped area is constantly present between the two anterior tubercles situated on the gastric area, and in fresh specimens it is always lighter in colour than the rest of the carapace. Lastly, *M. picta* reaches a considerable size, whereas *M. Miersii* is one of the smaller species of the genus. A *Sacculina* frequently occurs on the abdomen, and I have not noticed this in the case of the two other species of the genus which occur commonly at Madras.

The largest specimen I have seen, out of several hundred examples, is a male with the carapace 26·5 mm. long and 27 mm. wide (not including the spines), while the average size is considerably less.

Distribution. South India and Ceylon.

Genus LEUCOSIA, Fabr.

173. LEUCOSIA CRANIOLARIS (Linn.).

L. craniolaris (Linn.), Bell, Trans. Linn. Soc. vol. xxi. p. 283 (1855).

Rameswaram and Muttuwartu Par (*Thurston*); Ceylon (*Haly*); Gulf of Martaban (*Oates*); Madras (*J. R. H.*).

Distribution. Indian Seas, Malay Archipelago, China.

174. LEUCOSIA WHITMEEI, Miers.

L. Whitmeei, Miers, Ann. Mag. Nat. Hist. ser. 4, vol. xvi. p. 342 (1875); id. Trans. Linn. Soc. ser. 2, Zool. vol. i. p. 238. pl. xxxviii. figs. 16–18 (1877).

Gulf of Martaban, two males (*Oates*).

The thoracic sinus is deep and well-defined, with two large flattened reniform tubercles, placed immediately over the base of the chelipede (not mentioned by Miers though shown in his figure); the anterior tubercle is somewhat larger than the posterior. The front is excavated superiorly and tridentate, with the median tooth very minute. The anterior half or more of the carapace is sparingly punctate, and towards the posterior border there are four dark spots (five according to Miers). arranged in a semilunar line, and the ground-colour of the carapace is light in the vicinity of the spots. The hand is compressed, both towards its inner and its outer margin. The male abdomen is constricted between the penultimate and antepenultimate segments; on the latter there is a T-shaped sulcus, and on the former a distal median ridge.

The carapace is 12·5 mm. long and 10 mm. broad.

Distribution. Samoa; Fijis (*Miers*). Shark's Bay, W. Australia (*Brit. Mus.*).

Genus PSEUDOPHILYRA, Miers.

175. PSEUDOPHILYRA MELITA, De Man.

P. Melita, De Man, Mergui Crust. p. 199 (1888).

Muttuwartu Par, a female with ova and a male (*Thurston*); Gulf of Martaban, two females with ova and two males (*Oates*).

I have compared these and found them identical with one of De Man's original specimens (a young male). As the colour markings have not been described, and as they are still visible in the above examples, I add the following brief account as a supplement to the original description :—The front is dark brown, and a large irregularly circular brown ring is seen on the anterior part of each branchial region, the two being connected posteriorly by a line which passes back in the middle of the carapace as far as the hinder margin; the hepatic region has a brownish border. The merus, carpus, and propodus of the chelipedes have each a proximal brown band, and the fingers are crossed by a similar band near their bases; the ambulatory legs show bands of pale brown.

A female is 14·5 mm. long and 13·3 mm. wide; the right chelipede 24 mm. long.

Leucosia orbicularis, Bell, ought, I think, to be placed in the genus *Philyra*; it has the epistome much more prominent than the front, a character which distinguishes it at once from the present species. *Pseudophilyra Perryi*, Miers, is distinguished from *P. Melita* by having a ridge on the frontal part of the carapace, passing back from the median frontal tooth. *Leucosia pubescens*, Miers, is, I think, correctly placed in the genus *Leucosia*, as it has a distinct thoracic sinus; De Man suspects its identity with his *Pseudophilyra Hoedtii*. There is some confusion in regard to the genus *Pseudophilyra*, which undoubtedly comes very near to *Philyra* and the two can scarcely be separated; at the same time *Pseudophilyra* may conveniently be retained for those species with the general facies of *Leucosia*, but with no thoracic sinus.

Distribution. Mergui (*De Man*).

176. PSEUDOPHILYRA PUSILLA, n. sp.   (Pl. XXXVII. figs. 13–15.)

Gulf of Martaban, five females with ova, two males (*Oates*).

This species—one of the smallest of known Leucosiids—has the carapace smooth, and excavated antero-laterally, with a very slight hepatic swelling. The front is straight, except for the presence of a small obtuse median tooth, from which a faint carina runs back in the middle line of the anterior third of the carapace; the internal orbital angle is but little prominent. A finely granulated marginal line is seen bordering the carapace laterally and posteriorly. The epistome is very short and is covered by the front. The exognath of the external maxillipedes has its outer margin very slightly curved.

The chelipedes are moderately long in the male, but much shorter in the female. The merus is provided with small rounded tubercles on its proximal two thirds, which are arranged in rows and best seen on the inner surface; the carpus and propodus are smooth with the exception of a series of minute granules on the inner surface of the hand. A small articular tubercle is seen on both the inner and outer margins of the propodus at the carpal articulation.

The fingers are faintly sulcate externally, and separated by a slight basal hiatus in both sexes, which occupies slightly more than half the interval; they are feebly toothed in the male, but without teeth in the female. The ambulatory legs are smooth. The male abdomen gradually tapers to the apex and is smooth externally, with the lateral margins of the basal segments slightly wavy or irregular in outline; the female abdomen is smooth and very convex.

The front is dark brown in colour, and a short distance behind on the surface of the carapace, but separated by an uncoloured band, is an irregular semilunar mark on each branchial region, with the convexity of the curve outwards, and a few small spots are seen towards the middle of the carapace. Some transverse markings occur on the chelipedes at the middle and distal end of the merus, and about the middle of the hand. The legs are uncoloured.

The largest male is 6 mm. long and 5 mm. broad, with the chelipede 10 mm. long; the largest female is 5·8 mm. long and 5 mm. broad, the chelipede 8·5 mm. long.

The species is distinguished at once by its small size, and there can be no doubt that the Martaban examples are adult. The nearest ally appears to be *P. tridentata*, Miers, from Japan, in which, however, in addition to the difference in size, the median frontal projection is much more prominent, and the carapace is punctulated.

Genus PHILYRA, Leach.

177. PHILYRA SCABRIUSCULA (Fabr.).

P. scabriuscula (Fabr.), Bell, Trans. Linn. Soc. vol. xxi. p. 299 (1855).

Rameswaram and Tuticorin, many specimens (*Thurston*). Abundant at Madras and on the S. Indian coast generally (*J. R. H.*).

There is considerable variation as regards the amount of tuberculation on the carapace : very commonly there is a smooth rounded area on the cardiac region, and a smooth longitudinal area on each branchial region. On the post-gastric region the tubercles may be absent, but they are usually present in this locality, and some of them may be larger than those met with elsewhere. In young specimens the fingers are armed with more prominent teeth towards the apices than in adults, and are also slightly setose.

Distribution. E. Africa, Indian Seas, Malay Archipelago.

178. PHILYRA VERRUCOSA, n. sp. (Pl. XXXVII. figs. 10-12.)

Madras, an adult male (*J. R. H.*).

This species is so closely allied to *P. scabriuscula* that only the points of difference between the two need be pointed out. The carapace is more convex, with deeper branchio-cardiac grooves, and, excepting the surface of the frontal lobes, it is everywhere uniformly covered with smooth, rounded tubercles, one of which in the centre of the post-gastric area is larger than the others. The tubercles on the anterior half of the carapace are smaller than those on the posterior half. The external orbital angle is scarcely represented, while in *P. scabriuscula* it is prominent, and the front is narrower between the eyes in our species. The small blunt lobe seen on the hepatic area in *P. scabriuscula* is not present, but this surface is crossed obliquely by a continuous tuberculated line. The external maxillipedes are uniformly granulated externally, including even the exognaths, while in *P. scabriuscula* they are almost smooth, there being at most a few granules on the endognath; the exognath is broader than the ischial joint of the endognath, and its outer margin is strongly convex, distinctly indenting the lateral margin of the carapace ; in the longer known species the exognath is decidedly less convex.

The chelipedes are shorter and stouter in the new species, and with more numerous but smaller tubercles on the merus; the fingers are without small teeth or setæ. The sternum is uniformly tuberculate, whereas in *P. scabriuscula* there are merely lines of small tubercles along the margins of the sternal segments. The basal abdominal segment is narrower and more ⊥-shaped in the new species. The colour is brownish, whereas in *P. scabriuscula* it is usually grey.

The carapace is 8·7 mm. long and 10 mm. broad, the merus of the chelipedes 7·5 mm. long by 3 mm. in width, the propodus 7 mm. long and 2·8 mm. wide.

I have examined several hundred specimens of *P. scabriuscula* from different localities, including Madras where the new species was taken, and have never seen a specimen approaching the form just described; I may add that I have never seen a specimen of *P. scabriuscula*, variable as that species is in regard to tuberculation, with the anterior half of the carapace uniformly covered with tubercles or granules.

179. PHILYRA ADAMSII, Bell.

P. Adamsii, Bell, Trans. Linn. Soc. vol. xxi. p. 301, tab. xxxiii. fig. 1 (1855).

Rameswaram and Silavaturai Par, several specimens (*Thurston*); Gulf of Martaban, a female (*Oates*).

I have compared these with the type in the British Museum. The grooves separating the branchial from the cardiac and intestinal regions of the carapace are deeper than usual, and the regions which they define are in consequence apparently swollen. The carapace in its posterior two thirds, especially on the more elevated parts, and towards the lateral and posterior margins, is covered with small rounded granules. The whole front, as in most species of the genus (but not as in *P. scabriuscula* and *P. cervacosa*), projects in advance of the eyes, and is scarcely shorter than the epistome; the median frontal projection is distinctly visible when the carapace is viewed from above. The external maxillipedes are much less dilated than in *P. scabriuscula*, and the exognath is granulated. The granules on the merus of the chelipedes are more numerous, but not so large as in *P. scabriuscula*; both the inner and outer surfaces of the hand are granulated, and there is a distinct line of granules towards the upper limit of the inner surface. In the adult male there are two distinct granules on the upper surface of the palm, opposite the base of the immobile finger.

	Adult ♂. millim.	Adult ♀ (with ova). millim.
Length of carapace	9·5	7
Breadth ,,	10	7·5
Length of right chelipede	23	11

Distribution. Borneo (*Brit. Mus.*).

180. PHILYRA PLATYCHEIRA, De Haan.

P. platycheira, De Haan, Crust. Japon. p. 132, tab. xxxiii. fig. 6 (1850).

Silavaturai Par, three males and three females with ova (*Thurston*).

The immobile finger of the chelipedes bears on its inner margin a very characteristic fringe of hairs, both shown in De Haan's figure and mentioned in his description, by means of which the species is easily recognized.

Distribution. Japan (*De Haan*); Hong Kong (*Stimpson*); Philippines (*Bell*); Mergui (*De Man*).

181. PHILYRA GLOBOSA (Fabr.).

P. globosa (Fabr.), De Man, Mergui Crust. p. 202 (1888).

Rameswaram and Tuticorin (*Thurston*). Common at Madras and on the South Indian coast generally (*J. R. H.*).

Distribution. Indian Seas.

182. PHILYRA POLITA, n. sp. (Pl. XXXVIII. figs. 1–3.)

Madras, a series, not uncommon (*J. R. H.*).

This species is closely allied to *P. globosa*, but distinguished as follows :—The carapace is smooth, shining, punctate, and regularly convex, without grooves, the margin defined by a finely granulated line, which in the hepatic region is not perceptibly indented. In *P. globosa*, on the other hand, the carapace is finely granulated on the branchial regions, not shining, and with branchio-cardiac grooves; the marginal line carries tubercles of varying size, and is distinctly indented at the hepatic area.

The hand and carpus of the chelipedes are smooth, whereas in *P. globosa* they are granulated along the inner surface, and the granules are partly arranged in linear series. The fingers are smooth on their upper and lower surfaces, and the opposing margins are only sparingly toothed; in *P. globosa* the surfaces are finely sulcate. The inner margin of the hand and immobile finger is almost straight; in *P. globosa* it is strongly curved. The penultimate segment of the male abdomen is smooth externally, and nearly twice the length of the last segment; in *P. globosa* it carries a prominent tubercle near the distal end, and is only about one fourth of its length longer than the terminal segment. The meropodites of the ambulatory legs are smooth underneath, whereas in *P. globosa* they are finely granulated, especially those of the first pair.

The largest specimen, a male, has the carapace 19·5 mm. both in length and in breadth, the hand 18·5 mm. long, and the dactylus 10·5 mm.; in the female the carapace is very slightly broader than long.

This species has probably been confused with *P. globosa*. It is almost certainly the one referred to *Leucosia porcellana* of Fabricius, by Leach, Bell, and Milne-Edwards; but De Man, who has examined the type, has shown that Fabricius's species is a true *Leucosia*. Both Leach and Bell considered the species they examined as scarcely distinct from *P. globosa*. In the British Museum, under the name "? *Philyra porcellana*, Fabr.," there are three specimens, two of the present species, and a third of a distinct undescribed form; all three carry a second label " *P. globulosa*," probably in Bell's handwriting.

In some specimens of *P. polita* the carapace is encrusted with *Membranipora Savartii*, Aud., and a species of *Hydractinia* occurs on the arms both of this species and of *P. globosa*. I have not met with these commensals on *P. scabriuscula*, which probably burrows in the sandy bottom, while their presence in the two former indicates that they live above ground.

Genus Myra, Leach.

183. Myra fugax (Fabr.).

M. fugax (Fabr.), Bell, Trans. Linn. Soc. vol. xxi. p. 296 (1855).

Rameswaram (*Thurston, J. R. H.*); Ceylon (*Haly*); Gulf of Martaban (*Oates*).

In most of the specimens I have examined there is a distinct median row of granules on the carapace.

Distribution. Mascarenes, Malay Archipelago, China, Japan.

184. Myra australis, Haswell.

M. australis, Haswell, Catal. Austral. Crust. p. 122 (1882); Miers, ' Challenger ' Brachyura, p. 315 (1886).

Gulf of Martaban, four males (*Oates*).

These agree on the whole with the description, and with specimens in the British Museum from Australia. The granules on the carapace are most strongly marked along the median line, so as to give rise to a semicarinated appearance; as noted by Haswell, the intestinal region is capped by a cluster of granules, one of which is more prominent than the rest. I do not think it can be the young of *M. mamillaris*, Bell, as suggested by Miers, for the hepatic regions are quite different in the two forms.

Distribution. N. Australia (*Haswell, Miers*). Singapore (*Walker*).

Genus Ebalia, Leach.

185. Ebalia Pfefferi, De Man.

E. Pfefferi, De Man, Brock's Crust. p. 390, taf. xvii. fig. 4 (1888).

Muttuwartu Par, a female with ova (*Thurston*).

The surface is everywhere finely granulated, and the carapace rises immediately behind the front to form a convex swelling, the smaller elevations on which are less distinct in my specimen than indicated in De Man's figure, or seen in a specimen from Mauritius in the British Museum. The fingers are slightly shorter than the palm. The abdomen is covered externally with smooth rounded granules. This species comes very near and is perhaps not distinct from *Ebalia* (*Nucia*) *speciosa*, Dana, from the Sandwich Islands.

The carapace is 11 mm. long and 12 mm. wide.

Distribution. Amboina (*De Man*); Mauritius (*Brit. Mus.*).

186. Ebalia fallax, n. sp. (Pl. XXXVIII. figs. 4–6.)

Muttuwartu Par, a female (*Thurston*); Gulf of Martaban, a male (*Oates*).

The carapace is very convex, with the hepatic areas deeply excavated, and the surface everywhere covered with circular flat-topped polished tubercles of varying size, which are closely crowded in most places, but in the hepatic hollows are few and small. On either side of the carapace, bounding the hepatic hollow, is a rounded granulated swelling; the remainder of the lateral margin is simply rounded, and without teeth or projections of any kind. On the most elevated part of the carapace, i. e. the post-gastric area, are four prominent granulated swellings or tubercles, the two anterior placed directly in front of the two posterior, which are slightly smaller. On the cardiac area there is a single median swelling, which is smaller than those in front of it. On the intestinal region are two slightly marked median elevations, and a similar slight elevation is seen on either side of the short posterior margin of the carapace. The front is narrow, and there is a deep concavity between the two rather prominent inner orbital angles. The whole under surface of the body, including the abdomen and external maxillipedes, is covered with flattened tubercles.

In the male the chelipedes are moderately long; they have been lost in the female specimen. The arm is subcylindrical, and covered on all sides with flattened tubercles; the carpus and hand are finely granulated. The fingers are about one and a half times the length of the palm (measured along the lower margin); they are compressed and carry finely granulated carinæ on both surfaces. The ambulatory legs at first sight appear smooth in both sexes, but examination with a lens shows that they are minutely granulated. The male abdomen gradually tapers to its apex, and has a prominent recurved granular tooth on the penultimate segment; in the same position on the female abdomen there is a rounded swelling.

The Muttuwartu example has the carapace 18 mm. long and 19 mm. wide. The Martaban example is 10 mm. long and 10·2 mm. wide; the right chelipede is 14 mm. long, and the hand 8 mm.

The flat-topped tubercles which characterize this species probably give it a protective resemblance to a piece of eroded coral. Its general appearance is very different from that of any species known to me, but it apparently comes nearest to E. erosa, A. Milne-Edw., from the Pacific, and E. fragifera, Miers, from the Canaries. The fingers are longer and more slender than is usual in the genus; in this respect they bear a slight resemblance to those of Arcania.

Genus ARCANIA, Leach.

187. ARCANIA SEPTEMSPINOSA (Fabr.).

Iphis septemspinosa (Herbst), Bell, Trans. Linn. Soc. vol. xxi. p. 311 (1855); nec *Arcania septemspinosa*, Bell.

Gulf of Martaban (*Oates*); Madras (*J. R. H.*).

One of the Martaban specimens belongs to what is at least a distinct variety, but as it appears to be young it need not be specially characterized. It differs from a specimen of the typical form at the same stage of growth in having a well-defined sulcus on the carapace, separating the branchial regions from each side of the intestinal, cardiac, and post-gastric areas, and a slight transverse sulcus between the cardiac and intestinal regions. The front is narrower and more prominent than in the typical form. The spines at the postero-lateral margin of the carapace are represented merely by rudiments, while the chelipedes and legs are more slender than usual, especially the fingers. The male abdomen tapers gradually to its apex. There are specimens of this variety in the

British Museum from China; it is perhaps a distinct species, but at any rate may be termed provisionally *A. septemspinosa*, var. *gracilis*.

Distribution. Indian Seas, Malay Archipelago, China.

188. ARCANIA UNDECIMSPINOSA, De Haan.

A. undecimspinosa, De Haan, Crust. Japon. p. 135, tab. xxxiii. fig. 8 (1850); Miers, ' Alert ' Crust. p. 548 (1884).

(= *A. granulosa*, Miers).

Gulf of Martaban (*Oates*).

The single specimen, a male, 9 mm. long and 9·5 mm. wide, is identical with specimens in the British Museum from Moreton Bay, Australia.

Distribution. Japan (*De Haan*); Moreton Bay; Seychelles (*Miers*).

Genus NURSIA, Leach.

189. NURSIA PLICATA (Herbst).

N. plicata (Herbst), Miers, Trans. Linn. Soc. ser. 2, Zool. vol. i. p. 240, pl. xxxviii. fig. 28 (1877).

Gulf of Martaban, an adult female overgrown with *Membranipora Savartii*, Aud. (*Oates*); Rameswaram (*J. R. H.*).

Distribution. Indian Ocean, Malay Archipelago, China, Australia (?).

190. NURSIA ABBREVIATA, Bell.

N. abbreviata, Bell, Trans. Linn. Soc. vol. xxi. p. 308, tab. xxxiv. fig. 5 (1855).

Silavaturai Par (*Thurston*); Rameswaram (*J. R. H.*); Gulf of Martaban (*Oates*).

The carapace is slightly narrower and the chelipedes longer in the male; the ridges on the carapace are also more elevated in this sex. The largest male is 9·5 mm. long and 10 mm. wide.

Distribution. Indian Ocean (*Bell*); Moreton Bay, Australia (*Miers*).

Genus DORIPPE, Fabr.

191. DORIPPE DORSIPES (Linn.).

D. dorsipes (Linn.), Miers, ' Alert ' Crust. p. 257 (1884), *ubi synon.*

(= *D. quadridens*, Fabr.).

Rameswaram and Silavaturai Par (*Thurston*); Ceylon (*Haly*); Madras, not uncommon (*J. R. H.*).

This species reaches a larger size than *D. facchino*. The upper surface of the carapace is roughened; the eye-stalks are rather long. I have never met with an individual protected by a shell.

Distribution. Red Sea, E. Africa, Indian Ocean, Malay Archipelago, China, Japan, Australia.

192. DORIPPE FACCHINO (Herbst).

D. facchino (Herbst), Miers. ' Challenger ' Brachyura, p. 328 (1886).
(= D. sima, Milne-Edw.)

Rameswaram and Tuticorin (*Thurston*). Very common at Madras, and on the S. Indian coast generally (*J. R. H.*).

The upper surface of the carapace is usually smooth, and individuals are often met with protected by the valve of some flat Lamellibranch, e. g. *Placuna*, to which an Actinia is attached. The eye-stalks are short. A *Lepas* is frequently found attached to the legs, and occasionally a *Balanus* on the under surface of the abdomen.

Distribution. From India to China and Japan.

193. DORIPPE ASTUTA, Fabr.

D. astuta (Fabr.), Milne-Edwards, Hist. Nat. Crust. t. ii. p. 157 (1837).

Madras, several specimens (*J. R. H.*).

The carapace is narrow and remarkably flattened, with the regions well mapped out. The legs are long and slender, and the right chelipede in the male has the hand swollen.

	Adult ♂. millim.	Adult ♀ (with ova). millim.
Length of carapace	11	13
Breadth ,,	12	14
Length of second ambulatory leg	38	40

Distribution. Seas of Asia (*Milne-Edwards*); Indian Ocean, Philippines (*White*); Port Denison, Australia (*Haswell*); Singapore (*Walker*).

Genus CYMOPOLIA, Roux.

194. CYMOPOLIA JUKESII, White.

C. Jukesii, White, Append. Jukes's Voyage ' Fly,' p. 338, pl. ii. fig. 1 (1847) ; Miers, ' Erebus' and ' Terror ' Crust. p. 4, pl. iii. fig. 4 (1874) ; Miers, ' Challenger' Brachyura, p. 335 (1886).

Gulf of Martaban, a female with ova, and a young male (*Oates*).

I have compared these and found them identical with White's type in the British Museum, dredged off Sir C. Hardy's Is., Torres Strait, 11 fathoms, coarse sand. The carapace of the female is 6·7 mm. long and 8 mm. broad.

Distribution. N. Australia (*White, Haswell*). Celebes Sea (*Miers*).

Suborder ANOMURA.

Group DROMIDEA.

Genus DROMIDIA, Stimpson.

195. DROMIDIA UNIDENTATA (Rüppell).

D. unidentata (Rüpp.), De Man, Mergui Crust. p. 207. pl. xiv. figs. 4, 5 (1888).

Tuticorin, two females with ova, and two males (*Thurston*); Ceylon (*Haly*).

The largest specimen, a female, is covered by a sponge; its carapace is 19·5 mm. long and 19 mm. in breadth.

Distribution. Red Sea (*Rüppell*); Mozambique (*Hilgendorf*); Mergui (*De Man*).

196. DROMIDIA AUSTRALIENSIS (Haswell).

D. australiensis (Haswell), De Man, Brock's Crust. p. 396, Taf. xvii. fig. 6 (1888).

Silavaturai Par, three males (*Thurston*).

These certainly belong to the species as figured and described by De Man. One specimen is covered by a sponge; the largest is only 9 mm. long.

Distribution. E. Australia (*Haswell*); Amboina (*De Man*).

Genus CRYPTODROMIA, Stimpson.

197. CRYPTODROMIA PENTAGONALIS, Hilgendorf.

C. pentagonalis, Hilgendorf, Monatsb. Ak. Wissensch. Berlin, p. 811, Taf. ii. figs. 1, 2 (1878).

Muttuwartu Par, four specimens (one covered by a sponge); Silavaturai Par, two specimens (*Thurston*).

I refer these with some uncertainty to this species, as the antero-lateral margin of the carapace is scarcely so long as represented by Hilgendorf; otherwise they agree well with it, and are identical with specimens from Mauritius named *C. pentagonalis* in the British Museum. The Silavaturai examples have a rudimentary tooth or almost an indentation on the lateral margin of the carapace, between the antero-lateral angle and the tooth which marks the cervical groove. A trace of this may also be seen in the Muttuwartu examples, but it is not represented by Hilgendorf. A more prominent tooth is seen in the same position in *C. tomentosa*, Heller (= *C. canaliculata*, Stm., fide De Man), and as the latter species otherwise resembles *C. pentagonalis* perhaps the two are not distinct.

Distribution. Ibo, E. Africa (*Hilgendorf*); Mauritius (*Brit. Mus.*).

Genus DROMIA, Fabr.

198. DROMIA RUMPHII, Fabr.

D. Rumphii (Fabr.), De Haan, Crust. Japon. p. 107, tab. xxxii. (1850).

Ceylon (*Italy*).

Distribution. Red Sea, E. Africa, Mauritius, Malay Archipelago, Japan.

Genus PSEUDODROMIA, Stimpson.

199. PSEUDODROMIA INTEGRIFRONS, Henderson. (Pl. XXXVIII. figs. 7–9.)

P. integrifrons, Henderson, 'Challenger' Anomura, p. 16, footnote (1888).

Tuticorin, two females with ova (*Thurston*).

The carapace is smooth and polished, very sparingly pubescent, and regularly convex, both from side to side and from end to end. The surface is a little uneven, and the branchio-cardiac and cervical grooves are well marked, the latter indenting the lateral margin of the carapace behind its middle. The front is entire and subacute, without any trace of lateral teeth; it is somewhat deflexed and the upper surface is not channelled or hollowed out, but continuous with that of the carapace. The antero-lateral margin is very short, merely corresponding to the superior orbital margin; it is regularly curved and without teeth. The lateral margin is very long and entire, somewhat ill-defined, *i. e.* rounded, for the first or most anterior fourth of its length. The subhepatic region has two slight and subparallel sulci, the upper of which is very short, and contains a fissure passing back from the poorly marked external orbital angle; the pterygostomial region is membranous. The eyes are somewhat elongated, and the lower orbital margin is formed simply by the antennal peduncle. The rostrum when viewed from below is seen to have an inferior vertical extension, which partly separates the antennules, but which in this genus is not joined to the epistome, although it comes very close to it.

The chelipedes and ambulatory legs are covered with a short brown pubescence, most dense on the former. The chelipedes, with the exception of their fingers, are devoid of teeth or tubercles, and the hand is only slightly dilated. The first three pairs of ambulatory legs have strongly curved horny dactyli, and the third pair have a prominent lobe at the outer distal end of the carpus. The elongated last pair of legs have the carpal joint lying on the branchial region of the carapace in the cervical groove; the dactylus, unlike that of the other legs, is straight, and the distal end of the propodus carries three spinules. The abdominal segments in the female are smooth, with a broad rounded median carina. The sternal sulci commence opposite the coxae of the last legs, and, converging opposite the oviductal openings, run parallel as far as the interspace between the bases of the chelipedes and first pair of legs, where they are separated by a double or saddle-shaped tubercle.

The larger specimen is without chelipedes, and has the carapace 19 mm. long, and 15 mm. broad immediately in front of the cervical groove, the distance between the external orbital angles is 7 mm.; the first leg is 20 mm. long, second leg 21 mm., third leg 14·5 mm., fourth or last leg 22 mm. (all the legs measured from below and stretched as far as possible). The smaller specimen, although also bearing ova, is only 14 mm. long.

Both specimens are enveloped in a membranous covering apparently formed by an ascidian. From *P. latens*, Stm. (Simon's Bay, Cape), the only other known species of this genus, the one just described may be distinguished at once by its entire front, whereas in Stimpson's species as is usual in the group, the rostrum is tridentate.

Genus CONCHŒCETES, Stimpson.

200. CONCHŒCETES ARTIFICIOSUS (Fabr.).

Dromia artificiosa, Fabricius, Suppl. Ent. Syst. p. 360 (1798).
Cancer artificiosa, Herbst, Naturg. Krabben u. Krebse, Bd. iii. Heft 3, p. 54, tab. lviii. fig. 7 (1803).
Conchœcetes artificiosus, Stimpson, Proc. Acad. Nat. Sci. Philad., Dec. 1858, p. 226.
Dromia conchifera, Haswell, Catal. Austral. Crust. p. 141, pl. iii. fig. 1 (1882).

Madras, not uncommon (*J. R. H.*).

58*

The whole surface of the body and limbs is covered with a short dense pubescence. The carapace is flattened, and smooth under the pubescence, except towards the lateral margins where a few granules occur ; the whole under surface is finely granulated. The amount of granulation on the palm of the chelipedes varies in different individuals ; the granules are polished and are sometimes arranged in lines. The fingers and the granules on the palm are crimson, a character mentioned by Haswell. The sternal sulci of the female end in tubercles opposite the bases of the first pair of ambulatory legs. In Herbst's figure the lateral teeth of the carapace are exaggerated in size.

In the British Museum there are specimens from Moreton Bay, Australia, labelled *Concharcetes conchifera*, Haswell, which are not specifically distinct from those described above, and my examples also agree completely with Haswell's description and figure; so his species must therefore, I think, be united with *C. artificiosus*.

The largest male is 23 mm. long and 24 mm. broad ; the right chelipede is 38 mm. long.

Distribution. China (*Stimpson*); N.E. Australia (*Haswell, Brit. Mus.*); Singapore (*Walker*).

Group RANINIDEA.

Genus RANINOIDES, Milne-Edw.

201. RANINOIDES SERRATIFRONS, n. sp.   (Pl. XXXVIII. figs. 10–12.)

Cheval Par, a female (*Thurston*).

The carapace is minutely granulated in front, especially along a line connecting the two lateral spines of the carapace and in the space between this line and the frontal margin. Fainter granulations are also seen towards the sides of the carapace, but they disappear entirely about half-way back ; the remainder of the upper surface is smooth and glabrous. The median frontal projection is broad and its apex obtuse, but scarcely rounded, while the margins are armed with small spinose teeth ; the rest of the frontal margin or upper orbital margin is finely serrated and presents two subequal fissures, the lobe between which is drawn out into a short spine or tooth. The outer fissure is bounded externally by the prominent antero-lateral spine. On the upper surface of the rostrum and in the middle line a slight carina runs from the apex as far back as the granulated transverse line connecting the two lateral spines. A single lateral spine occurs on each side of the carapace, a short distance behind the antero-lateral spine, and it is slightly smaller than the latter. The basal joint of the antennal peduncle, which forms the lower boundary of the orbit, is finely spinulose.

The chelipedes have the ischium unarmed and the merus dilated externally at its base ; the carpus is finely granulated above, and has a short spine at the distal end of the upper and inner margins. The hand is finely granulated, and the lower margin carries three spines, of which the first or proximal is small and the other two larger and subequal ; on the upper surface are two fine subparallel ridges, separated by a narrow interval. The fingers are slender, curved, and compressed ; the immobile one with five denticles on its inner margin. The external maxillipedes have the merus faintly granular, and the ischium is about one third of its length longer than the merus, and almost smooth.

The pterygostomial regions are faintly granulated. The sternal region resembles that of *R. personatus*, but is narrower between the second pair of legs.

The total length of the body, with the abdomen extended, is 20 mm.; the carapace is 14 mm. long and 7·3 mm. wide.

In the British Museum there is a single specimen of this species, taken by H.M.S. 'Penguin' on Holothuria Bank, N.W. Australia, at a depth of 39 fathoms. It also is a female, but considerably larger than the Ceylon example, having a total length of 31 mm., with the carapace 22 mm. long and 11·7 mm. wide. Its nearest ally is *R. personatus*, Henderson, from Amboina, but the two are readily distinguished. In *R. personatus*, the carapace is scarcely granulated even in front, the rostrum is entire, and there is no spine or tooth between the fissures ; on the chelipedes there is a spine at the inferior distal end of the ischium, two spines on the upper distal end of the carpus, and one on the propodus over the base of the mobile finger; the immobile finger also is much broader than in the new species. *R. lævis*, Latr., is a much larger species, with very deep frontal fissures, and the lateral spine larger than the antero-lateral, besides other points of difference.

Group HIPPIDEA.

Genus HIPPA, Fabr.

202. HIPPA ASIATICA, Milne-Edw.

H. asiatica (Milne-Edw.), Miers, Journ. Linn. Soc., Zool. vol. xiv. p. 325, pl. v. fig. 11 (1877).

Rameswaram (*Thurston*). Abundant at Madras and on the S. Indian coast generally, burrowing in sand at low water (*J. R. H.*).

Distribution. Indian Seas, Ceylon, Malay Archipelago.

Genus ALBUNEA, Fabr.

203. ALBUNEA SYMNISTA (Linn.).

A. symnista (Linn.), Miers, Journ. Linn. Soc., Zool. vol. xiv. p. 326 (1877).

Rameswaram (*Thurston*). Common on the S. Indian coast in sand at low water ; less common at Madras than *Hippa asiatica* (*J. R. H.*).

Distribution. Mascarenes, Indian Seas, Malay Archipelago.

204. ALBUNEA THURSTONI, n. sp. (Pl. XXXVIII. figs. 13–15.)

Cheval Par. five specimens (*Thurston*).

The carapace is glabrous and faintly carinated in the middle line, with the same lines marking it which are seen in the other species of the genus. The surface is slightly pubescent between the frontal margin and the most anterior line on the carapace. The median frontal spine is acute, and does not extend as far as the apices of the submedian spines which bound the central concavity in which the median spine is placed. On either side of the central concavity are eight or nine spinules ; the first or submedian is of moderate size, the second to fifth inclusive are small, the sixth to eighth are larger even than the first, and the ninth is small or even absent. The second, third, and fourth spinules are rudimentary or even absent in some specimens. The antero-lateral or sub-hepatic spine is prominent (much more so than in *A. microps*). The eye-peduncles are narrow and elongated, the length exceeding twice the breadth at the base; the breadth is slightly greater at the middle than at the base, the outer margin is convex, and the apex is pointed. The cornea is minute and not placed on any special lobe.

The chelipedes and legs resemble those of the other species of the genus. The outer surface of the hand has comparatively few short pubescent ridges or lines, the longest being one which runs obliquely across nearly two thirds of the outer surface and ends on the immobile finger. The telson is ovate in outline, with the outer margin regularly arcuate and the apex subobtuse; the upper surface is non-pubescent, and has three faint carinæ confined to its middle portion, *i. e.* not running from end to end.

The largest specimen, a male, is 14·5 mm. long when the abdomen is extended, and the carapace is 7·5 mm. in breadth at the front.

This species is most nearly allied to *A. microps*, Miers (Sooloo Sea and Celebes Sea), in which species, however, the eye-peduncles are shorter and broader, with the cornea on a small constricted lobe ; the telson is not regularly arcuate externally, and its upper surface is pubescent. *A. speciosa*, Dana, from the Sandwich Islands, has the eye-peduncles slender, but their outer margins concave. The eye-stalks of our species resemble most those of *A. Gibbesii*, Stm., a very distinct species from the south-east coast of the United States.

I have pleasure in naming this interesting species after my friend Mr. Thurston, of the Madras Museum, by whom it was discovered.

Group PAGURIDEA.

Genus CŒNOBITA, Latr.

205. CŒNOBITA RUGOSA, Milne-Edw.

C. rugosa (Milne-Edw.), Henderson, ' Challenger ' Anomura, p. 51 (1888), *ubi synon.*

Rameswaram, Tuticorin, and Silavaturai Par (*Thurston*). Common on the S. Indian coast (*J. R. H.*).

Distribution. From the Red Sea, E. Africa, and Natal to Japan, Australia, and the Pacific.

206. CŒNOBITA COMPRESSA, Milne-Edw.

C. compressa (Milne-Edw.), Ortmann, Zoolog. Jahrbücher, Bd. 6, Abth. f. Syst. p. 318, Taf. xii. fig. 23 (1892), *ubi synon.*

(= *C. violascens*, Heller).

Not uncommon in the back waters along the Madras coast (*J. R. H.*).

Distribution. E. Africa (*Hilgendorf, Hoffmann*); Ceylon (*Ortmann*); Nicobars (*Heller*); Mergui (*De Man*); Malay Archipelago (*Miers, De Man*); Japan (*De Haan*).

Genus DIOGENES, Dana.

Great confusion exists as to the nomenclature of the commonest and longest known members of this genus. I have therefore drawn up in tabular form below, a synopsis of the species described by last-century writers, arranged according to order of publication, and showing the probable interpretation of each, or the name which the species now bears.

Linnæus, 1767 .... Syst. Nat. tom. i. pars 2.	*Cancer Diogenes*	Probably several species included under this name.
Fabricius, 1775 .... Syst. Ent.	*Pagurus Diogenes*	Description copied from Linnæus.
Fabricius, 1787 .... Mantissa Insect. tom. i.	*Pagurus Diogenes*	Species unrecognizable, perhaps a *Pagurus **.
	Pagurus miles	*D. miles* (Herbst). Fabricius had evidently seen the then unpublished figure of Herbst, for he refers the species to *Cancer miles*, Herbst.
Herbst, 1791 † .... Naturges. Krabben u. Krebse, Bd. ii. Heft 1.	*Cancer Diogenes*	*D. Diogenes* (Herbst).
	Cancer miles	*D. miles* (Herbst).
Fabricius, 1793 .... Ent. Syst. tom. ii.	*Pagurus Diogenes*	Species unrecognizable.
	Pagurus miles ..	*D. miles* (Herbst). (Both the above are copied from the 'Mantissa Insectorum.')
Fabricius, 1798 Suppl. Ent. Syst.	*Pagurus Diogenes* ...	Species unrecognizable.
	Pagurus miles	Probably *D. Diogenes* (Herbst).
	Pagurus custos	Probably *D. custos* (Fabr.), Milne-Edw.
	Pagurus diaphanus	*D. miles* (Herbst).

The first writer to definitely characterize any of the species is Herbst, and on Taf. xxii. of his work he gives clear and unmistakable figures of two of the commoner forms, which I shall redescribe in the following pages as *Diogenes Diogenes* ‡ (Herbst) and *D. miles* (Herbst). The short diagnoses of Fabricius, published four years earlier in the 'Mantissa Insectorum,' were probably intended to characterize the same species, and in the case of the second, viz. *Pagurus miles*, Fabricius makes reference to the then unpublished figure of Herbst. In the 'Supplementum Entomologiæ Systematicæ,' published seven years after Herbst's description of the two above-named species, confusion is apparent — Herbst's *Cancer*

---

* De Haan referred this species to *P. aspersus*, Berthold.

† Herbst's work appeared in parts published between 1782 and 1804; the date given is that of the part in which the two species of *Diogenes* are described.

‡ Identical generic and specific names are perhaps objectionable, but the other alternative, of changing a long-established specific name because it has at some later period been adopted for the genus, appears to me still more objectionable. The latter plan was adopted by Dana in the Paguridæ, and his species *Clibanarius vulgaris* and *Aniculus typicus* should, in my opinion, stand as *Clibanarius clibanarius* (Herbst) and *Aniculus aniculus* (Fabr.).

miles is now termed *Pagurus diaphanus*, and what is probably the *Cancer Diogenes* of Herbst is termed *Pagurus miles*. A new species, *Pagurus custos*, appears in this work for the first time, and there can be little doubt that it represents the very common Indian species which Milne-Edwards and others identified from Fabricius's short diagnosis. De Man, in his Report on the Mergui Crustacea, has referred to the *Pagurus miles* of Fabricius the species which I follow Milne-Edwards in regarding as *P. custos*, Fabr. ; this determination was based on an examination of the type of the former, which is unfortunately in a fragmentary state and some of the most important parts are missing, but I imagine there has been some mistake in connexion with the labelling of the specimen, for it does not agree with Fabricius's later diagnosis of *P. miles*. An examination of types is not likely to be of much service in this case, for it appears almost certain that Fabricius described two distinct species under the name of *P. miles*.

The species described by Milne-Edwards in the 'Histoire Naturelle des Crustacés' as *P. miles*, *P. custos*, and *P. diaphanus* are, in my opinion, identical with those so named by Fabricius in the 'Supplementum Entomologiæ Systematicæ,' and, as I have pointed out, Herbst's earlier names must be adopted in the case of two of these.

207. DIOGENES DIOGENES (Herbst).

Cancer Diogenes, Herbst, Naturges. Krabben u. Krebse, Bd. ii. Heft 1, p. 17, Taf. xxii. fig. 5 (1791).

Pagurus miles, Fabricius, Suppl. Ent. Syst. p. 412 (1798) ; Milne-Edwards, Hist. Nat. Crust. t. ii. p. 235 (1837).

Diogenes miles. Dana, Crust. U.S. Explor. Exped. pt. i. p. 439, pl. xxvii. fig. 9 (1852) ; nec *D. miles*, De Man.

Rameswaram and Tuticorin (*Thurston*). Common at Madras and on the S. Indian coast generally (*J. R. H.*).

The ophthalmic process is narrow and elongate, exceeding the ophthalmic scales by almost half its length, and the distal half is armed with well-developed lateral spinules. The eye-stalks are slender and faintly curved, slightly exceeding the penultimate joint of the antennal peduncle ; the outer border of the ophthalmic scales is straight for the greater part of its course, and armed with minute spinules which increase in size towards the apex of each scale. The antennal peduncle is elongated ; the antennal acicle is bifurcate and minutely spinose, with the outer process considerably longer than the inner, and extending almost to the distal end of the penultimate peduncular joint ; the flagellum is rather long and sparingly pubescent. The antennular peduncle is elongated, exceeding the antennal peduncle by almost half the length of its terminal joint.

The hand of the left chelipede is armed externally and on its upper and lower margins with strong, blunt, pointed spines, which are, however, deficient on an oblique area extending from the carpo-propodal articulation to the base of the immobile finger ; the dactylus is armed with two rows of similar spines—one on the upper border and the other on the outer surface. The ambulatory legs are strongly pubescent, more especially their dactyli, and the anterior surface of the three terminal joints is armed with short horny-tipped spinules, which are arranged in three rows on the propodus.

The total length of the body in a full-grown adult is about 60 mm.

Distribution. Indian Seas (*Fabricius, Milne-Edwards, &c.*); Madras and Nicobars

(*Heller*); Sooloo Sea (*Dana*); New South Wales (*Dana, Hess*). Krauss records the species from Natal, and Richter records it from Madagascar, but their specimens were perhaps referable to some other *Diogenes* *.

208. DIOGENES MERGUIENSIS, De Man.

D. merguiensis, De Man, Mergui Crust. p. 228, pl. xv. figs 1–6 (1888).

Muttuwartu Par, an adult male (*Thurston*); not uncommon at Madras (*J. R. H.*).

This species has been so fully described by De Man that only the more important differences between it and the foregoing species—to which undoubtedly it is closely allied—need be pointed out. The ophthalmic process is narrow and slender, but not twice the length of the ophthalmic scales ; it ends in a pointed spine and is sparingly provided with lateral spinules, which appear to arise from the dorsal surface. The eye-stalks, antennal and antennular peduncles, are comparatively shorter than those of *D. Diogenes*. The ophthalmic scales are somewhat narrow, with the marginal spinules rather prominent towards the apex. The antennal acicle is deeply cleft, the outer process passing beyond the distal end of the penultimate peduncular joint, while the inner process scarcely extends so far; both processes are sparingly spinose on the inner margin. The antennular peduncle exceeds that of the antenna only by about one-fourth of its last joint.

The chelipedes and ambulatory legs are covered with short hairs or setæ, which in most places radiate from tubercles. The hand of the left chelipede is short and broad, and the outer surface is covered with subacute setigerous tubercles, which are somewhat deficient on the immobile finger. The upper margin of the whole chelipede is distinctly spinose. The anterior margin of the ambulatory legs is also spinose, the spines being most strongly developed on the carpi ; the dactyli are shorter and less strongly curved than those of *D. Diogenes*, with the posterior surface hollowed out from side to side, and the spinules of the anterior margin almost obsolete.

The largest specimen I have seen was 53 mm. in total length. In a young specimen only 14 mm. long, all the distinctive features are recognizable, but as usual there is a tendency to exaggerated spinulation.

Although this is perhaps the species figured by Milne-Edwards as *Pagurus miles* (Ann. Sci. Nat. sér. 2, Zool., t. vi. pl. xiv. fig. 2, 1836), yet his description applies much better to *D. Diogenes*.

Distribution. Mergui (*De Man*).

209. DIOGENES MILES (Herbst).

Cancer miles, Herbst, Naturges. Krabben u. Krebse, Bd. ii. Heft 1, p. 19, Taf. xxii. fig. 7 (1791).

Pagurus diaphanus, Fabricius, Suppl. Ent. Syst. p. 412 (1798) ; Milne-Edwards, Hist. Nat. Crust. t. ii. p. 236 (1837).

Rameswaram and Silavaturai Par (*Thurston*); common at Madras (*J. R. H.*).

This species lives invariably in shells with a narrow aperture, and its marked peculiarities of form are due to this fact ; at Madras it is nearly always found in *Oliva* shells, and the adult, so far as I know, always selects the shell of *Oliva gibbosa*, Born. The

* In the British Museum collection there are examples of a large and perfectly distinct species from Natal.

body is remarkably flattened, and the hand of the left chelipede is bent almost at a right angle to the rest of the limb; the left carpus is produced into a strong blunt lobe on the inner margin. The ophthalmic process is narrow and exceeds the ophthalmic scales by nearly half its length; the distal two thirds are laterally spinulose. The ophthalmic scales are very slightly arcuate externally, and spinulose, the largest spinule being situated at the apex. The antennular peduncles are short, the eyes reaching almost to the middle of the last peduncular joint. The antennal acicle reaches the distal end of the penultimate peduncular joint; it is very slightly produced internally, but not bifurcate, and the inner margin is spinulose. The eyes slightly exceed the end of the antennal acicle on each side. The antennal flagellum is short and fringed with long hairs.

The hand of the left chelipede is almost smooth externally, but granulated on the upper and lower margins; the upper margin of the mobile finger is serrate. The ambulatory dactyli are faintly serrate along the anterior margin and are very long, being exactly twice the length of the propodi when both are measured along the anterior margin.

It attains a somewhat smaller size than the last species.

Distribution. Indian Seas (*Herbst, Fabricius, Miers*); Ceylon (*Miers*).

10. DIOGENES CUSTOS (Fabr.).

Pagurus custos, Fabricius, Suppl. Ent. Syst. p. 412 (1798); Milne-Edwards, Hist. Nat. Crust. t. ii. p. 236 (1837); nec *Diogenes custos,* Dana.

Diogenes miles, De Man, Mergui Crust. p. 232, pl. xv. figs. 7–9 (1888).

Rameswaram (*Thurston*). Abundant on the S. Indian coast; at Madras it is the commonest species of the genus (*J. R. H.*).

The ophthalmic process is narrow and elongated, exceeding the ophthalmic scales by half its length, and the distal three-fourths are armed with lateral spinules which increase in size towards the apex. The eye-stalks scarcely exceed the penultimate joint of the antennal peduncle; the ophthalmic scales are subtriangular, with the outer border spinulose and the largest spinule situated at the apex. The antennal acicle is spinulose and bifurcated, the inner process scarcely reaching the middle of the penultimate peduncular joint, while the outer process extends quite to the end of this joint; the antennal flagellum is moderately long and fringed with long hairs. The antennular peduncle scarcely exceeds the antennal peduncle.

The hand of the left chelipede is granulated externally, the granules being often less strongly marked in adults on a circular area at the lower proximal surface. The lower margin of the hand is somewhat flattened proximally, and usually this part is strongly granulated, while the upper margin is dentate; the dactylus is granulated externally, but dentate above, and both fingers are provided with bundles of setæ on their inner margins. The left merus is broad, and the antero-external margin (at the carpal articulation) is armed with a row of short spinules; the left carpus is convex externally and strongly granulated. The ambulatory legs are pubescent, more especially their dactyli; the anterior surface of the meri and carpi is armed with short stout spines; the propodi are granulated externally, and their anterior margin, as well as that of the dactyli, is armed with short subspinose tubercles.

The total length of an adult is about 55 mm.

There is considerable variation in this species as regards the amount of granulation on the larger chela; indeed, I have met with a few specimens in which the granules are almost subspiniform. The marginal teeth of the carpus, hand, and finger are much more prominent in some individuals than in others, but are never absent; the form of the hand also varies slightly. I met with a specimen in which the left chela had the characters of a fully-developed right chela; it had probably been repaired, but in any case illustrated a reversion to the primitive state of equal and similar chelipedes. De Man has recently described an allied species *D. intermedius*, from Celebes (Max Weber's Crust. p. 352), which is apparently distinguished among other characters by its more deeply cleft antennal acicle, the inner fork of which extends beyond the middle of the penultimate peduncular joint, and by the granules on the outer surface of the larger chela being less numerous, but sharp and subspiniform.

Distribution. Indian Seas (*Fabricius, Milne-Edwards*); Mergui (*De Man*).

211. DIOGENES AFFINIS, n. sp. (Pl. XXXIX. figs. 1, 2.)

D. custos, Dana, Crust. U.S. Explor. Exped. pt. i. p. 439, pl. xxvii. fig. 10 (1852); Henderson, 'Challenger' Anomura, p. 53 (1888), nec *D. custos*, Fabr.

Madras, eight specimens; not common (*J. R. H.*).

This species is closely allied to *D.custos*, but distinguished as follows :—The ophthalmic process is short, and broad especially towards its distal end, extending only to the ends of the ophthalmic scales, or very slightly beyond these, with the lateral spinules almost obsolete, but the terminal ones well developed and in line with the spinules of the scales. The eye-stalks, antennal and antennular peduncles, are relatively shorter and stouter than in *D. custos*; the antennal flagellum is stout and not twice the length of the peduncle, with long fringing hairs, whereas in *D. custos* it is considerably longer. The antennal acicle does not reach the end of the penultimate peduncular joint, and is scarcely produced internally at its base, certainly not bifurcate as in *D. custos*. The antennular peduncles are barely as long as the antennal peduncles, whereas in *D. custos* they are slightly longer.

The hand of the left chelipede is shorter and broader, also more compressed and the fingers more abbreviated than in *D. custos*, while the lower margin of the immobile finger is thin and slightly sinuous. In other respects the two species closely agree.

The largest specimen is 35 mm. long, and a female with ova is only 20 mm. in total length.

All my specimens share the above characters and do not vary to any great extent from each other. I have compared them with a large series of *D. custos* of similar size, from Madras. The species may be recognized at once by the characters of the ophthalmic process, but as a general shortening seems to have taken place in connection with the eye-stalks, antennal and antennular peduncles, it may possibly come to be regarded as merely a variety of *D. custos*; I do not, however, think this probable, and in any case it is worthy of a distinctive name. There can be no doubt that it is the species figured by Dana as *D. custos*; I have re-examined the Australian specimen which I referred to *D. custos*, in the Report on the 'Challenger' Anomura, and I find it identical with the

59*

Madras examples. The *D. custos* of Stimpson, Hess, and Ortmann, from New South Wales and Queensland, is also probably referable to the present species.

Distribution. New South Wales (*Dana, Henderson*); Madras (*J. R. H.*).

212. DIOGENES VIOLACEUS, n. sp.   (Pl. XXXIX. figs. 3, 4.)

Madras, common; many specimens (*J. R. H.*).

The ophthalmic process is elongated, exceeding the ophthalmic scales by nearly half its length, with the distal two thirds laterally spinulose, and the terminal spinules rather long. The outer margin of the ophthalmic scales is straight and spinulose, the distal spinule being larger than the others. The antennal acicle is short, with a very slightly produced inner process, and the outer process scarcely reaches the commencement of the last peduncular joint. The eye-stalks slightly exceed the penultimate joint of the antennal peduncle. The antennular peduncles are short, and do not extend beyond the antennal peduncles. The antennal flagellum is short, with comparatively few long fringing hairs.

The left chelipede has the carpus, hand, and fingers elongated, and the outer surface of all uniformly and finely granulated; a faint dentate line is seen on the upper margin of the carpus, hand, and mobile finger, and the lower and outer surface of the carpus is subsulcate. The lower margin of the immobile finger is placed in the same straight line as the lower margin of the hand. On the outer surface of the hand, at the carpal articulation, starting from the proximal and lower angle, is an oblique subcristiform elevation. The fingers are slightly incurved, their apices are acute, and a few small tufts of hair are seen on the opposing edges. The ambulatory legs have the anterior margin of the carpi and propodi faintly dentate and pubescent; the dactyli are slender.

Length of body 26 mm., of left chelipede 28 mm., carpus 7 mm., propodus 12 mm. long and 6 mm. in height, dactylus 7·5 mm. long, and the second ambulatory leg 28 mm. long.

The colour in fresh specimens is violet. This species differs from *D. custos* in size, colour, and the form of the left chelipede. It is distinguished from all the smaller species of the genus by its spinulose ophthalmic process.

213. DIOGENES PLANIMANUS, n. sp.   (Pl. XXXIX. figs. 5, 6.)

Rameswaram, one specimen (*J. R. H.*); Madras, not common, four specimens (*J. R. H.*).

The ophthalmic process is narrow and lanceolate, tapering towards the apex, and only exceeding the ophthalmic scales by about one third of its length; it is sparingly armed with minute lateral spinules, of which a subapical pair are most prominent. The ophthalmic scales have the lateral margin straight and spinulose, the spinules slightly increasing in size towards the apex. The antennal acicle is short, not reaching the end of the penultimate peduncular joint; it is slightly produced internally, but scarcely bifurcate, and the spinulose inner margin appears regularly concave. The eye-stalks reach the middle of the last antennal peduncular joint, and the antennal peduncles are about equal in length to the antennular peduncles.

The left chelipede has the merus more distinctly trigonal than usual, the upper border being rather thin and compressed, and armed with acute teeth, the most distal of which is most prominent. The carpus has a longitudinal row of pointed tubercles on its outer surface, from four to seven in number, and of which one near the distal end is most prominent; between this row and the dentate inner margin, on which there are about thirteen teeth, is a comparatively smooth and almost sulcate surface; the remainder of the outer surface is slightly tuberculate, and on the antero-external margin bounding the carpo-propodal articulation are three well-marked spinose tubercles. The left hand is slightly bent at an angle to the carpus, as in *D. miles*. The palm is covered externally with small glabrous granules, which are most crowded along the lower margin; the outer surface is flattened, more especially on the lower half, and the flattened portion is bounded proximally by a short ridge, which runs parallel to the carpal articulation, and on which the granules are almost subspinose. The upper margin of the hand and mobile finger is finely dentate. The ambulatory legs are comparatively smooth, the most prominent spinules being seen on the carpi, and especially towards their distal ends; the dactyli are rather broad, and only about one third longer than the propodi. The propodus of the second left leg presents glabrous tuberculiform elevations on its upper margin.

A female is 30 mm. long, the left chelipede (which cannot be fully straightened) is 18 mm. long, carpus 6 mm., hand 11 mm. long and 6 mm. in height, dactylus 6·5 mm. long; second ambulatory leg 28 mm. long, its propodus 7 mm., and its dactylus 10·5 mm.

This species is sufficiently characterized by the form of its ophthalmic process, the flattened hand of the left chela, and the armature of the carpus.

214. DIOGENES AVARUS, Heller.

D. avarus, Heller, ' Novara ' Crust. p. 83, Taf. vii. fig. 2 (1865).

Tuticorin (*Thurston*); Rameswaram, between tide-marks; Madras and Ennore, not uncommon (*J. R. H.*).

This small species is easily recognized by its narrow elongated left chelipede, the carpus of which is longer than the palm. The antero-lateral margins of the carapace are either unarmed, or at most provided with nearly imperceptible spinules. The ophthalmic process is narrow and entire, scarcely reaching the apices of the ophthalmic scales. The ophthalmic scales are subentire, with merely a few marginal spinules towards the apex. The antennal acicle is short and straight.

The carpus and hand of the larger chela are finely granulated externally, and minutely dentate along the upper margin. The hand is subcostate externally, the costa being ill-defined; the immobile finger is deflexed and not in the same straight line as the lower margin of the hand. The ambulatory legs are smooth.

The largest specimen I have examined is only 20 mm. in length ; Heller's type was 22 mm. long.

The specimen from Singapore, figured by Walker as perhaps a variety of *D. acarus*, is not, I think, referable to this species.

Distribution. Bay of Bengal—Nicobars (*Heller*); Mergui (*De Man*).

215. DIOGENES COSTATUS, n. sp.   (Pl. XXXIX. figs. 7, 8.)

Rameswaram, one specimen ; Tuticorin, one specimen (*Thurston*); Madras, not common, twelve specimens (*J. R. H.*).

The ophthalmic process is very narrow and entire, not reaching the apices of the ophthalmic scales. The ophthalmic scales are subtriangulate, with merely two or three spinules towards the apex. The antennal acicle is straight, scarcely reaching the distal end of the penultimate peduncular joint, with no trace of bifurcation, and with from six to eight well-marked spinules on the inner margin. The eye-stalks scarcely reach the middle of the last antennal peduncular joint. The antennular peduncles are longer than the antennal peduncles by nearly half the length of their last (antennular) joint. The antero-lateral margin of the carapace is armed with about seven spinules.

The left chelipede has the merus dentate along its inferior margin. The carpus is granulated externally, and the upper margin carries about twelve short teeth, of which the distal one is larger than any of the others ; the antero-external margin, bounding the carpo-propodal articulation, carries about six small teeth, and a few are also seen on the lower distal margin. The hand is almost smooth externally, but has a prominent, though short, oblique granulated ridge, commencing at the proximal inferior angle and passing for some distance parallel to the carpal articulation ; the upper margin is provided with subspiniform granules, and a few more slightly marked granules are seen on the lower margin, which is faintly concave, *i. e.* the immobile finger is not in the same straight line, but is somewhat deflexed. The upper margin of the mobile finger is finely crenated. The ambulatory legs are almost smooth, with the anterior margins pubescent and very faintly toothed.

Length of body 18 mm., of left chelipede 20 mm., of carpus 5·5 mm. ; the propodus is 8·8 mm. long and 4·8 mm. in height, the dactylus 5·8 mm. long, and the second ambulatory leg 21 mm. long.

This species is distinguished by the ridge on the proximal outer surface of the hand. It is separated from *D. acarus*, which has a faint longitudinal ridge, by the very different form of the left chelipede, and by other characters. A trace of the hand ridge is also seen in the Atlantic *D. varians* (Costa), but although this species agrees in some respects with ours, the form of the left chelipede, the armature of the carpus, and the proportions of this joint are quite different in the two species. *D. granulatus*, Miers (from West Australia), judging from the type, which is dried and not in very good order, is an allied species, but in it the ophthalmic scales are entire, the antero-lateral margin of the carapace is unarmed, the carpus is less strongly toothed, and has no antero-external spinules, while the hand is uniformly granulated externally, and has only a very slight carina.

216. DIOGENES RECTIMANUS, Miers.

D. rectimanus, Miers, 'Alert' Crust. p. 262, pl. xxvii. fig. C (1884).

Madras, common; a large series (*J. R. H.*).

The ophthalmic process is narrow and entire, not exceeding the ophthalmic scales; the latter are rounded, and with few marginal spinules. The antennal acicle is undivided, with the inner margin spinulose. The lower margin of the left hand is straight and spinose; the outer surface of this joint is flattened and slightly pubescent, with a few spinules chiefly arranged along an oblique line near the upper margin, which is itself dentate; the fingers are very short, and the lower border of the immobile one is in a straight line with the lower border of the hand.

The average length is about 25 mm.

Distribution. Prince of Wales Channel, N. Australia; 7 fathoms (*Miers*).

Genus PAGURUS, Fabricius.

217. PAGURUS PUNCTULATUS, Olivier.

P. punctulatus (Oliv.), Milne-Edwards, Hist. Nat. Crust. t. ii. p. 222 (1837); Dana, Crust. U.S. Explor. Exped. pt. i. p. 451, pl. xxviii. fig. 4 (1852).

Tuticorin (*Thurston*); common on the reef at Rameswaram (*J. R. H.*).

This common species reaches a considerable size. The eye-stalks, even in spirit specimens, are of a very deep red colour, and the corneae are defined by a white line.

The *Cancer megistos* figured by Herbst is undoubtedly a representation of the present species, but the draughtsman has supplied it with an altogether fanciful abdomen.

Distribution. From the Red Sea and E. Africa to China, Australia, and the Pacific.

218. PAGURUS HESSII, Miers.

P. Hessii, Miers, 'Alert' Crust. p. 264, pl. xxviii. fig. A (1884).

P. similimanus, Henderson, 'Challenger' Anomura, p. 59, pl. vi. fig. 6 (1888).

Gulf of Martaban, two specimens (*Oates*); Madras, not uncommon (*J. R. H.*).

This species, in regard to its chelipedes, has the general appearance of a *Clibanarius*, but its cephalic region is that of a true *Pagurus*. The colour-markings are characteristic, the hands being red, especially on the under surface, while the under surface of the propodus of the first and second ambulatory legs, and the sides of the eye-stalks, are banded with reddish brown. The figure in the 'Alert' Crustacea somewhat exaggerates the size of the eyes, and Miers states that the antennular peduncles scarcely reach the end of the eye-stalks, whereas they slightly exceed these, and this arrangement is shown in his figure. I have re-examined my type of *P. similimanus*, and find it identical with that of *P. Hessii*.

The largest specimen, a male, is 65 mm. long, the right chelipede 50 mm., and the eye-stalks 10 mm. long.

Distribution. Arafura Sea (*Miers*); Celebes Sea (*Henderson*).

219. PAGURUS DEFORMIS, Milne-Edw.

P. *deformis*, Milne-Edwards, Ann. Sci. Nat. sér. 2, Zool. t. vi. p. 272, pl. xiii. fig. 4 (1836) ; id. Hist. Nat. Crust. t. ii. p. 222 (1837).

Tuticorin (*Thurston*) ; Rameswaram (*J. R. H.*).

Distribution. From E. Africa to the Pacific (Ousima, Fijis, Tahiti &c.).

220. PAGURUS VARIPES, Heller.

P. *varipes*, Heller, Sitzungsb. Akad. Wiss. Wien, Bd. xliv. p. 244, Taf. i. fig. 1, Taf. ii. figs. 2, 3 (1862) ; De Man, Brock's Crust. p. 436 (1888).

(= ? *Cancer pedunculatus*, Herbst).

Tuticorin, a male in the shell of a *Bulla* ; Muttuwartu Par, a male in the shell of a *Fusus* (*Thurston*).

In both cases the shells carry several examples of an Actinia. As noted by Miers and De Man, this species is distinguished from *P. deformis* mainly by the absence of a carina from the immobile finger of the larger chelipede, and by having the penultimate joint of the third left leg rounded and not ridged on its outer surface. Both specimens present a white band on a reddish background, encircling the eye-stalks, and in one the larger chelipede is mottled with violet. *P. dearmatus*, Henderson, from the Admiralty Is., is a closely allied species, but distinguished by the elongated form of the larger hand, the outer surface of which is uniformly and finely granulated, without tubercles. Herbst's figure of *Cancer pedunculatus* is not recognizable.

Distribution. Red Sea (*Heller, De Man*) ; E. Africa (*Hilgendorf*) ; Malay Archipelago (*Miers, De Man*) ; Australia (*White*).

221. PAGURUS SETIFER, Milne-Edw.

P. *setifer*, Milne-Edwards, Hist. Nat. Crust. t. ii. p. 225 (1837) ; De Haan, Crust. Japon. p. 209 (1850) ; non *P. setifer*, Hilgendorf, nec De Man, nec Ortmann.

P. *sculptipes*, Stimpson, Proc. Acad. Nat. Sci. Philad. Dec. 1858, p. 246 ; Ortmann, Zool. Jahrb. Bd. vi. Abth. f. Syst. p. 287 (1892).

P. *pavimentatus*, Hilgendorf, Monatsb. Akad. Wiss. Berlin, p. 816, Taf. iii. figs. 1–5 (1878).

Tuticorin (*Thurston*) ; Gulf of Martaban (*Oates*) ; Madras, not uncommon (*J. R. H.*).

Much confusion is apparent in regard to this widely distributed and probably common species. I sent a Madras specimen to Prof. A. Milne-Edwards, who kindly informed me that it was referable to *P. setifer*, Milne-Edw., and that in his opinion *P. sculptipes*, Stm., is the same species. I had formerly referred my specimens to *P. pavimentatus*, Hilgendorf, with the description and figures of which they closely agree, except that in Hilgendorf's figure the left hand is somewhat shorter in proportion to its breadth than is usual in Indian examples. The sculpture of the two terminal joints of the second left ambulatory leg is very characteristic.

Distribution. E. Africa (*Hilgendorf*) ; Japan (*De Haan, Stimpson, Ortmann*) ; Australia (*Milne-Edwards, Brit. Mus.*) ; "Isle of Pines" (*Brit. Mus.*).

Genus TROGLOPAGURUS, n.

The front is scarcely produced in the middle. The eyes are moderately slender, the ophthalmic scales narrow, triangular, and closely approximated. The antennal acicle is short and robust ; the antennal flagellum rather short, and fringed with long hairs. The chelipedes are shorter than the ambulatory legs, and the left is larger ; the fingers are almost vertical, and their apices are calcareous. The ambulatory legs are slender, and similar on the two sides.

The species described below inhabits small holes in coral. The genus comes nearest to *Pagurus*, in which, however, the chelipedes are longer, and the fingers have corneous apices, the antennal flagellum is long and not ciliated, the ophthalmic scales are broader, and separated by a wide interval which is occupied by a calcified nodule or sclerite ; the ambulatory legs are usually dissimilar on the two sides, and the species are of much larger size. In some respects it resembles *Paguristes*, but in this genus the chelipedes are subequal, and the first, or first and second abdominal segments, carry genital appendages. *Gryllopagurus*, Zietz (Trans. Roy. Soc. S. Austral. vol. x. 1888), which inhabits cavities in loose stones, has the ophthalmic segment exposed, and provided with a mobile scale (presumably as in *Diogenes*), and its structure is otherwise very different.

222. TROGLOPAGURUS MANAARENSIS, n. sp. (Pl. XXXIX. figs. 9–11.)

Tuticorin and Muttuwartu Par (*Thurston*).

The carapace is well calcified anteriorly, and somewhat rugose, with a rather deep semicircular impressed line a short distance behind the front. The median projection of the front is obtuse, and but slightly produced. The ophthalmic scales are narrow and triangular, with about six spinules on the outer margin, of which the apical one is largest. The eye-stalks are slender, reaching the middle of the last antennal peduncular joint. The antennular peduncles are slightly larger than the antennal peduncles. The antennal acicle is short and broad, scarcely extending beyond the commencement of the penultimate peduncular joint, with about five small spinules on its inner or subterminal margin ; the antennal flagellum is about twice the length of the peduncle, and fringed inferiorly with very long hairs.

The left or larger chelipede has the carpus, hand, and fingers spinose and pubescent above. On the carpus the spines are almost confined to the inner margin and the upper anterior margin ; on the hand they occur chiefly along the inner margin, extending on to the border of the dactylus, while on the upper surface and outer margin, especially towards the immobile finger, some smaller ones are seen. The fingers are finely and irregularly toothed, with their inner margins practically in contact when closed. The right chelipede reaches as far as the commencement of the dactylus of the left chelipede ; it is strongly pubescent, but has fewer spines than the left. The ambulatory legs are slender, and similar on the two sides, with the joints moderately pubescent, but otherwise smooth ; the dactyli have horny tips, and are almost as long as the propodi. The margin of the telson is finely dentate. The abdomen and its appendages are similar to those of a *Pagurus*.

The largest specimen, a female with ova, is about 20 mm. long; the chelipedes cannot be fully straightened, but measured from below the left is 8·3 mm. long, and the right 7 mm.; the first ambulatory leg is 11 mm. long.

Of about thirty specimens the majority are females carrying eggs, and many are considerably smaller than the above. Mr. Thurston informed me that the species lived in minute cavities in coral.

Genus ANICULUS, Dana.

223. ANICULUS ANICULUS (Fabr.).

Pagurus aniculus (Fabr.). Milne-Edwards, Hist. Nat. Crust. t. ii. p. 230 (1837).
Aniculus typicus, Dana, Crust. U.S. Explor. Exped. pt. i. p. 461, pl. xxix. fig. 1 (1852).

Tuticorin and Muttuwartu Par (*Thurston*).

In addition to the transverse strigose lines on the chelipedes and ambulatory legs, many long marginal hairs are present, especially on the upper margin of the hands and on the ambulatory dactyli. The eye-stalks are slightly constricted towards the middle. The ophthalmic scales are somewhat approximate, and each ends in a single acute spinule. The rostral projection is separated by a distinct transverse groove from the rest of the carapace, and, as pointed out by Dana, the median areolet of the anterior portion of the carapace is distinctly defined, and fusiform in shape. Long hairs are present at the sides of the carapace, on the antennal and antennular peduncles, and even on the eye-stalks.

Distribution. From E. Africa to Japan, Australia, and the Pacific (Wake Is., Paumotu Is., Samoa, Fijis, New Zealand, &c.).

224. ANICULUS STRIGATUS (Herbst).

Cancer strigatus, Herbst, Naturges. Krabben u. Krebse, Bd. iii. Heft 4, p. 25, tab. lxi. fig. 3 (1804).
Pagurus strigatus, Hilgendorf, Monatsb. Akad. Wiss. Berlin, p. 820, Taf. ii. fig. 8 (1878) ; Ortmann, Zool. Jahrb. Bd. vi. Abth. f. Syst. p. 285 (1892).

Tuticorin, two specimens (*Thurston*).

This species evidently lives in shells with a narrow aperture—probably in Cones—and its body has, in consequence, undergone great flattening. It is distinguished from *A. typicus* by the absence of long hairs from the chelipedes and legs, its front is obtuse, the apex of the ophthalmic scales is bidentate, and the general form and colour are different. The colour when fresh is very brilliant, the ground tint a deep red becoming orange in spirit, with the legs and chelipedes encircled by blue lines which soon fade and disappear. Herbst's figure gives a fair idea of the form, and colour in a faded specimen.

This species, along with three others belonging to different genera of Paguridæ, one of which has already been referred to in this paper, illustrates a remarkable modification in the body-form of these hermit-crabs, brought about by a habit which has become constant, of the species selecting a shell with a narrow elongated mouth or aperture.

In each the body has become greatly compressed, with the carapace, thoracic sterna, and abdominal tergites proportionately widened, and the chelipedes so formed as to adapt themselves to the closing of the aperture. They are :—*Diogenes miles* (Herbst). *Aniculus strigatus* (Herbst), *Pagurus platythorax**. Stm., from the Loo Choo Is., and *Clibanarius eurysternus*, Hilgendorf, from Mozambique and the Malay Archipelago. In the last-mentioned species the flattening is less apparent.

Distribution. East Indies (*Herbst*); Ilo. E. Africa (*Hilgendorf*); Tahiti (*Ortmann*).

Genus CLIBANARIUS. Dana.

225. CLIBANARIUS CLIBANARIUS (Herbst).

Pagurus clibanarius (Herbst), Milne-Edwards, Hist. Nat. Crust. t. ii. p. 227 (1837).
Clibanarius vulgaris, Dana, Crust. U.S. Explor. Exped. pt. i. p. 462 (1852).

Madras, not uncommon (*J. R. H.*).

The colour (in spirit) is a reddish orange, and the legs show indistinct and pale longitudinal bands. My largest specimen, a male, is 70 mm. long, the right chelipede 45 mm. long.

Distribution. ? E. Africa (*Bianconi. Krauss*); Penang (*Brit. Mus.*); Singapore (*Walker*); Borneo (*Miers*); ? Hong Kong and Gaspar Strait (*Stimpson*).

226. CLIBANARIUS INFRASPINATUS, Hilgendorf.

C. infraspinatus (Hilg.), De Man, Mergui Crust. p. 237 (1888).

Madras, less common than the former species (*J. R. H.*).

De Man proposes to unite this species with the preceding, but in my opinion they are probably distinct. I have never seen a specimen that I had any difficulty in referring to one or the other form; they occur in the same locality, and in examining a number of specimens I find the characters of each constant at all stages of growth. In *C. infraspinatus* the ground-colour is paler, the banding more distinct, a strong conical tubercle is present on the under surface of the merus of the chelipedes, at the inner proximal margin of the joint, and the size is much less than in the other species. In *C. clibanarius* the body and legs, generally, carry much more numerous and longer hairs, the spinose tubercles on the upper surface of the chelipedes are more strongly marked, and there is no trace of the inferior meral tubercle.

Distribution. Red Sea (*Ortmann*); Bombay (*Brit. Mus.*); Mergui (*De Man*); Singapore (*Hilgendorf, Brit. Mus.*); Philippines (*Brit. Mus.*); Sydney (*Ortmann*).

227. CLIBANARIUS PADAVENSIS, De Man.

C. padavensis, De Man, Mergui Crust. p. 242, pl. xvi. figs. 1–5 (1888).

Tuticorin (*Thurston*); Rameswaram, Eunore, Madras (*J. R. H.*).

* This species presents many of the characters of *A. strigatus* (Herbst), to judge from Stimpson's short diagnosis, but, as no mention is made of the strigose lines on the chelipedes and legs, it is probably distinct.

This species is very common in the backwaters along the Madras coast; I do not
know whether or not it also lives in the sea. Young specimens are found in great
numbers inhabiting the shells of a common brackish-water Cerithiid. The largest
example I have seen is about 40 mm. long.

Distribution. Mergui (*De Man*).

228. CLIBANARIUS ARETHUSA, De Man.

C. Arethusa, De Man, Mergui Crust. p. 252 (1888).

Muttuwartu Par (*Thurston*); Rameswaram; Madras, living among large stones in
the harbour (*J. R. II.*).

The following characteristic colouring is observable :—The cephalothorax is grey, the
eye-stalks, antennal peduncles, chelipedes, and ambulatory legs deep brick-red, without
bands; the chelipedes and ambulatory legs are tipped with black, and several minute
black spinules are seen on the under margin of the propodi of the second and third legs.
The largest specimen is 35 mm. long. One example has the right eye-stalk only half
the length of the left, probably in process of repair.

Distribution. Mergui (*De Man*).

Genus CATAPAGURUS, A. Milne-Edwards.

229. CATAPAGURUS ENSIFER, n. sp.   (Pl. XXXVIII. figs. 16-19.)

Gulf of Martaban; three females with ova, and two males in shells of *Nassa*, sp., and
Natica, juv. (*Oates*).

The carapace is glabrous, with merely a few hairs towards the margins; the frontal
projections are obtusely rounded. The eye-stalks are moderately long and stout, being
little shorter than the antennal peduncles. The ophthalmic scales are narrow, but well
developed, and with the inner edge slightly convex. The antennal acicle is short and
almost straight, not reaching the distal end of the penultimate peduncular joint; the
flagellum is more than twice the length of the body. The antennular peduncle exceeds
the antennal peduncle by nearly the two distal peduncular joints.

The chelipedes are longer than usual, the right being considerably stouter but not
much longer than the left, with the surface very faintly granulated, but the granules
subspinulose on the carpus. The hands are glabrous above, merely a few granules
being seen with a lens. The right carpus is nearly equal in length to the right palm,
and the fingers are about half this length; the left carpus is much shorter than the
left palm, and on this side the fingers are about equal in length to the palm. The
ambulatory legs are almost smooth, with merely a few slight hairs on the anterior
margin of the broad flattened meri; the propodi and dactyli, which are about equal in
length, are elongated and flattened, without fringing hairs. Each dactylus bears a
strong resemblance to a curved sword-blade (hence the specific name), and is slightly
broader than the propodus, measuring both at the broadest point. The male copulatory
organ (protruded vas deferens or ductus ejaculatorius) is very long and slender; com-

mencing at the base of the fifth right leg, it curves completely over the abdomen as far as the base of the fifth left leg.

Length of body in a male 9 mm., right chelipede 12 mm., left chelipede 10·5 mm. A female is about the same size.

This small species comes nearest to *C. Sharreri*, A. Milne-Edw., common in deep water off the east coast of the United States, but is distinguished at once from the American form by its non-ciliated ambulatory (or perhaps swimming) dactyli and propodi, and by its longer and more slender male organ. The only previously known Indo-Pacific species is *C. australis*, Henderson, from the Arafura Sea and Fiji, in which the chelipedes are shorter and quite differently armed, with the ambulatory legs not specially flattened.

Genus SPIROPAGURUS, Stimpson.

230. SPIROPAGURUS SPIRIGER (De Haan).

Pagurus spiriger, De Haan, Crust. Japon. p. 206, tab. xlix. fig. 2 (1850).

Gulf of Martaban (*Oates*); Madras, not uncommon (*J. R. H.*).

Distribution. Malay Archipelago, China, Japan, Torres Strait, Admiralty Is.

Genus EUPAGURUS, Brandt.

231. EUPAGURUS ZEBRA, n. sp. (Pl. XXXIX. figs. 12–15.)

Muttuwartu Par, a single specimen 13 mm. long (*Thurston*).

This specimen is preserved in the same bottle with a Hydroid, *Aglaophenia urens*, Kirchenpauer, to which several examples of *Aricula zebra*, Reeve, are attached, and which have a similar coloration, so that the Mollusc and Crustacean probably live together, and are protected by the similarity of their markings to the dark ramuli of the Hydroid. In the British Museum there is a much larger specimen, taken by H.M.S. 'Penguin,' on Holothuria Bank, N.W. Australia, at a depth of 53 fathoms, from which the following description and also the figures are taken.

The colour-markings of this very beautiful species are so striking as to distinguish it at once from all other known species. They take the form of dark blood-red parallel lines along both surfaces of the two pairs of ambulatory legs, on the left or smaller chelipede, on the merus and inner margin of the right chelipede, on the sides of the anterior portion of the carapace, on the upper surface of the antennal peduncles, and as a thin line, interrupted on each segment, along either side of the entire antennal flagella. The ocular corneæ are dark green, and the contiguous portion of the eye-stalk is encircled by a yellow band. The median frontal projection and the ophthalmic scales are yellow.

The median frontal projection is prominent and acute, reaching to about the middle of the ophthalmic scales, which latter are small, subtriangular, and entire. The eye-stalks are long, and but little shorter than the antennal peduncles. The antennal acicle is slender and slightly curved, reaching the level of the end of the eye-stalks. The antennular peduncles exceed those of the antennæ by nearly half the length of their terminal joint.

The right or larger chelipede gradually increases in width, as far as the base of the mobile finger, where it is widest ; the fingers open transversely. The merus has a rather prominent inferior projection. The upper surface of the carpus and propodus is somewhat flattened, and armed with not very numerous spinose granules, which are most prominent on the anterior margin of the carpus, bordering the articulation with the hand, and along an area near the middle of the hand surface. The outer margin of the hand is thin and finely serrated, while internally there is a deep or vertical finely granulated surface. The fingers are considerably shorter than the palm and somewhat deflexed, with the mobile one strongly carinated along its inner margin, which is also finely serrated. There are no prominent teeth on the opposing margins of the fingers. The left chelipede is slender, and smooth but for the presence of a few hairs ; its carpus is longer than the hand and fingers taken together. The ambulatory legs are smooth and very sparingly pubescent ; the second pair are unequally developed, that of the right side being longer and proportionately broader than the left, and the two terminal joints are faintly sulcate longitudinally, an arrangement which is not seen on the left side. On both sides the dactyli are longer than the propodi.

The Australian example, a female, is about 21 mm. long ; the right chelipede (which cannot be fully extended) is 18 mm. long, the left chelipede 14 mm., the second left ambulatory leg 20 mm., and the second right ambulatory leg 23 mm.

Group GALATHEIDEA.

Genus PETROLISTHES, Stimpson.

232. PETROLISTHES DENTATUS (Milne-Edw.).

Porcellana dentata (Milne-Edw.), De Man, Mergui Crust. p. 216 (1888).
(= *P. bellis*. Heller ; *P. Haswelli*, Miers).

Tuticorin and Muttuwartu Par (*Thurston*) ; Rameswaram, common under coral blocks between tide-marks (*J. R. H.*).

I have compared my specimens with examples from Mergui examined by De Man and with the types of *Petrolisthes Haswelli*, and find that all belong to the same species. According to Ortmann, *Porcellana dentata* of De Man is not the *P. dentata* of Milne-Edwards, but is synonymous with *P. speciosa*, Dana ; he seems to have overlooked the fact, however, that the Mergui specimens were examined by Prof. A. Milne-Edwards and pronounced identical with *P. dentata*, Milne-Edw. The carpus of the chelipedes is usually about twice as long as broad, though sometimes shorter. There is considerable variation in regard to the number and form of the denticles on the anterior and posterior margins of the carpus ; as a rule, there are three on the hind margin. The lobe on the inner margin of the merus is always obtuse.

Distribution. Nicobars (*Heller*) ; Mergui (*De Man*) ; Singapore (*Walker*) ; Java (*Milne-Edwards*) ; Malay Archipelago (*De Man*) ; N. and N.E. Australia (*Miers*).

233. PETROLISTHES BOSCII (Audouin).

Porcellana Boscii (Aud.), De Man, Mergui Crust. p. 217 1888,.

= *P. rugosa*, Milne-Edw.)

Rameswaram and Muttuwartu Par (*Thurston*); Rameswaram, not uncommon (*J. R. H.*).

This species is allied to the last, but distinguished by the very different sculpture, especially of the chelipedes. The carpal denticles are liable to considerable variation. The lobe at the inner distal end of the merus is acute, and on the upper distal margin of the same joint one or occasionally two spinules are met with.

Distribution. Red Sea (*Audouin, Heller, Kossmann, De Man*); Mergui (*De Man*); Kurachi (*Brit. Mus.*); N. Australia (*Brit. Mus.*).

234. PETROLISTHES MILITARIS (Heller).

Porcellana militaris (Heller), De Man, Brock's Crust. p. 410 (1888).

Petrolisthes annulipes, Miers, 'Alert' Crust. p. 270, pl. xxix. fig. B (1884).

Muttuwartu Par and Cheval Par (*Thurston*); Rameswaram (*Thurston, J. R. H.*).

My specimens are identical with the types of *P. annulipes*, and at the same time are referable to *P. militaris*, as defined by De Man. A supra-orbital spinule is present, but the lateral frontal margins are simply crenulated and not spinulose. Behind the outer orbital angle are two or three spines, the first placed on the margin and the others on the branchial surface, while about the middle of the branchial margin are from two to four spinules. De Man regards *P. annulipes* as identical with *P. scabricula*, Dana ; but in the latter the frontal margins are spinulose. I have, however, seen examples of the present species in which the normal crenulations have become almost spinulose, so that this identity may yet be established by further research ; in the meanwhile the two are perhaps best kept apart.

Distribution. Nicobars (*Heller*); Seychelles (*Miers*); W. coast of Java (*De Man*); Philippines (*White*); N. Australia (*Miers, Henderson*); Loo Choo Is. (*Ortmann*).

Genus RAPHIDOPUS, Stimpson.

235. RAPHIDOPUS INDICUS, n. sp. (Pl. XXXIX. figs. 19-22.)

Madras, a male (*J. R. H.*).

The carapace is convex from side to side and from before backwards, with the regions ill-defined and almost smooth, there being merely a few faint elevations on the branchial areas, some of which, in particular posteriorly, form short granulated lines; two very slight elevations rise almost in the centre of the carapace. The front is nearly straight when viewed from above, but looked at from before three projections can be seen, of which the median is slightly the most prominent. On the lateral margin of the carapace about a quarter of the distance back, is a well-defined notch, and between this and the external orbital angle is a sharp obscurely crenulated margin. Behind the notch the margin is convex and distinctly crenulated, but terminates abruptly by passing on to the surface of the carapace, leaving the posterior fourth of the side of the carapace simply rounded and marked by some of the elevated lines already referred to. The eyes are small.

The antennal peduncle is elongated, the penultimate joint being longest; the flagellum is long and naked.

The chelipedes are long and subequal, the right being but slightly larger. The merus is short and massive, granulated above, and with a small projecting lobe on the inner distal end of the upper surface; on the right side there is a sharp moderately long spine on the middle of the lower anterior surface. The carpus is about twice the length of the merus, with the upper surface uneven but scarcely granulated, the anterior margin moderately sharp and crenulated but without teeth, and the posterior margin rounded. The hand is slightly granulated above, the granules being more numerous on the smaller chela; the lower and outer surfaces, including both fingers, are densely pubescent. The fingers are strongly curved at their apices, and even when closed there is a considerable intervening hiatus; a single tooth is present on the immobile finger slightly beyond the middle; the mobile finger has a small basal tooth and is crenulated along the inner margin, its upper surface is rounded and granulated chiefly in the smaller chela. The ambulatory legs are long and slender, with the joints simply pubescent; the dactyli are entire, slender, and straight, about two thirds the length of the propodi, densely hairy above, and with a sulcus on the anterior surface.

The carapace is 6·5 mm. long and 9·5 mm. broad, the right chelipede 23 mm. long, the first ambulatory leg 14·5 mm. long.

This little-known genus bears some resemblance to *Polyonyx*, from which it is distinguished by the form of the front, the smaller eyes, the longer antennal peduncle, longer legs, and especially by the form of the ambulatory dactyli. The only previously known species, *R. ciliatus*, Stm., from China and Japan, has the carapace flatter and narrower, with the regions well defined; the postero-lateral margin of the carapace carries two or three spines, and the carpus of the chelipedes has a median row of tubercles on its outer surface.

Genus PACHYCHELES, Stimpson.

236. PACHYCHELES TOMENTOSUS, n. sp.   (Pl. XXXIX. figs. 16–18.)

Kurachi; four males, and five females all bearing ova (*Brit. Mus.*).

The carapace is flattened, glabrous, and depressed anteriorly, with the regions not defined, the protogastric lobules slightly prominent, and the surface slightly uneven towards the sides of the anterior branchial regions, which are raised above the level of the lateral margin. A few faint lines or wrinkles cross the posterior rounded lateral margin in passing to the under surface, and the remainder of the lateral border is defined by a somewhat sharp entire convex edge; opposite the penultimate joint of the antennal peduncle is a shallow depression or notch in the margin. The front is depressed, obscurely tridentate, and most prominent in the middle, with its upper surface densely tomentose. The upper orbital margin is obtusely rounded, and the eyes are of moderate size.

The chelipedes are unequal, and either may be the larger; they are granulated and densely tomentose above, the hairs being arranged in short tufts. The merus has a denticulated lobe on its inner and superior distal margin. The carpus is slightly convex and densely hairy above, with three longitudinal rows of white polished tubercles on the proximal half, and usually four or five tubercles in each row; the anterior or inner margin has three denticulated lobes or teeth, the first two of which are subequal and the distal one smaller, but in some cases the denticulations normally present on the edges of the primary teeth are absent, and the first tooth may be double, making four in all. The hand is flattened above, with a few tubercular granules scattered over the entire surface, most of which give rise to hairs; the long outer margin is denticulated, while the under surface is glabrous and finely granulated, especially on the outer side. The mobile finger is denticulated along its upper margin, finely tubercular and tomentose above, sparingly granulated and glabrous below, with a rounded tooth near the base on the inner margin; the fingers show a wide hiatus when closed, and the tip of the mobile one is bent underneath the tip of the other. The smaller chelipede is similar to the one just described, *i. e.* the larger, except that the margins of the hand and fingers are more strongly denticulate. The ambulatory legs are short and fringed with hairs, the under surface of the propodus presents two spinules at its distal end, and the dactyli have three minute horny spinules on the posterior margin of their proximal half.

The carapace of a female is 11·3 mm. long and 13 mm. broad, the left or larger carpus is 6·5 mm. long and 6 mm. broad, the propodus 12 mm. measured along its outer margin, the first ambulatory leg 15 mm. long.

It is distinguished from *P. grossimanus* (Guérin) by its densely tomentose and sparingly granulated chelipedes, and by the denticulated fingers. *P. pertinicarpus,* Stm., is very briefly characterized and agrees in some respects, but its carpus is described as having the anterior margin " pectinated with eight small equal spiniform teeth," and no mention is made of hairs on the chelipedes, while the carpus is much broader than long. In *P. Stereasii,* Stm., the chelipedes are not described as hairy, and the hand of the smaller chela is longitudinally bisulcate.

Genus PORCELLANELLA, White.

237. PORCELLANELLA TRILOBA, White.

P. triloba, White, in Macgillivray's Voyage H.M.S. ' Rattlesnake,' vol. ii. Appendix. p. 391, pl. v. fig. 2 (1852).

Rameswaram (*Thurston*).

I have examined White's type of *P. triloba,* as well as original specimens of *P. picta,* Stm., from Hong Kong, in the British Museum, and can find only the following differences :— In White's species the median frontal projection but slightly exceeds the lateral ones, and its apex is rounded, while the first or most proximal of the four spinules on the ambulatory dactyli is very small ; in Stimpson's species the median frontal tooth is slightly longer and subacute, and the four spinules on the dactyli are subequal. The two species may yet be united, but at present may be kept separate.

Distribution. N. Australia (*White*); Celebes Sea (*Henderson*) ; Falkland Is. (*Henderson*).

Genus POLYONYX, Stimpson.

238. POLYONYX OBESULUS, Miers.

P. obesulus (White), Miers, 'Alert' Crust. p. 272, pl. xxix. fig. D (1884).

Rameswaram and Tuticorin (*Thurston*). Common at Rameswaram, both free and in sponges (*J. R. H.*).

I have compared my specimens with the types in the British Museum. The median frontal projection is obtusely rounded and but little prominent. The ambulatory dactyli are triunguiculate, the middle claw being slightly stouter and larger than the distal one, whereas the proximal one is much smaller. Sexual dimorphism is seen in regard to the chelipedes and the width of the carapace. In both sexes the right chelipede (which is usually the smaller of the two) has the hand more or less carinated inferiorly, and the carina often minutely dentate; the fingers are in contact throughout, or almost so, in males, the opposing margins being finely dentate and without any prominent tooth. In females and young males the left chelipede, which is as a rule slightly the larger, is similar to the right, whereas in adult males it is more strongly developed; the fingers have a wide gape, and are not in contact even at the apices when closed; while a prominent tooth is present on the inner margin of the lower finger. The male probably holds the chelipede of the female during copulation.

In *P. biunguiculatus* (Dana) the median frontal projection is prominent and acute, while the ambulatory dactyli are biunguiculate, the first or proximal claw, present in *P. obesulus*, being scarcely visible and represented merely by a minute seta. On the chelipedes the lobe of the inner margin of the merus is more prominent, and the carpus is usually longer than in Miers's species. In some specimens the outer surface of the hand is granulated. There are examples in the British Museum of Dana's species from the Gulf of Suez, the Seychelles, and the Amirantes. De Man has suggested that *P. obesulus* is identical with *P. biunguiculatus*, and that the *P. biunguiculatus* described by Miers is a distinct species; but I cannot agree with this suggestion.

The following measurements are taken from Rameswaram specimens :—

	Male.	Female.
Length of carapace	6·7 mm.	6·2 mm.
Breadth ,,	8·3 ,,	8·5 ,,
Length of left hand	11·5 ,,	8·5 ,,
Breadth ,,	5·5 ,,	4·3 ,,
Length of left carpus	7·5 ,,	5·7 ,,

The colour is a pale red, turning white in spirit. One individual—a male—carries a *Sacculina*.

Distribution. Madjicosima Is. (*White*); N. Australia (*Miers, Henderson*); Amboina (*De Man*); Singapore (*Walker*).

239. POLYONYX TUBERCULOSUS, De Man.

Porcellana (Polyonyx) sp. *(tuberculosa* in text), De Man, Brock's Crust. p. 424, pl. xiii. fig. 1 (1888).

Cheval Par (*Thurston*); Rameswaram, common (*J. R. H.*).

I doubtfully refer to the above species a large series of specimens with the following characters :—The median frontal projection is subacute when viewed from before. The chelipedes are tuberculate on the upper surface of the carpus and hand; the merus is produced internally into a finely-toothed lobe ; the inner margin of the carpus has a few subacute teeth, while the outer margin of the hand is carinated and finely serrated. The ambulatory dactyli are four-clawed, the two proximal spinules being very minute, while the terminal claw is longer and slightly stouter than the penultimate one. The ambulatory legs are fringed anteriorly with hairs. This species is certainly distinct from *P. obesulus* or *P. biunguiculatus*, and, as De Man represents his species with the carpus smooth above, and with very few tubercles present on the hand, our specimens may also be distinct from *P. tuberculosus*. The ambulatory dactyli of the last species are not described by De Man. I have noticed in one or two specimens of *P. obesulus* a slight tendency towards tuberculation on the hand, chiefly in small individuals; but our species may be distinguished from this variety by the greater tuberculation and the different ambulatory dactyli. De Man had only a single small specimen, and it may have belonged to this variety of *P. obesulus*, in which case a new name will be necessary for the form which is here briefly characterized.

A male is 7·3 mm. long and 8 mm. broad.

Distribution. Amboina (*De Man*).

Genus GALATHEA, Fabricius.

240. GALATHEA ELEGANS, White.

G. elegans (White), Adams & White, 'Samarang' Crust. pp. i, ii, pl. xii. fig. 7 (1848).

Tuticorin, four specimens (*Thurston*); Gulf of Martaban, two specimens (*Oates*).

There appears to be considerable variation in the coloration and in the form of the rostrum ; perhaps *G. grandirostris*, Stm., and *G. deflexifrons*, Haswell, are merely varieties of this species.

Distribution. Philippines and Borneo (*Adams & White*) ; Singapore (*Walker*) : Amboina (*De Man*) ; Celebes Sea (*Henderson*) ; N. Australia (*Miers, Haswell*).

241. GALATHEA SPINOSIROSTRIS, Dana.

G. spinosirostris, Dana, Crust. U.S. Explor. Exped. pt. i. p. 480, pl. xxx. fig. 9 (1852) ; De Man. Brock's Crust. p. 456 (1888).

Muttuwartu Par, two females with ova (*Thurston*) ; Gulf of Martaban, a male (*Oates*).

I refer these with some doubt to this species. The Muttuwartu specimens, the larger of which is only 10 mm. in total length, are without gastric spinules at the base of the rostrum, and in this respect agree with *G. corallicola*, Haswell, which was regarded by Miers as a variety of *G. australiensis*, Stm. The Martaban specimen has a rudimentary pair of gastric spinules, but otherwise closely agrees with the Muttuwartu examples. It seems probable that *G. australiensis* is identical with Dana's species, so I refer my specimens to the latter.

Distribution. Sandwich Is. (*Dana*)?; E. Australia (*Stimpson, Haswell, Miers*); Amirantes (*Miers*); Amboina (*De Man*); Mauritius (*Richters*); Arafura Sea (*Henderson*).

Genus MUNIDA, Leach.

242. MUNIDA SPINULIFERA, Miers.

M. spinulifera, Miers, ' Alert ' Crust. p. 279, pl. xxxi. fig. B (1884).

Muttuwartu Par, a female with ova (*Thurston*) ; Gulf of Martaban, a male (*Oates*).

The male is 13 mm. long and the female somewhat smaller ; in both specimens the abdominal segments are without dorsal spinules.

Distribution. Arafura Sea (*Miers*); Amboina (*Henderson*).

Suborder MACRURA.

Group THALASSINIDEA.

Genus GEBIOPSIS, A. Milne-Edw.

243. GEBIOPSIS DARWINII, Miers.

G. Darwinii, Miers, ' Alert' Crust. p. 281, pl. xxxii. fig. A (1884).

G. intermedia, De Man, Mergui Crust. p. 256, pl. xvi. fig. 2 (1888) ; id. Brock's Crust. p. 462 (1888).

Rameswaram, Tuticorin, and Cheval Par (*Thurston*). Common at Rameswaram, usually living in sponges (*J. R. H.*).

I have compared my specimens with (1) a single type-specimen of De Man's species in the British Museum, (2) the types of Miers's species, and in my opinion the two species are identical. The antennal and antennular peduncles are alike in both, and are incorrectly figured by Miers. I find, however, on examining a number of specimens, that there is some variation in the length of the penultimate antennal peduncular segment. The row of minute spinules (or tubercles) on the meropodites of the chelipedes, mentioned by De Man, occurs also in Miers's species. The two spines described by De Man as present on the carpopodites are liable to variation ; sometimes the lower one is rudimentary or even absent (it is rudimentary in De Man's specimen in the British Museum), while the upper one is often similarly reduced. The last pair of legs are wrongly figured by Miers; his specimens agree perfectly with De Man's—*i. e.* the last legs are chelate, and the carpus is but slightly longer than the propodus.

The only differences I can find are—(*a*) in size De Man's specimens are much larger than Miers's, but this is evidently of little importance, for one of the Rameswaram males is 36 mm. long, while a female with eggs from the same locality is only 23 mm. long; (*b*) in Miers's specimens the inferior spine of the carpopodite is absent or represented by a mere rudiment, and the upper one is greatly reduced, but, as previously noted, these characters vary. De Man has more recently described a variety *amboinensis* in which the lower carpal spine is wanting.

Distribution. N. Australia (*Miers*); Amboina (*De Man*); Singapore (*Walker*); Mergui (*De Man*).

Group ASTACIDEA.

Genus THENUS, Leach.

244. THENUS ORIENTALIS (Fabr.).

T. orientalis (Fabr.), Milne-Edwards, Hist. Nat. Crust. t. ii. p. 286 (1837).

Common at Madras and on the South Indian coast generally (*J. R. H.*).

The three teeth in the mid-dorsal line of the carapace are prominent and subacute in young individuals, blunt and ill-defined in adults.

Distribution. Madagascar, Seychelles, Indian Seas, Malay Archipelago, China, W. Australia.

Genus PANULIRUS, Gray.

245. PANULIRUS ORNATUS (Fabr.).

Palinurus ornatus (Fabr.), Milne-Edwards, Hist. Nat. Crust. t. ii. p. 296 (1837).
Panulirus ornatus (Fabr.), Stimpson, Proc. Acad. Nat. Sci. Philad. Jan. 1860, p. 24.
Senex ornatus (Fabr.), Ortmann, Zool. Jahrb. Bd. vi. Abth. f. Syst. p. 34 (1892), *ubi synon.*

Ceylon (*Haly*).

Distribution. From E. Africa to Japan, N. Australia, and the Pacific (Samoa).

246. PANULIRUS PENICILLATUS (Olivier).

Palinurus penicillatus (Oliv.), Milne-Edwards, Hist. Nat. Crust. t. ii. p. 299 (1837).
Panulirus penicillatus (Oliv.), Stimpson, Proc. Acad. Nat. Sci. Philad. Jan. 1860, p. 24.
Senex penicillatus (Oliv.), Ortmann, Zool. Jahrb. Bd. vi. Abth. f. Syst. p. 28 (1892), *ubi synon.*

Ceylon (*Haly*).

Distribution. From the Red Sea and Mauritius to the Malay Archipelago, N. Australia, and the Pacific (Fijis, New Hebrides, Tahiti).

247. PANULIRUS DASYPUS (Latr.).

Palinurus dasypus (Latr.), Milne-Edwards, Hist. Nat. Crust. t. ii. p. 300 (1837).
Senex dasypus (Latr.), Ortmann, Zool. Jahrb. Bd. vi. Abth. f. Syst. p. 33, (1892), *ubi synon.*

Silavaturai Par (*Thurston*). Common at Madras (*J. R. H.*).

The Silavaturai example is very young, measuring only 15 mm. in length, but is apparently referable to this species. It has two pairs of spines, arranged as if at the angles of a square, on the antennal segment, the posterior pair being smaller than the anterior pair; at a later stage small spinules are developed towards the centre of the square.

Distribution. Indian Ocean (*Milne-Edwards*); Ceylon and Madras (*Heller*); Muscat (*Brit. Mus.*); Moluccas (*Herklot*).

Group C A R I D E A.

Genus CARIDINA, Milne-Edwards.

248. CARIDINA WYCKII (Hickson).

C. Wyckii (Hickson), De Man, Max Weber's Crust. p. 386, Taf. xxiv. fig. 29 (1891).

Madras, common in wells and in ponds with clear fresh water (*J. R. H.*).

I can find no difference, except in size, between Madras specimens and Hickson's types in the British Museum, the Indian examples being considerably larger, and reaching a length of about 35 mm., including the rostrum; they also completely agree with De Man's excellent description and figures. I first observed the species in a swimming-bath at Northwick, Madras, the residence of my friend the Rev. Dr. Miller. As De Man has pointed out, it is very closely related to *C. nilotica*, Roux (= *C. longirostris*, Milne-Edw.), from N. and E. Africa, and perhaps the two species are not distinct.

A *Caridina* from Roorkee, in the Day collection, is represented by a single damaged specimen which cannot be satisfactorily identified.

Distribution. Celebes, in fresh water at an altitude of 2000 ft. (*Hickson*); Celebes, Saleyer, and Flores, in fresh and brackish water (*De Man*).

Genus ALPHEUS, Fabricius.

249. ALPHEUS MALABARICUS, Fabr.   (Pl. XL. figs. 1–3.)

A. malabaricus, Fabr. Suppl. Ent. Syst. p. 405 (1798); non *A. malabaricus*, De Haan, nec Hilgendorf, nec Ortmann.

Common in the backwater at Pulicat, and apparently burrowing in a muddy bottom (*J. R. H.*).

The ocular hoods are prominent, but simply rounded, and placed closer together than usual. The rostrum is acute, reaching the level of the basal antennular scales, and not extending back on the carapace behind the posterior limit of the eyes, though clearly distinct from the latter. The antennal and antennular peduncles are subequal in length. The antennular scales do not reach the end of the proximal peduncular joint by about one fourth the length of the latter, and the second peduncular joint is fully twice the length of the distal one. The antennal scales are about equal in length to both the antennal and antennular peduncles, and the outer distal spine is minute.

The larger chelipede, which may be either the right or the left, is slender proximally, but has a massive hand. The merus has a slight tooth on its upper distal surface, and a well-marked spine on the inner distal margin. The hand is moderately compressed, with a distinct sulcus crossing the upper margin behind the insertion of the mobile finger, and a second sulcus immediately underneath on the lower margin; both the upper and lower margins behind the sulci are well rounded. On both the inner and the outer surfaces of the hand a wide shallow furrow with ill-defined margins passes back from the upper sulcus; the outer of these furrows passes somewhat obliquely towards the proximal inferior angle of the joint, while the inner, which is scarcely so large, passes close to the upper margin. On the inner surface of the hand a shallow furrow connects the two marginal sulci and extends across the long axis of the joint. The dactylus is strongly curved and carinated dorsally, with the apex curving beyond that of the lower immobile finger. No ridges are present on the larger hand. The smaller chelipede is very long, slender, and unarmed; the fingers are slightly incurved and very long, being about three and a half times the length of the hand in adults, and in close apposition—*i. e.* they are parallel and with scarcely any hiatus at the base when closed. The mobile finger has a distinct basal tooth, and long hairs clothe the inner edges of both fingers. The second chelate legs have the first and second carpal joints long and subequal, the third and fourth short and subequal, and the fifth slightly longer than either the third or the fourth. The ambulatory legs are slender and unarmed. The apex of the telson is obtusely rounded, with the terminal lateral spinules very minute.

An adult male is 30 mm. long, the larger chelipede 27 mm. long, the hand 11 mm. long, and the fingers 7 mm.; the smaller chelipede is 29 mm. long, the hand 4 mm., and the fingers 13·5 mm. In the female the chelipedes are slightly smaller.

This species, originally collected by Daldorff in South India, has apparently been lost sight of for nearly a hundred years. I think there can be little doubt that the species just described is identical with that of Fabricius; it completely agrees with his short diagnosis, while the Japanese species referred to *A. malabaricus* by De Haan and others does not conform to the original description in one important respect—it exhibits a wide gape or hiatus between the fingers of the smaller chela, which Fabricius expressly states are parallel. De Haan's species is termed *A. malabaricus* in the description (Crust. Japon. p. 177), but *A. brevicristatus* on the plate (tab. xlv. fig. 1), so that the latter designation may be conveniently retained for it, provided that the earlier described *A. dispar*, Randall, should not prove to be synonymous, as some writers have supposed. In the British Museum is a specimen of our species from Pondicherry, bearing a MS. name, "*A. forceps*," White. *A. dolichodactylus*, Ortmann, from Japan, is nearly allied, and has both the hand sulci present, but it has a wide gape between the fingers of the smaller chela, and the dactylus is apparently without a tooth; it has also a distinct tooth on the upper margin near the base of the larger dactylus, which is not seen in our species. *A. brevicristatus*, De Haan, is easily distinguished by its larger hand, which is ridged externally; the inferior marginal sulcus is absent, and there is a wide gape between the fingers of the smaller chela.

Distribution. South India (*Fabricius*).

250. ALPHEUS EDWARDSII (Audouin).

A. Edwardsii (Aud.), Miers, ' Alert ' Crust. p. 281 (1884 , *ubi synon.*

Rameswaram, Tuticorin, and Muttuwartu Par (*Thurston*); Gulf of Martaban (*Oates*); Kurachi (*Brit Mus.*). Very common on the reef at Rameswaram (*J. R. H.*).

Distribution. Atlantic Region—from N. Carolina to Brazil, West Indies, Cape Verd Is. Indo-Pacific Region—from the Red Sea and E. Africa to Japan, California, Samoa, the Fijis, Tahiti, &c.

251. ALPHEUS HIPPOTHOË, De Man.

A. Hippothoë, De Man, Mergui Crust. p. 268, pl. xvii. figs. 1-5 (1888).

Rameswaram, six specimens (*J. R. H.*).

This species is allied to *A. Edwardsii,* which it resembles in size, the rounded ocular hoods, and the general form of the chela, but is distinguished by its stouter ambulatory legs, those of the second and third pairs with the meral joints broad and flattened, and armed with a distal spine on the lower margin; the rostrum is more strongly marked than in *A. Edwardsii,* and in some cases extends back on the carapace, though faintly, almost to the middle.

Distribution. Mergui; Pulo Edam and Amboina (*De Man*).

252. ALPHEUS FRONTALIS, Say.

A. frontalis (Say), Milne-Edwards, Hist. Nat. Crust. t. ii. p. 356 (1837); id. Atlas, Cuv. Règne Anim. pl. liii. fig. 2 (1849).

Tuticorin (*Thurston*).

Distribution. Australia (*Milne-Edwards*); Tahiti (*Heller*); Loo Choo Is.; Samoa; South Sea (*Ortmann*).

253. ALPHEUS LÆVIS, Randall.

A. lævis (Rand.), Ortmann, Zool. Jahrb. Bd. v. Abth. f. Syst. p. 487 (1891), *ubi synon.*

Rameswaram and Tuticorin (*Thurston*). Not uncommon on the reef at Rameswaram (*J. R. H.*).

Distribution. From the Red Sea and E. Africa to Japan, Sydney, and the Pacific (Tonga, Fijis, Tahiti, Sandwich Is., &c.).

254. ALPHEUS NEPTUNUS, Dana.

A. Neptunus, Dana, Crust. U.S. Explor. Exped. pt. i. p. 553, pl. xxxv. fig. 5 (1852).

Kurachi (*Brit. Mus.*). Common on the reef at Rameswaram (*J. R. H.*).

Both Miers and De Man regard this as merely a variety of *A. minor,* Say, which is common on the east coast of the United States.

Distribution. From the Red Sea to China, Japan, Port Jackson, and the west coast of Central America.

Genus DORODOTES, Bate.

255. DORODOTES LEVICARINA, Bate.

D. levicarina, Bate, 'Challenger' Macrura, p. 680, pl. cxii. fig. 5 (1888).

Gulf of Martaban (*Oates*).

The single specimen is a female with ova, measuring 51 mm. in length, including the rostrum, which is 11 mm. long.

Distribution. Arafura Sea, 28 fathoms (*Bate*).

Genus ANGASIA. Bate.

Angasia, Bate, Proc. Zool. Soc. p. 498 (1863).

Tozeuma, Stimpson, Proc. Acad. Nat. Sci. Philad. p. 26, Jan. 1860.

I propose to substitute this generic name for the older *Tozeuma*, Stimpson, which, in its correctly spelt form *Toxeuma*, had been previously applied by Walker to a genus of Hymenoptera. Stimpson gives the derivation of his name, so that the spelling has perhaps been due to a printer's error which he has allowed to pass.

256. ANGASIA STIMPSONII, n. sp. (Pl. XL. figs. 18-20.)

Gulf of Martaban, two specimens (*Oates*).

The body is compressed laterally, with the rostrum about equal in length to the abdomen, omitting the telson. The rostrum is slightly upturned, with an obtuse or rounded dorsal carina, bounded on either side by a slight groove, but thin or laminar, and finely serrated, below ; seen from the side it is deepest immediately in front of the eyes, from which point it gradually tapers to the apex. The carapace is provided with an acute antero-lateral spine. The eyes occupy orbits, which are formed partly by the rostrum, and partly by the antennal peduncles. The antennular peduncles are not half the length of the antennal scales, and their flagella, which otherwise agree with Stimpson's description of those in *A. lanceolata*, reach only to about the middle of the scale ; the basal peduncular segment has an external flattened acute process. The antennal peduncle has an acute spine on the under surface of its basal joint, about equal in size to the antero-lateral spine of the carapace ; the flagellum extends considerably beyond the rostrum, although incomplete in both specimens. The antennal scale is very long and narrow, being almost half the length of the rostrum.

The abdominal segments are obtusely carinated, and the third, fourth, and fifth are each prolonged posteriorly into a dorsal tooth. The telson is very long, narrow, and acuminate, slightly exceeding the last appendages, and with three pairs of lateral spinules. The legs are as described by Stimpson in *A. lanceolata*, the wrist of the second pair being three-jointed.

The larger specimen, a female with ova, is imperfect, but the smaller gives the following measurements :—length of body, measured from the eye to the tip of the telson, 43 mm., rostrum 22 mm., antennal scale 9·7 mm. long and 1·2 mm. in greatest breadth, telson 9·3 mm. long.

In some respects this species seems to agree with *A. lanceolata* (Stm.) from Hong Kong, but Stimpson, in his short description of the latter, states that the rostrum is "scarcely a fourth part shorter than the body," and that the antennulæ equal in length the antennal appendices or scales ; he also describes the antennæ as shorter than the rostrum, the antennal scales as one third the length of the rostrum, and the breadth of each scale as being equal to one fourth of its length. Our species may therefore be distinguished at once by its very much longer and narrower antennal scale. *A. paronina*, Bate, from South Australia, has the rostrum with only four teeth below, the antennal scale reaching nearly to the end of the rostrum, and the apex of the telson obtuse. The only other species known, so far as I am aware, is *A. carolinensis* (Kingsley), from the east coast of the United States. The *Tozeuma serratum* of A. Milne-Edwards, from the West Indies, is probably, as Bate has remarked, referable to some other genus, for in it the carpus of the second legs is multiarticulate.

Genus RHYNCHOCINETES, Milne-Edwards.

257. RHYNCHOCINETES RUGULOSUS, Stimpson.

R. rugulosus, Stimpson, Proc. Acad. Nat. Sci. Philad. Jan. 1860, p. 36.

Tuticorin, four specimens (*Thurston*).

The body is marked dorsally by fine transverse or somewhat concentric impressed striæ. The rostral formula in three specimens is $\frac{3+2+2}{9}$, and in the fourth $\frac{3+2+2}{8}$, the first three upper teeth being situated on the carapace; whereas according to Stimpson the rostrum is tridentate above near the apex, and has twelve teeth below. These differences may be due to local variation, or possibly the Tuticorin examples are referable to a distinct and new species, but I do not venture to separate them. A few spinules are present on the meral joints of the last three pairs of legs, and the first pair have a spine at the upper distal end of both the merus and the carpus, while the latter joint is carinated superiorly along its entire length. The apex of the telson is acuminate, and carries two pairs of subterminal spinules, of which the inner pair exceed the terminal portion of the telson, and are about three times the length of the outer pair.

Distribution. Port Jackson (*Stimpson*).

Genus PONTONIA, Latreille.

258. PONTONIA TRIDACNAE, Dana.

P. tridacnae, Dana, Crust. U.S. Explor. Exped. pt. i. p. 571, pl. xxxvii. fig. 1 (1852).
(= *Conchodytes tridacnae*, Peters).

Tuticorin (*Thurston*); Rameswaram, in the mantle-chamber of a large *Pinna* (*J. R. H.*).

Distribution. Red Sea (*Hilgendorf*); E. Africa (*Peters*, *Hilgendorf*); N. and N.E. Australia (*Miers*); Samoa (*Dana*, *Ortmann*); Fijis (*Miers*).

Genus LEANDER, Desmarest.

This genus was founded by E. Desmarest in 1849 (Ann. Soc. Ent. de France, sér. 2 t. vii. p. 91), but poorly characterized, most stress being laid on the gibbosity of the abdomen; indeed, the characters furnished by this writer might apply to either the fresh-water or the marine forms. He, however, figures as the type an undoubted marine form, *L. erraticus*, Desm. (= *L. natator*, Milne-Edw. fide Spence Bate). Stimpson, in 1860, was the first to separate *Leander* and *Palæmon*, and to properly characterize them, placing the marine species in *Leander* and the fluviatile species in *Palæmon*, an arrangement which has been followed by most subsequent writers. Spence Bate, in his Report on the 'Challenger' Macrura, partially reverses this arrangement and refers the marine species to *Palæmon*, partly because he regarded Desmarest's diagnosis as valueless, and because Leach, Milne-Edwards, Bell, and others had termed the common

European marine species *Palæmon*, while he places the freshwater forms in the genus *Bithynis*, founded by Philippi in 1860. A reference to Fabricius's writings shows that he, without naming any special type, described the freshwater forms first, and his name *Palæmon* ought therefore to be taken for these; this is the plan adopted by Dr. Ortmann, who has recently prepared a useful and much needed revision of the genus. Ortmann correctly limits the genus *Bithynis* to a single species, *B. Gaudichaudii* (Milne-Edw.), from Chili and Peru, in which the hepatic spine is absent, and the chelipedes are unequal and greatly enlarged.

259. LEANDER LONGIROSTRIS (Say).

Palæmon longirostris (Say), Milne-Edwards, Hist. Nat. Crust. t. ii. p. 394 (1837).

Kurachi, four specimens (*Brit. Mus.*); Sunderbunds, four specimens; Mergui, one specimen (*Day*); Gulf of Martaban, three specimens (*Oates*).

The rostrum, which is upturned distally, exceeds the antennal scales by half or more of its length; the basal crest ends opposite the articulation between the last two joints of the antennular peduncle. The first lower rostral tooth is placed under the most distal tooth of the basal crest. The shortest of the three antennular flagella exceeds the antennal scales by more than half its length. On the carapace the antennal or upper spine is minute, while the branchiostegal or lower one is well developed. The spine on the outer margin of the antennal scale is placed at some distance from the apex, the distance equalling nearly one third of the total length of the outer margin.

The first pair of legs reach to or slightly exceed the antennal scales. The second legs have the ischium and merus cylindrical and subequal, the carpus slightly shorter and dorsally dilated; the propodus is shorter than the carpus, and considerably swollen in the adult of both sexes, with its outer surface sulcate, and the sulcus bounded by two ridges, an arrangement which is best seen on the distal two thirds of the hand, terminating opposite the base of the mobile finger. The fingers are very long and slender, being about half its length longer than the palm; they have sharp cutting-edges, but no teeth, and are strongly curved at their apices. The remaining feet are slender and slightly longer than the first pair. The last four abdominal segments are dorsally more or less carinated. The telson is dorsally smooth and rounded, with the very slender and acute apex placed opposite the spine on the outer margin of the exopodite of the sixth pair of abdominal appendages; the two minute subterminal spinules are greatly exceeded in length by the apex of the telson.

A female from the Sunderbunds is 64 mm. long from the orbit to the apex of the telson, the rostrum 20 mm. long, the second leg 68 mm. long.

The following are the rostral formulae in specimens from the different localities:—

Kurachi.—$\frac{5+3}{9}, \frac{6+3}{9}, \frac{6+3}{8}$.

Sunderbunds.—Three specimens $\frac{6+2}{9}$, one specimen $\frac{5+2}{8}$.

Martaban.—$\frac{6+1}{7}, \frac{6+1}{8}$.

Mergui.—$\frac{6+1}{8}$.

The *L. longirostris*, var. *japonicus*, of Ortmann, which is distinguished by the form of its telson and rostrum, is, I think, a distinct species, while the var. *carinatus*, of the same author, from China, founded on the carination of the abdominal segments which is seen in Milne-Edwards's species, may or may not be distinct. De Man (Notes Leyden Museum, vol. iii. p. 141, 1881) describes the branchiostegal spine as smaller than the antennal spine in the Chinese examples which he referred to *L. longirostris*, but this is probably an error of description.

Distribution. Sunderbunds (*Milne-Edwards*); China (*De Man, Ortmann*).

260. LEANDER TENUIPES, n. sp.   (Pl. XL. figs. 14, 15.)

Bombay, two imperfect specimens (*Day*); Gulf of Martaban, five specimens (*Oates*); Madras, ten specimens (*J. R. H.*).

The rostrum is slender, and exceeds the antennal scales by about half its length, with the distal two thirds styliform and upturned; the basal crest scarcely reaches the end of the proximal antennal peduncular joint. The first lower rostral tooth is minute, and placed under or in front of the distal tooth of the basal crest; both the upper and lower distal teeth are placed at some distance from the apex of the rostrum. The shortest of the three antennular flagella does not reach the end of the antennal scales. The spine on the antennal scale is placed much nearer the apex than in *L. longirostris.* The antennal spine is minute, but the branchiostegal one is well developed.

The first pair of legs are slightly longer than the antennal scales. The second legs have the merus more than twice the length of the ischium, and the former joint is proximally compressed, with an ill-defined sulcus on the upper surface, but its distal half is narrow and less compressed; the carpus is about equal in length to the ischium, while the palm, which is slightly dilated and smooth, is a little longer than the carpus. The fingers are nearly twice the length of the palm, but otherwise similar to those of *L. longirostris.* The remaining feet are extremely long and slender, more especially due to a lengthening of their terminal joints, which are more slender than even the antennal and antennular flagella; they increase in length on passing back, the last pair being longest. It is impossible to give accurate measurements of these legs, as in most cases they appear to be imperfect. This extraordinary lengthening is not confined to the legs, but is seen also in the antennal and antennular flagella, which are certainly more than twice the length of the body. The last three abdominal segments are strongly compressed laterally, and narrowed above but not carinated. The telson is smooth and rounded dorsally, except for the presence of a shallow sulcus towards the apex; the apex is blunt, and not produced to the level of the spine on the exopodites of the last appendages, with the subterminal pair of spinules considerably longer than the free end of the telson.

The colour noted in fresh specimens is grey, with the thoracic viscera presenting an orange hue under the carapace, and the attached or fertilized ova in the female yellowish green.

A Madras specimen, measured like the last species, is 55 mm. long, the rostrum 19 mm., the second leg 36 mm., and the last leg 75 mm. Although the dactylus of the last leg in this example is broken at the tip, it still measures 15 mm. in length.

The rostral formulæ are as follows :—

Martaban.—Three specimens $\frac{5+1}{4}$, two specimens $\frac{5+1}{3}$.

Madras.—Five specimens $\frac{6+1}{4}$, two specimens $\frac{5+1}{4}$, one specimen $\frac{5+1}{3}$, one specimen $\frac{6+1}{5}$.

This species in some respects, as in the form of the rostrum, the compressed abdominal segments, the small antennal spine, and the form of the hand and fingers, is allied to *L. longirostris*, but may be distinguished at once by its greatly elongated and excessively slender legs, the form of the second legs, telson, antennal scales, &c. I at first felt inclined to establish a new genus for its reception, but on further consideration I think it better to regard it as an aberrant species of *Leander*, for all its more important structural features are such as vary considerably among the different known species of this genus.

261. LEANDER MODESTUS, Heller.

L. modestus, Heller, ' Novara' Crust. p. 111, Taf. x. fig. 6 (1865).

Madras, six specimens (*J. R. H.*).

The apical third or more of the rostrum is edentulous and upturned, while the proximal part carries eight or nine small teeth ; three teeth are found on the lower margin, the most distal of which in all my specimens is placed in advance of the most distal upper tooth, while in Heller's figure the two are represented as placed opposite each other.

Distribution. Shanghai (*Heller*).

Genus PALÆMON *, Fabricius.

262. PALÆMON CARCINUS (Fabr.).

P. carcinus (Fabr.), Ortmann, Zool. Jahrb. Bd. v. Abth. f. Syst. p. 700, Taf. xlvii. fig. 1 (1891).

A large series from Bombay ; Ganjam ; Calcutta ; Sunderbunds ; Sittoung, Burmah ; Tavoy (*Day*) ; Burmah (*Oates*).

The colour is characteristic, the chelipedes, carapace, and abdomen being marked with purple, as indicated in the figure of Herbst.

The examination of a large series from different localities has left me in considerable doubt as to the limitations of this species. I find great variation as regards the length of the chelipedes in adult males, and the length and toothing of the rostrum, in specimens taken along with, and which I cannot separate from, the typical form. In some specimens from Bombay, Madras, and Ganjam, in both sexes the rostrum is scarcely longer than the antennal scales, while the number of teeth is greatly reduced ; and, as

* There are several species of *Palæmon* in the Day collection which are probably new, but I have not ventured to characterize them, owing to deficiency of material ; nor have I as yet attempted to identify my Madras specimens. An example from Ganjam (*Day*), without chelipedes, and which, therefore, cannot be satisfactorily identified, carries a Bopyrid parasite, and some time ago I forwarded a specimen, taken in fresh water at Madras, to Prof. Giard and M. Bonnier, with a similar parasite. These authors have recorded two freshwater Bopyrids from the Malay Archipelago.

they are normal in other respects, I am forced to regard them as belonging to a variety in which the apical growth of the rostrum has been arrested.

I refer to the *P. Lamarrei*, of Milne-Edwards, described from Bengal, certain specimens from Ganjam, in which the rostrum exceeds the antennal scales by about half its length, and is upturned distally, with six or more teeth below, and the upper teeth most marked proximally, in which the telson is narrow and acute, with the subterminal spinules at some distance from the apex. These were taken with typical examples of *P. carcinus*, and I regard them as being merely the young of this species. De Man and Ortmann regard *P. Lamarrei* as identical with a species found in Brazil; but it seems to me improbable that, in a freshwater genus apparently so plastic as *Palæmon*, the same species should occur in such widely separate localities.

Distribution. India, Burmah, Siam, Malay Peninsula, and the Malay Archipelago (Sumatra, Java, Borneo, Philippines, Celebes, New Guinea).

263. PALÆMON DISPAR, von Martens.

P. dispar (v. Mart.), Ortmann, Zool. Jahrb. Bd. v. Abth. f. Syst. p. 718 (1891), *ubi synon.* ; De Man, Max Weber's Crust. p. 427, Taf. xxvi. fig. 34 (1891).

Calcutta, several specimens (*Day*).

I refer these with some hesitation to this species. The rostrum is almost straight, reaching the end of the antennal peduncles, and in some specimens even the end of the antennal scales, with from nine to thirteen teeth above, and four or more, rarely five, below, the first two upper teeth separated by a wider interval than the others, and the third placed above the orbital margin. The carapace is slightly scabrous. The chelipedes are very long, slender, and unequal, with the surface scabrous; the carpus exceeds the palm by half its length, and the fingers are about half the length of the palm. Both fingers in the male have a row of tubercles on the inner margin, while in the female there is simply a sharp edge. The telson is rather broad towards the apex, but pointed, with the inner subterminal spinules more than twice the length of the outer ones, or of the apical spine of the telson; the terminal setæ are slightly longer than the inner spinules. The largest specimen is 73 mm. long, not including the rostrum, and the larger chelipede 145 mm. long.

Distribution. Réunion, Mauritius, Rodriguez, Malay Archipelago (Adonara, Timor, Flores, Saleyer, Celebes, Amboina), Samoa.

264. PALÆMON SCABRICULUS, Heller.

P. scabriculus, Heller, 'Novara' Crust. p. 117, Taf. x. fig. 9 (1865) ; Ortmann, Zool. Jahrb. Bd. v. Abth. f. Syst. p. 710 (1891) ; De Man, Max Weber's Crust. p. 462, Taf. xxvii. fig. 41 (1891).

Kotri, on the River Indus, several specimens (*Brit. Mus.*).

The rostrum is deep, and scarcely reaches the end of the antennal scales ; the teeth are more erect than usual, and in number $\frac{11-15}{2}$, the fourth or fifth upper tooth placed above the orbital margin. The carapace is scabriculate anteriorly and on the branchial areas, but punctate behind. The chelipedes in the male are about equal in length to the body, pubescent and slightly scabriculate, with the carpus about equal to the palm; the fingers are longer than the palm, and slightly curved in the male, with their opposed margins finely toothed and pubescent. The right chelipede is usually larger than the left. In the female the chelipedes are less elongated, and the fingers may be slightly shorter than the palm. The telson is truncated, but obtusely pointed at the apex, with the inner spinules and the setæ very long.

A male is 42 mm. long, not including the rostrum, the right chelipede 45 mm., and the left chelipede 33 mm.

Distribution. Ceylon (*Heller*); Saleyer and Celebes (*De Man*).

265. PALÆMON DAYANUS, n. sp. (Pl. XL. figs. 7–13.)

A large series from Orissa, Jubbulpore. Calcutta, Beerbhoom, Debroo *, Delhi, Roorkee, Hurdwar, Loodiana, River Jumna, Lahore (*Day*).

The rostrum is usually almost straight, and extends to the end of the antennal scales, with the formula $\frac{7-9}{5-6}$; on the upper margin the six proximal teeth are equidistant, and separated by a wider interval from two, or more rarely three, smaller subapical teeth, which are placed close together, while the second, occasionally the third, proximal tooth is placed above the orbital margin; on the lower margin the teeth are equidistant, and slightly decrease in size towards the apex. The free end of the antennal scale is rounded, and scarcely angulated internally. The carapace is smooth, with the hepatic spine rather small, and a faint sulcus which commences below the level of the latter extends back almost to the middle of the side wall of the carapace.

The first legs exceed the antennal scales by the length of their fingers. The second legs are of equal size, and rather short, being shorter than the body, but moderately stout; they are pubescent, and very slightly scabrous. The merus and carpus are subequal in length, the latter being very slightly the longer; the carpus widens slightly towards its distal end, and is equal in length to the palm or occasionally a little longer; the palm is practically cylindrical, and slightly wider than the carpus. The fingers are two thirds or more the length of the palm, and pubescent, with sharp cutting-edges in both sexes, and one or two minute basal teeth; when examined with a lens after removal of the hairs, they are seen to be finely ridged longitudinally on all sides, and punctate between the ridges. The ambulatory legs are rather slender. The telson is shorter than the terminal appendages; its apex is rather broad, but with a short median spine; the inner spinules are considerably longer than the median point, and more than twice the length of the outer spinules. The fertilized eggs carried by the female are remarkably large (in some specimens nearly 2 mm. in diameter), and this perhaps points to direct development occurring in the species.

An adult male from Roorkee is 48 mm. long, not including the rostrum; the first legs are 19·5 mm. long, and the second legs 36 mm. long. An adult female from the same locality is 45 mm. long, the first legs are 17·5 mm., and the second legs 29 mm. The largest specimen is a male from Beerbhoom 55 mm. long; and a female with ova from the

* The locality thus expressed on the label of the bottle is probably the River Dibru in Assam.

Punjab is 38 mm. long. The second legs give the following measurements in the best preserved examples:—

	Roorkee ♂. mm.	Roorkee ♂. mm.	Lahore ♂. mm.
Length of merus	7·8	. 7·6	8·3
,, carpus	8	8	9
,, palm	8	7·8	9
,, fingers	5·3	5·6	6·7

This species, which is apparently very common in North India, exhibits considerable variation in the length, form, and toothing of the rostrum. In some specimens the rostrum is considerably shorter than the antennal scales, while in others it exceeds these by nearly one third of its length, and is somewhat upturned distally; the most diverse forms occur, however, in the same localities, and are connected by transitional forms. The upper rostral teeth vary in number from five to ten, according to the length of the rostrum, but in nearly all cases two are subterminal, and the distance between these and the proximal teeth depends upon the length of the rostrum, i. e. it is greatest in the long-rostrum forms; the lower teeth are much more constant, their number being from five to seven.

P. Dayanus belongs to that small section of Ortmann's group *Eupalæmon* in which the carpus and merus are subequal, or the carpus only slightly longer, and it is distinguished from the other species by the characters of its rostrum, second legs, and especially by the peculiar ridging of the fingers. *P. Malcolmsonii*[*], Milne-Edw. (Jacquemont's Voyage dans l'Inde, Crust. p. 8, pl. iii. 1844), from Nagpore, has the rostrum elevated proximally, with a single subapical tooth, the chelipedes longer than the body, the mobile finger with a velvety covering of hair, and it is a much larger species, attaining a length of 155 mm.

266. PALÆMON ALTIFRONS, n. sp. (Pl. XL. figs. 4–6.)

Delhi, three specimens; River Jumna, six specimens; Lahore, six specimens (*Day*).

The rostrum reaches the end of the antennal peduncles, and is vertically deep, with the teeth $\frac{9-12}{2-3}$. The upper teeth are subequal and more erect than usual, with their interspaces ciliated, and the fourth tooth, occasionally the third, placed above the orbital margin; the three, or more rarely two, lower teeth are subequal in size. The upper margin of the rostrum is convex, but the apex is placed in the same horizontal line as the surface of the carapace; the apex forms an acute and slightly upturned tooth. The free end of the antennal scale is rounded internally. The carapace is slightly scabriculate anteriorly, and the hepatic spine is rather small.

The first legs have the middle of the palm opposite the end of the antennal scale.

[*] This species has, so far as I am aware, not been referred to since Milne-Edwards published his description, nor is it included by Ortmann in his revision of the genus. In the characters of its rostrum it bears considerable resemblance to *P. Weberi*, De Man, from Celebes.

The second legs are subequal, or slightly unequal, in the adult male; they are about equal in length to the body, with all the joints roughened by small thorny points, and practically cylindrical. The carpus is a little shorter than the merus, and the former is slightly expanded distally ; the palm is longer than the merus, though scarcely broader than the distal end of the carpus; the fingers are more than half the length of the palm, and smooth above and below, with two or three small teeth on the inner surface of the proximal half of each, the distal halves with a sharp cutting edge, and the apices yellow, horny, and incurved. The thorny spinules, though fewer in number here, are specially developed on the inner surface of the hand and immobile finger. The ambulatory legs are robust, and the posterior margin of the propodi is furnished with setæ. The apex of the telson is rather broad and obtusely pointed ; the subterminal spinules are short, the inner pair being only slightly longer than the outer pair, while the terminal setæ are very long.

An adult male from Delhi is 52 mm. long, second legs 50 mm., merus 10·5 mm., carpus 9·5 mm., palm 14 mm., fingers 7·8 mm. An adult female from the Jumna is 50 mm. long, and the second legs 40 mm. long.

In adult females the fingers are not toothed internally, and the entire inner edges are thin ; in young individuals the chelipedes are almost smooth, and in one specimen the fingers are even slightly longer than the palm. The carapace is much more scabriculate in some examples than in others.

In some respects this species resembles *P. scabriculus*, but in the latter the fingers are longer than the palm, and there are other important differences. It comes nearest to *P. equidens*, Dana, as defined by De Man (= *P. acutirostris*, De Man, Mergui Crust.), with which it agrees in having the carpus shorter than the merus, but in Dana's species the rostrum is not nearly so deep, and has usually four teeth below, while the inner subterminal spinules of the telson are very long. *P. asperulus*, v. Mart., from Shanghai, has a similar rostral formula, and also a short carpus, but its rostrum is longer and not so deep, with the upper margin straight. Our species belongs to that small section of *Eupalæmon* in which the carpus is shorter than the merus; it is characterized by the form of its rostrum, particularly the great depth and acute apex. *P. lanceifrons*, Dana, from the Philippines and Ceylon, has a somewhat similar rostrum, but the carpus in this species is much longer than the merus.

Genus NIKA, Risso.

267. NIKA PROCESSA, Bate.

N. processa, Bate, 'Challenger' Macrura, p. 527, pl. xcv. (1888).

Gulf of Martaban, live specimens (*Oates*).

This species may be distinguished from *N. macrognatha*, Stm., recorded from Mergui by De Man, by its longer rostrum, which equals or is even slightly longer than the eye-stalks. It is very nearly allied to the European *N. edulis*, Risso, and distinguished, according to Bate, merely by its smaller size and longer legs. A female with ova is 31 mm. long.

Distribution. Amboina, 15 fathoms (*Bate*).

Genus ÆGEON, Risso.

268. ÆGEON ORIENTALIS, n. sp. (Pl. XL. figs. 16, 17.)

Gulf of Martaban, a female (Oates).

The rostrum is shorter than the eyes, and excavated dorsally, with the apex obtuse and minutely bidentate ; a small tooth is placed on either side of the middle of the rostrum. The carapace has a median and three lateral rows of teeth on each side, running the entire length from end to end. The median row is composed of five equal teeth, the first placed at a short distance from the rostrum. The submedian row is composed of seven subequal teeth, the most anterior of which is placed in front of the first of the median row. The lateral row is also composed of seven teeth, but they gradually diminish in size on passing backwards, and the most anterior is placed on the same level as the first tooth of the median row. The lateral marginal row is composed of seven teeth, the first placed immediately behind the large antero-lateral spine of the carapace, and well developed ; the second is smaller, and the rest are minute, becoming almost imperceptible behind. A prominent spine occurs on the anterior margin of the carapace, external to the eye, but it is only about half the size of the antero-lateral spine.

The first legs are rather stout ; the second pair slender and chelate, scarcely reaching the middle of the propodus of the first pair ; the third pair very slender, and slightly longer than the first pair ; the last two pairs rather stout. The antennal scale is short and broad, only slightly longer than the antennular peduncle, with a dense fringe of long hairs on its inner margin. The terminal segment of the antennular peduncle extends to the middle of the last joint of the antennal peduncle. The external maxillipedes are slightly longer than the first legs. The abdominal segments have a series of submedian and lateral dorsal keels ; on the first segment a submedian pair, and a lateral pair on either side ; on the next three segments a single median keel, with a single lateral one on either side ; and on the fifth and sixth segments a submedian pair, with a single lateral keel on each side. The submedian keels on the third and fourth segments are more pronounced than any of the others. The telson is acuminate, and faintly channelled dorsally.

The single specimen is 27·5 mm. long, measured between the apices of the rostrum and telson.

The Burmese species bears a general resemblance to A. cataphractus (Oliv.), from the Mediterranean, but the latter has the teeth of the carapace both more prominent and more numerous, while there is a concavity on each hepatic region, in addition to other differences. There can be no doubt, however, that the two species are congeneric.

Group PENÆIDEA.

Genus PENÆUS, Fabricius.

I have included all the species of Penæus referred to in this paper, provisionally at least, in a single genus, though, so far as I know, only P. monodon and P. indicus belong to that genus, as restricted by Prof. S. J. Smith; most of the species are probably referable to *Parapenæus*, Smith, which is characterized chiefly by the absence of branchiæ from the last thoracic segment *. A revision of the Penæidæ, based on a large collection both of shallow-water and deep-water forms, is much needed, for at present the genera are in a state of considerable confusion, and Spence Bate appears to have worked independently of the results previously arrived at by Smith. Too much stress has perhaps been laid on certain features of the branchial arrangement, as, for instance, the number of epipodites, in drawing up generic characters.

269. PENÆUS MONODON, Fabr.

P. monodon (Fabr.), Bate, 'Challenger' Macrura, p. 250, pl. xxxiv. fig. 1 (1888).

(= *P. semisulcatus*, De Haan).

Bombay, Madras, Ganjam, many specimens (*Day*); very common on the South Indian coast and the chief edible species (*J. R. H.*).

The rostrum is about equal to the antennal peduncles, though sometimes longer, and is continued as a sulcate ridge almost to the hind margin of the carapace; the tooth-formula is $\frac{6-8}{1-3}$, with usually three teeth below. The antennular flagella are about equal in length to the peduncle. A short longitudinal ridge occurs on the carapace below the hepatic spine, and parallel to the free margin. The basal joint of the first legs is bispinose, that of the second legs unispinose. The fourth, fifth, and sixth abdominal segments are carinated. The species reaches a length of about a foot. *P. tahitensis*, Heller, and *P. carinatus*, Dana, are perhaps referable to this species.

Distribution. From the Red Sea and E. Africa to Japan, Australia, and the Pacific (Fijis).

270. PENÆUS INDICUS, Milne-Edw.

P. indicus (Milne-Edw.), Bate, 'Challenger' Macrura, p. 249, pl. xxxiii. fig. 2 (1888).

(= *P. merguiensis*, De Man).

Kurachi, Madras, Ganjam, Calcutta, Akyab, many specimens (*Day*); very common at Madras (*J. R. H.*).

The rostrum is styliform distally, and varies considerably in length: in young examples it is usually considerably longer than the antennular peduncles, whereas in adults it is generally shorter than in the young, and is continued as a prominent crest to about the middle of the carapace: the tooth-formula is $\frac{7-9}{3-7}$, with, as a rule, four to six small teeth below. On the carapace the rostrum forms a faint and obscurely sulcate ridge posteriorly, which, however, does not reach the hind margin. The antennular flagella

* The genus *Metapenæus*, Wood-Mason (Ann. Mag. Nat. Hist. ser. 6, vol. viii. p. 271, 1891), is separated from *Parapenæus* by very slight characters, the most important of which is the presence of a rudimentary anterior arthrobranch on the penultimate thoracic segment, a character which is absent in one of the species referred by Wood-Mason to the genus.

apparently vary in length, but are usually longer than the peduncles. There is no hepatic ridge on the carapace. The species reaches a length of about eight inches.

Distribution. Indian Seas, Malay Archipelago.

271. PENÆUS AFFINIS, Milne-Edw.

P. affinis (Milne-Edw.), Bate, Ann. Mag. Nat. Hist. ser. 5, vol. viii. p. 179, pl. xii. fig. 6 (1881).

(=? *P. monoceros*, Fabr.).

Kurachi (*Brit. Mus.*); Bombay, Canara, Madras, many specimens (*Day*); common at Madras (*J. R. H.*).

The rostrum is straight, or only slightly sinuous, reaching the end of the antennular peduncles, and continued back as a faint ridge almost to the hind margin of the carapace; the tooth-formula is $\frac{8-11}{0}$, the first tooth placed above the hepatic spine, and the second slightly behind the orbit. The antennular flagella are much shorter than the peduncle. The first three pairs of legs are unispinose at the base. The fourth, fifth, and sixth abdominal segments are carinated. A small sulcus is seen at the side of the base of the rostrum, termed by Stimpson the gastro-frontal sulcus. The fifth pair of legs in the male have a short projecting process bounding a notch near the proximal end of the ischium, but this is either faintly marked or absent in young males. Probably this species will prove to be synonymous with the older *P. monoceros*, Fabr. It is much smaller than either of the foregoing species.

Distribution. Indian Seas, Malay Archipelago.

272. PENÆUS SCULPTILIS, Heller.

P. sculptilis (Heller), De Man, Mergui Crust. p. 286 (1888).

(= *P. Hardwickii*, Miers).

Kurachi (*Brit. Mus.*); Malabar, Sunderbunds, many specimens (*Day*); Gulf of Martaban, several specimens (*Oates*); Madras (*J. R. H.*).

The rostrum is upturned and styliform distally, varying considerably in length, but usually a third or more of its length longer than the antennular peduncles, and continued back as a more or less sulcate ridge almost to the hind margin of the carapace; the tooth-formula is $\frac{6-10}{0}$, and the first two teeth are placed as in the last species. The antennular flagella vary considerably in length, but are usually longer than the peduncles. The first and second legs are unispinose at the base. All the abdominal segments may be carinated, but the first three indistinctly so, and sometimes not at all. This species bears some resemblance to *P. affinis*, but is distinguished at once from the latter by the presence of three crack-like marks or fissures in the integument, one (which may be absent) on the edge of the pleuron of the first abdominal segment, the second on the branchiostegite behind the middle of the carapace, and the third on the carapace, commencing above the antennal spine and running parallel to the rostral ridge, as far as a point beyond the middle of the carapace. In the adult male the meropodite of the fourth pair of legs is slightly dilated, but the fifth pair are not notched.

Considerable variation is seen in the length of the telson, and in some specimens the marginal spinules are well developed, especially the subapical pair, while in others the whole series is scarcely marked, or even altogether absent.

Distribution. Indian Seas, Malay Archipelago.

273. PENÆUS DOBSONI, Miers.

P. dobsoni, Miers, Proc. Zool. Soc. p. 302. pl. xvii. fig. 2 (1878).

Madras; a female specimen, probably from fresh water (*J. R. H.*).

The surface of the body is slightly pubescent. The rostrum is styliform and slightly upturned distally, with the dental formula $\frac{9}{0}$, the first tooth at some distance from the second, and the fourth above the orbital margin. The antennular flagella are about equal in length to the peduncle. The first three pairs of legs are unispinose at the base. The fifth pair of legs are rudimentary in the female, being represented merely by a basal protuberance on each side (while in males they are normal, according to Miers). The genital bursa or thelycum* in the female is trefoil-shaped, with a central depression. The total length of the Madras specimen is 103 mm.

Distribution. Mangalore, Western India (*Miers*).

274. PENÆUS VELUTINUS, Dana.

P. velutinus (Dana), Bate, ' Challenger ' Macrura, p. 253, pl. xxxiii. fig. 1 (1888).

Gulf of Martaban, a series (*Oates*).

The rostrum is straight, or rises slightly from the base to the apex, and scarcely reaches the end of the antennular peduncles, while posteriorly it does not extend behind the middle of the carapace; the dental formula is $\frac{6-8}{0}$, the lower margin with long cilia, and the first upper tooth separated by a wide interval from the second. The antennular flagella are very short, being scarcely as long as the two terminal joints of the peduncle. The entire surface of the body is pubescent. The eyes are of larger size than usual. The last four abdominal segments are carinated, and the distal half of the telson is armed with well-developed lateral spines. The petasma in the male is asymmetrical. The largest Martaban example is 65 mm. long.

Distribution. Red Sea (*Miers*); Mauritius (*Richters*); Singapore (*Walker*); Malay Archipelago (*Bate*); N. Australia (*Bate*); W. Australia (*Miers*); Loo-choo Is. (*Stimpson*); Japan (*Stimpson, Bate, Ortmann*); Sandwich Is. (*Dana*). It occurs also in the Atlantic region, on the coast of Senegambia (*Miers*), and in the West Indies is represented by the closely allied *P. pubescens*, Stm., which Miers regarded as scarcely distinct.

---

* Although good specific characters are probably to be obtained from this organ, and from the petasma in the male, I have not attempted to describe them in the other species, owing to the difficulty of doing so without reference to figures.

275. PENÆUS BREVICORNIS, Milne-Edw.

P. brevicornis, Milne-Edwards, Hist. Nat. Crust. t. ii. p. 417 (1837).
P. avirostris, Dana, Crust. U.S. Explor. Exped. pt. i. p. 603, pl. xl. fig. 3 (1852).

Kurachi, two specimens (*Brit. Mus.*); Calcutta, one specimen (*Day*).

The rostrum is short, only slightly exceeding the eyes, with the dental formula $\frac{6}{6}$; the distal half is styliform and unarmed, while the proximal half is slightly elevated above the level of the apical portion; the two proximal teeth are separated by a wider interval than any of the others. The antennular flagella are about equal in length to the peduncle. The hepatic spine is minute. The first three pairs of legs are unispinose at the base, while the fifth legs in the male are slender, with a proximal notch and ridge. The fourth, fifth, and sixth abdominal segments are carinated.

The specimens appear to belong to Dana's species, with which they closely agree, and they are probably also referable to Milne-Edwards's *P. brevicornis*. *P. Lysianassa*, De Man, from Mergui, is an allied species, but distinguished by its much shorter rostrum, which is also more elevated; the petasma has a different form, and the fifth leg in the male is not only notched, but provided with a hooked process.

Distribution. Indian Seas (*Milne-Edwards*); Mauritius (*Richters*); Singapore (*Dana*); Borneo (*Miers*).

276. PENÆUS CANALICULATUS, Olivier.

P. canaliculatus (Oliv.), Bate, 'Challenger' Macrura, p. 245, pl. xxxi., pl. xxxii. fig. 1, pl. xxxvii. fig. 2 (1888).

Gulf of Martaban, a single specimen (*Oates*).

The rostrum is slightly curved, and with the dental formula $\frac{12}{1}$ (in the species generally it is $\frac{9-12}{1}$); posteriorly it is continued to the hind margin of the carapace as a deeply sulcate ridge, on either side of which is a well-marked lateral sulcus. The first and second pairs of legs are unispinose at the base. The telson is unarmed, or provided with very minute lateral spinules. *P. coromote*, Risso, from the Mediterranean, and *P. brasiliensis*, Latr., from Eastern America, are closely allied.

Distribution. From the Red Sea and E. Africa to Japan, Australia, and the Pacific (Tahiti, Fijis).

277. PENÆUS COMPRESSIPES, n. sp.   (Pl. XL. figs. 21, 22.)

Gulf of Martaban, a female (*Oates*).

The rostrum is short and straight, only slightly exceeding the eyes, and continued as a faint ridge almost to the hinder margin of the carapace, with the dental formula $\frac{8}{0}$; the first tooth is placed some distance behind the level of the hepatic spine, almost half-way back on the carapace, and separated by a wide interval from the second, the third tooth nearly above the orbit; the upper teeth are continued to the apex, and the lower margin is ciliated. The eyes are rather small, with slender peduncles. The antennal scales are elongated and narrow; the flagella are wanting in the single specimen. The antennular peduncles are long, and about equal in length to the antennal scales, with the two flagella subequal, and slightly longer than the carapace. The cervical groove is faintly marked on the carapace.

The first four pairs of legs are rather short, with the meral and carpal joints broad and flattened, and the lower margin of all the joints fringed with moderately long but not very numerous hairs; no spines are visible at the bases of any of the legs. The second and third chelate pairs have the fingers long and slender, almost twice the length of the palm. The last pair of legs, in the female at least, are elongated and slender, especially the last three joints, which are cylindrical and very narrow. The thelycum shows two prominent parallel ridges bounding its lateral moieties internally. The last three abdominal segments are carinated, and there are traces of a carina on the third segment. The telson and last appendages are rather short, the former with a lateral basal notch on each side, but the margins otherwise entire, and without spinules, the apex not specially narrowed.

The branchial formula given below requires confirmation, as taken from a single specimen in which the gills readily became detached. There can be no doubt, however, that the last thoracic segment is without branchiæ, and the penultimate carries merely a single arthrobranch; the presence of a pleurobranch on segment VII. is unusual.

Segments	VI.	VII.	VIII.	IX.	X.	XI	XII.	XIII.	Total.
Epipodites	0	1	0	1	1	1	0	0	(1)
Podobranchiæ	0	1	0	0	0	0	0	0	1
Arthrobranchiæ ..	0	2	2	2	2	2	1	0	11
Pleurobranchiæ	0	1	1	1	1	0	0	0	4
Total	0	5	3	1	1	3	1	0	4+11+1+(1)

The length of body, not including the rostrum, is 39 mm., of the rostrum 3·3 mm., and of the antennal scales 7·5 mm.

Although there is only a single specimen of this species, I have ventured to describe it as new, for it possesses very decided characteristics, in the broad flattened feet, the narrow elongated last pair of legs, the long antennular flagella, and the toothing of the rostrum; these characters are sufficient to distinguish it from the other described species. It does not belong to the restricted genus *Penæus*, and is perhaps typical of a new generic division. In some respects it bears a resemblance to certain species of *Hemipenæus*, Bate, but in the diagnosis of this genus the hepatic spine is said to be absent, while it is present in our species.

Genus SOLENOCERA, Lucas.

278. SOLENOCERA CRASSICORNIS (Milne-Edw.).

Penæus crassicornis, Milne-Edwards, Hist. Nat. Crust. t. ii. p. 418 (1837).

Gulf of Martaban, a single specimen (*Oates*); Madras, a single specimen (*J. R. H.*).

The rostral formula is $\frac{10}{6}$, the first tooth situated on the gastric area at some distance from the others, the lower margin ciliated. The antennular flagella are longer than the carapace; the broad outer flagellum longitudinally grooved or concave along its inner surface, and enveloping the slender internal flagellum. The third pair of legs have the carpus elongated, with the proximal half swollen, and the distal half narrow and cylindrical.

Spence Bate, in his 'Challenger' Report, refers this species to his genus *Philonicus*, but in the latter the antennular flagella, though long, are otherwise normal.

Distribution. Shores of India (*Milne-Edwards*); Waltair, Madras Presidency (*Sir Walter Elliot*, fide *Spence Bate*).

Genus ACETES, Milne-Edwards.

279. ACETES INDICUS, Milne-Edw.

Acetes indicus (Milne-Edw.), Bate, 'Challenger' Macrura, pl. lxxv. fig. 1 (1888).

Gulf of Martaban, two specimens (*Oates*).

The larger specimen is 26 mm. long. In this aberrant genus the last two pairs of thoracic appendages are absent.

Distribution. Mouth of the Ganges (*Milne-Edwards*); India (*Sir W. Elliot*, fide *Spence Bate*); Singapore (*Dana, Walker*).

Order STOMATOPODA*.

Genus LYSIOSQUILLA, Dana.

280. LYSIOSQUILLA MACULATA (Fabr.).

L. maculata (Fabr.), Miers, Ann. Mag. Nat. Hist. ser. 5, vol. v. p. 5, pl. i. figs. 1, 2 (1880).

Madras (*Brit. Mus., J. R. H.*); Tuticorin (*Thurston*).

Distribution. Red Sea, Rodriguez, Indian Seas, Malay Archipelago, Japan, and the Pacific (Samoa, Fijis, Sandwich Is., &c.).

Genus SQUILLA, Fabricius.

281. SQUILLA NEPA, Latr.

S. nepa (Latr.), Miers, Ann. Mag. Nat. Hist. ser. 5, vol. v. p. 25, pl. ii. fig. 13 (1880).

Madras (*Brit. Mus.*); Ceylon (*Haly*); Tuticorin (*Thurston*). Very common at Madras (*J. R. H.*).

---

* Mr. Pocock has kindly furnished me with a list of the Indian Stomatopoda in the collection of the British Museum, and I have incorporated their localities with my own notes.

This is the commonest Stomatopod on the South Indian coast. My largest specimen is 147 mm. long.

Distribution. From India to China, Japan, Australia, and the Pacific generally, as far as New Zealand and the coast of Chili.

282. SQUILLA AFFINIS, Berthold.

S. affinis, Berthold. Abhandl. königl. Gesellsch. Wiss. Göttingen. Bd. iii. p. 26, Taf. iii. figs. 1, 2 (1847).

S. oratoria, De Haan, Crust. Japon. p. 223, pl. li. fig. 2 (1850) ; Heller, 'Novara' Crust. p. 121 (1865).

Madras; Sunderbunds (*Brit. Mus.*) ; Rameswaram (*J. R. H.*).

This species is closely allied to *S. nepa*, with which it has probably often been confused, and the two are not separated by Miers in his Revision of the Squillidæ ; the distinguishing characters, though slight, appear however to be constant. The two species are separated by Dr. H. J. Hansen, who has recently examined the Stomatopoda in the British Museum.

In *S. affinis* the eyes are much larger than in *S. nepa*, with their corneal portions greatly dilated and oblique ; the free thoracic and abdominal segments are more strongly carinated dorsally ; and very constantly the median line or sulcated carina of the carapace widens anteriorly to enclose a very short oval space, situated behind the frontal plate, whereas in specimens of *S. nepa*, of similar size, the space so enclosed is fully twice as long, and extends almost half-way back between the frontal plate and the transverse line which interrupts the median carina.

Distribution. Japan (*De Haan*) ; China (*Berthold, Brit. Mus.*) ; Port Curtis, Australia (*Brit. Mus.*) ; Ceylon (*Heller*). Probably some of the localities recorded for *S. nepa* refer to the present species.

283. SQUILLA SCORPIO, Latr.

S. scorpio (Latr.), Miers, Ann. Mag. Nat. Hist. ser. 5, vol. v. p. 18, pl. ii. fig. 7 (1880).

Madras, not uncommon (*J. R. H.*).

The colour-markings are characteristic. Four almost confluent dark spots are arranged transversely on the dorsal surface of the second abdominal segment, a large spot is seen on the proximal joint of the exopodite of the terminal abdominal appendages, and the lateral process of the first free thoracic segment is also dark in colour.

Distribution. From India to China and Australia.

284. SQUILLA RAPHIDEA, Fabr.

S. raphidea (Fabr.), Miers, Ann. Mag. Nat. Hist. ser. 5, vol. v. p. 27 (1880).

Sunderbunds (*Brit. Mus.*) ; Madras (*J. R. H.*).

A specimen from Madras in the Madras Central Museum measures thirteen inches in length.

Distribution. From East Africa to Japan.

Genus PSEUDOSQUILLA, Dana.

285. PSEUDOSQUILLA CILIATA (Fabr.).

P. ciliata (Fabr.), Miers. Ann. Mag. Nat. Hist. ser. 5, vol. v. p. 30, pl. iii. figs. 7, 8 (1880).

India (*Brit. Mus.*); Madras (*J. R. H.*).

Distribution. From the Red Sea to Australia and the Pacific (Fijis, Sandwich Is., &c.). It has also been recorded from the West Indies by Von Martens and Brooks.

Genus GONODACTYLUS, Latreille.

286. GONODACTYLUS CHIRAGRA (Fabr.).

G. chiragra (Fabr.), Miers, Ann. Mag. Nat. Hist. ser. 5, vol. v. p. 10 (1880).

India; Andamans; Galle, Ceylon (*Brit. Mus.*).

Distribution. From the Red Sea and East Africa to Australia, and the Pacific. It is also recorded from the Mediterranean, the West Indies, and the coast of Florida.

287. GONODACTYLUS GLABER, Brooks.

G. glabrous, Brooks, 'Challenger' Stomatopoda, p. 62, pl. xiv. fig. 5, pl. xv. figs. 7, 9 (1886).

Ceylon (*Brit. Mus.*); Tuticorin, Rameswaram, and Silavaturai Par, many specimens (*Thurston*); very common between tide-marks and on the reef at Rameswaram (*J. R. H.*).

G. glaber is closely allied to *G. graphurus*, Miers, but the differences appear constant in a large series; I have not met with the latter species, nor does the British Museum possess Indian specimens.

In *G. graphurus* the first five abdominal segments have a distinct dorsal impressed line or groove ("suture" of Brooks), which, commencing near the mid-dorsal line of each somite, passes to the lateral surface, and takes a rounded anterior curve so as to resemble a fish-hook; on the fourth and fifth segments the two lateral grooves almost meet in the middle line. Two smaller grooves are also present on the pleura of the same segments, one arising from the convex bend of the hook, the other rising from the anterior margin of the pleuron, and taking a curved course. In *G. glaber* the dorsal surface of the abdominal segments is perfectly smooth, and merely faint grooves are seen on the pleura. In *G. graphurus* there is a short median carina on the sixth abdominal segment, placed between the submedian longitudinal elevations; whereas in *G. glaber* this carina is usually absent, or at most but faintly indicated. According to Brooks the projections on the sixth abdominal segment and telson are more sharply defined and less swollen in *G. glaber*; but this character appears to be of doubtful value, for in the type-specimen of *G. graphurus* (originally named by White in MS.) the elevations are sharply defined, and even narrower than in my examples of *G. glaber*.

My series includes specimens from 15 mm. in length up to a length of 64 mm.

Distribution. Samboangan (*Brooks*); Aden; Massowah; Eastern Seas; Sooloo Sea; Sir C. Hardy's Island, N. Australia (*Brit. Mus.*).

288. GONODACTYLUS DEMANII, n. sp. (Pl. XL. figs. 23, 24.)

Gonodactylus, n. sp.? De Man, Brock's Crust. p. 571, Taf. xxii.*a*, fig. 7 (1888).

Rameswaram ; four females, two males (*J. R. H.*).

I have pleasure in naming this species after Dr. J. G. De Man, who, in his Report on the Crustacea collected by Dr. Brock in the Malay Archipelago, describes and figures a single specimen from Pulo Edam, pointing out that it is probably new, but without giving it a name. It is closely allied to *G. chiragra*, but the differences seem to me other than varietal, and are not due to the specimens being young, for the following comparison has been made with examples of *G. chiragra* of similar size, and from various localities, in the British Museum collection.

In *G. chiragra* the median of the three bosses or elevations on the dorsal surface of the telson is always narrow and longitudinally oval, with its distal end frequently embraced by a horse-shoe-shaped or semicircular elevation, but without spinules. In *G. Demanii* the central elevation is much broader, and indeed subglobular; when viewed in profile it is also seen to rise much higher above the level of the telson than in the other species. A series of from five to seven spinules is placed at the distal end of this elevation, usually arranged in a somewhat semicircular form, but there is no trace of the semicircular elevation seen in *G. chiragra*, unless the spinule-bearing region represents it. The narrow lateral bosses, which are not sufficiently defined in De Man's figure, carry one or two spinules at their distal ends, and two or three spinules also occur at the base of each of the two submedian terminal spines of the telson. None of these spinules occur in *G. chiragra*, and in this species the four inner longitudinal and spinule-tipped elevations on the sixth abdominal segment are subequal in size, or at most the median pair are only very slightly larger, whereas in all my specimens of *G. Demanii* the median pair are distinctly larger. The lateral processes of the frontal plate are more acute than in *G. chiragra*, but this part appears to vary slightly in the latter species. In all the specimens, round black pigment spots occur on the dorsal surface of the hinder portion of the carapace, on the second free thoracic segment, and on the first, third, fourth, and fifth abdominal segments; this may be a juvenile character, but in similar-sized examples of *G. chiragra* the mottlings, when present, are neither so well marked nor so regularly distributed.

The largest specimen, a female, is 23 mm. long, and the largest male 20·5 mm.; but the second male, although only 12 mm. long, has the sexual appendages developed. De Man's specimen, a female, was 17 mm. long.

Distribution. Pulo Edam (*De Man*).

Genus PROTOSQUILLA, Brooks.

289. PROTOSQUILLA TRISPINOSA (Dana).

Gonodactylus trispinosus (Dana), Miers, Ann. Mag. Nat. Hist. ser. 5, vol. v. p. 11, pl. iii. fig. 10 (1880).

Rameswaram (*Thurston*); Gulf of Martaban ; Ceylon (*Brit. Mus.*).

Distribution. Mauritius (*Hoffmann*); West Australia and Amboina (*Miers*): Auckland, New Zealand (*Heller*); Fijis (*Dana*).

EXPLANATION OF THE PLATES.

PLATE XXXVI.

Fig. 1. *Hoplophrys Oatesii*, gen. et sp. n.   × 3.
   2. Ditto, cephalic region from below.
   3. Ditto, chelipede.
   4. Ditto, abdomen.
   5. *Micippa margaritifera*, sp. n.   × 2.
   6. Ditto, deflexed region of carapace viewed from the front.
   7. Ditto, ambulatory leg.
   8. *Lophactea fissa*, sp. n.   × 2.
   8 a. Ditto, chelipede.
   9. *Hypocœlus rugosus*, sp. n.   × 2.
  10. Ditto, chelipede.   × 3.
  11. Ditto, pterygostomial cavity.
  12. *Hypocœlus granulatus*, de Haan, pterygostomial cavity.
  13. *Halimede Thurstoni*, sp. n.   × 2.
  14. Ditto, chelipede.
  15. *Actumnus verrucosus*, sp. n.   × 2.
  16. Ditto, chelipede.
  17. *Sarmatium indicum*, var. *malabaricum*, n., chelipede.
  18. *Xenophthalmus obscurus*, sp. n.   × 2.
  19. Ditto, cephalic region from before.

PLATE XXXVII.

Fig. 1. *Telphusa Masoniana*, sp. n., nat. size.
   2. Ditto, cephalic region from before.
   3. Ditto, external maxillipede.
   4. Ditto, abdomen of male.
   5. *Telphusa Pocockiana*, sp. n., nat. size.
   6. Ditto, cephalic region from before.
   7. Ditto, external maxillipede.
   8. Ditto, abdomen of male.
   9. *Kraussia nitida*, Stm., front of carapace.
  10. *Philyra verrucosa*, sp. n.   × 2.
  11. Ditto, cephalic region from below.
  12. Ditto, abdomen of male.
  13. *Pseudophilyra pusilla*, sp. n.   × 4.
  14. Ditto, cephalic region from below.
  15. Ditto, abdomen of male.

PLATE XXXVIII.

Fig. 1. *Philyra polita*, sp. n., nat. size.
  2. Ditto, cephalic region from below.
  3. Ditto, abdomen of male.
  4. *Ebalia fallax*, sp. n.   × 2.
  5. Ditto, abdomen of male.
  6. Ditto, chelipede.
  7. *Pseudodromia integrifrons*, sp. n.   × 2.
  8. Ditto, thoracic sternal region of female.
  9. Ditto, cephalic region from below.
  10. *Raninoides serratifrons*, sp. n.   × 2.
  11. Ditto, cephalic region from below.
  12. Ditto, chelipede.
  13. *Albunea Thurstoni*, sp. n.   × 2.
  14. Ditto, chelipede.
  15. Ditto, telson.
  16. *Catapagurus ensifer*, sp. n., front from above.
  17. Ditto, small chelipede.
  18. Ditto, large chelipede.
  19. Ditto, abdomen of male, showing copulatory organ.

PLATE XXXIX.

Fig. 1. *Diogenes affinis*, sp. n., front from above.   × 4.
  2. Ditto, large chelipede.   × 3.
  3. *Diogenes violaceus*, sp. n., front from above.   × 1.
  4. Ditto, large chelipede.   × 3.
  5. *Diogenes planimanus*, sp. n., front from above.   × 1.
  6. Ditto, large chelipede.   × 3.
  7. *Diogenes costatus*, sp. n., front from above.   × 1.
  8. Ditto, large chelipede.   × 3.
  9. *Troglopagurus manaarensis*, gen. et sp. n., front from above.   × 6.
  10. Ditto, large chelipede.
  11. Ditto, small chelipede.
  12. *Eupagurus zebra*, sp. n.   × 2.
  13. Ditto, front from above.
  14. Ditto, large chelipede.
  15. Ditto, small chelipede.
  16. *Pachycheles tomentosus*, sp. n.   × 2.
  17. Ditto, frontal region from before.
  18. Ditto, large chelipede.
  19. *Rhaphidopus indicus*, sp. n.   × 3
  20. Ditto, cephalic region from before.
  21. Ditto, large chelipede.
  22. Ditto, ambulatory leg.

PLATE XL.

Fig. 1 *Alpheus malabaricus* (Fabr.), front from above.
    2. Ditto, large chelipede.
    3. Ditto, small chelipede.
    4. *Palæmon altifrons*, sp. n., anterior portion of carapace.
    5. Ditto, chelipede.
    6. Ditto, apex of telson.
    7–10. *Palæmon Dayanus*, sp. n., anterior portion of carapace in four examples.
    11. Ditto, chelipede.
    12. Ditto, fingers, showing grooved surface.
    13. Ditto, apex of telson.
    14. *Leander tenuipes*, sp. n., nat. size.
    15. Ditto, apex of telson.
    16. *Ægeon orientalis*, sp. n., dorsal view.   × 2.
    17. Ditto, side view of cephalothorax.
    18. *Augasia Stimpsonii*, sp. n.   × 1½.
    19. Ditto, dorsal view of cephalothorax.
    20. Ditto, telson.
    21. *Penæus compressipes*, sp. n.   × 1½.
    22. Ditto, telson.
    23. *Gonodactylus Demanii*, sp. n., dorsal view.   × 3.
    24. Ditto, sixth abdominal segment and telson from above.

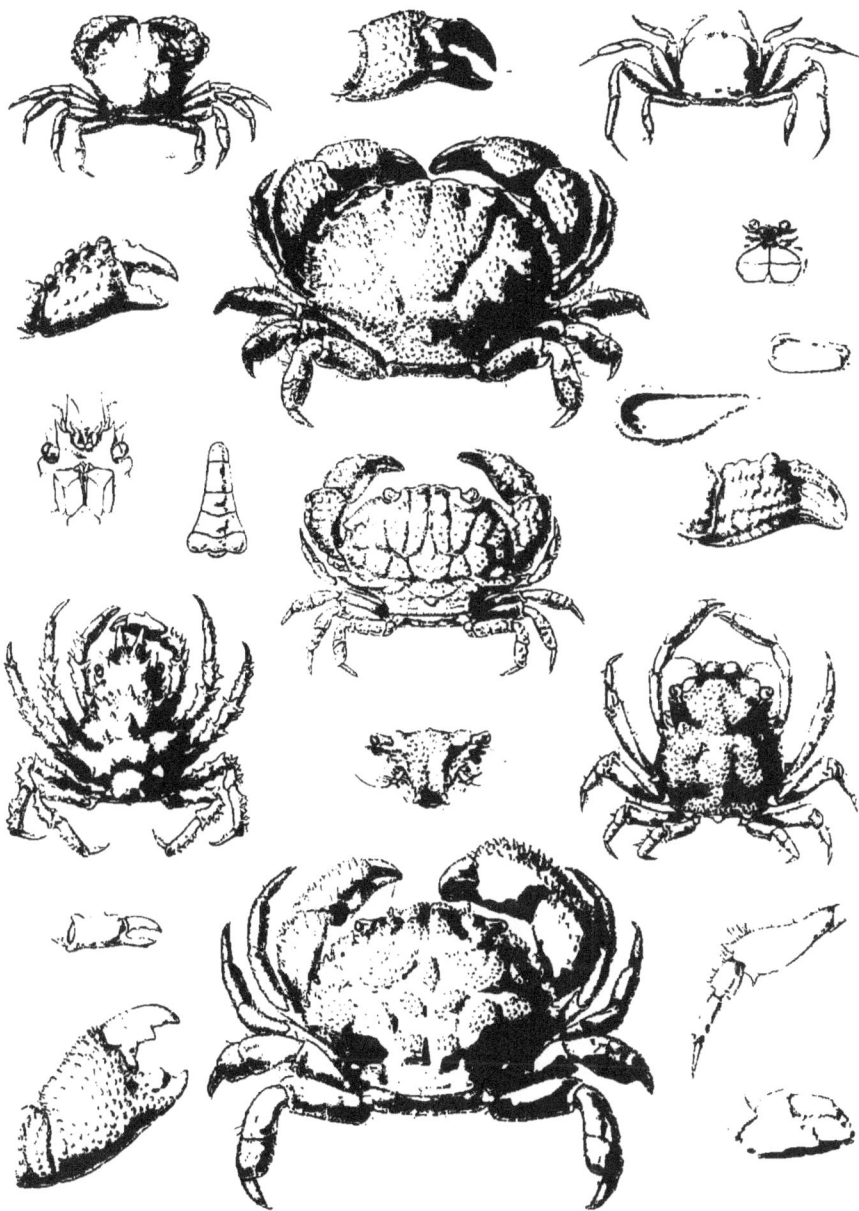

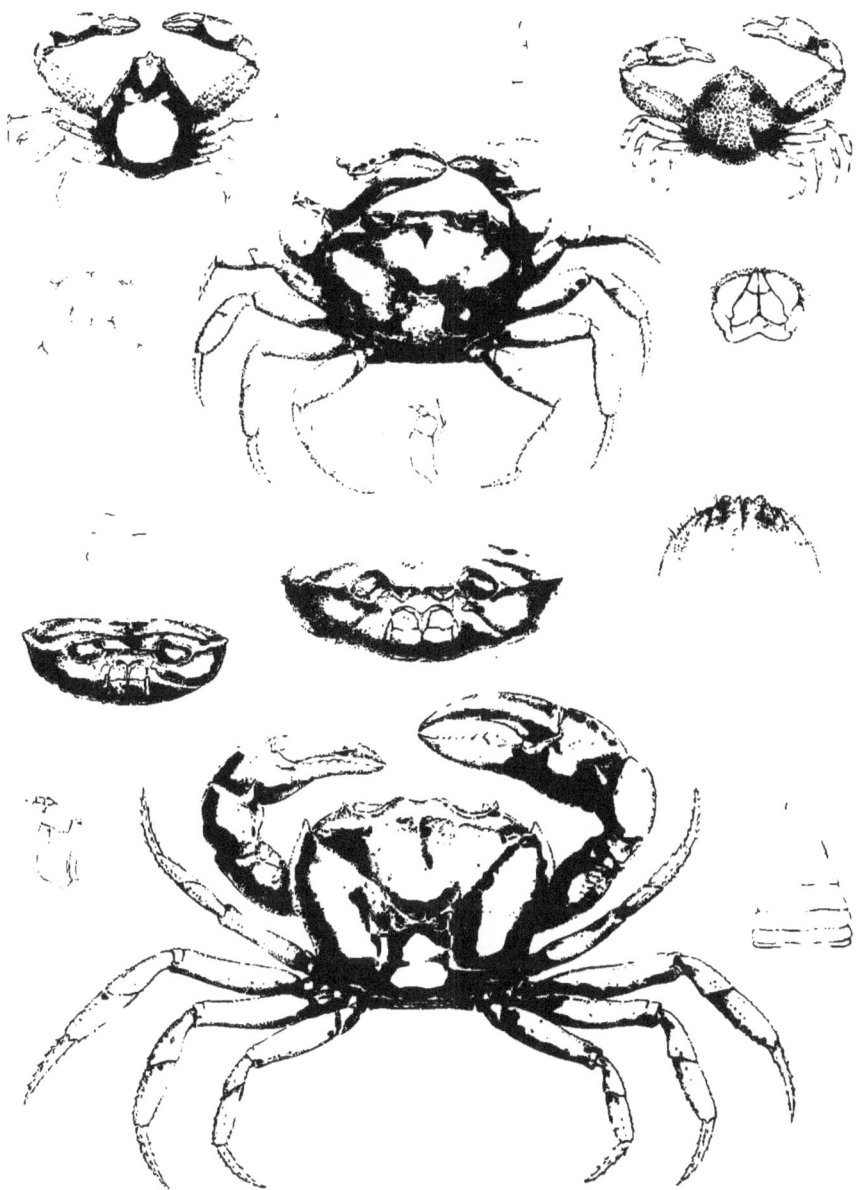

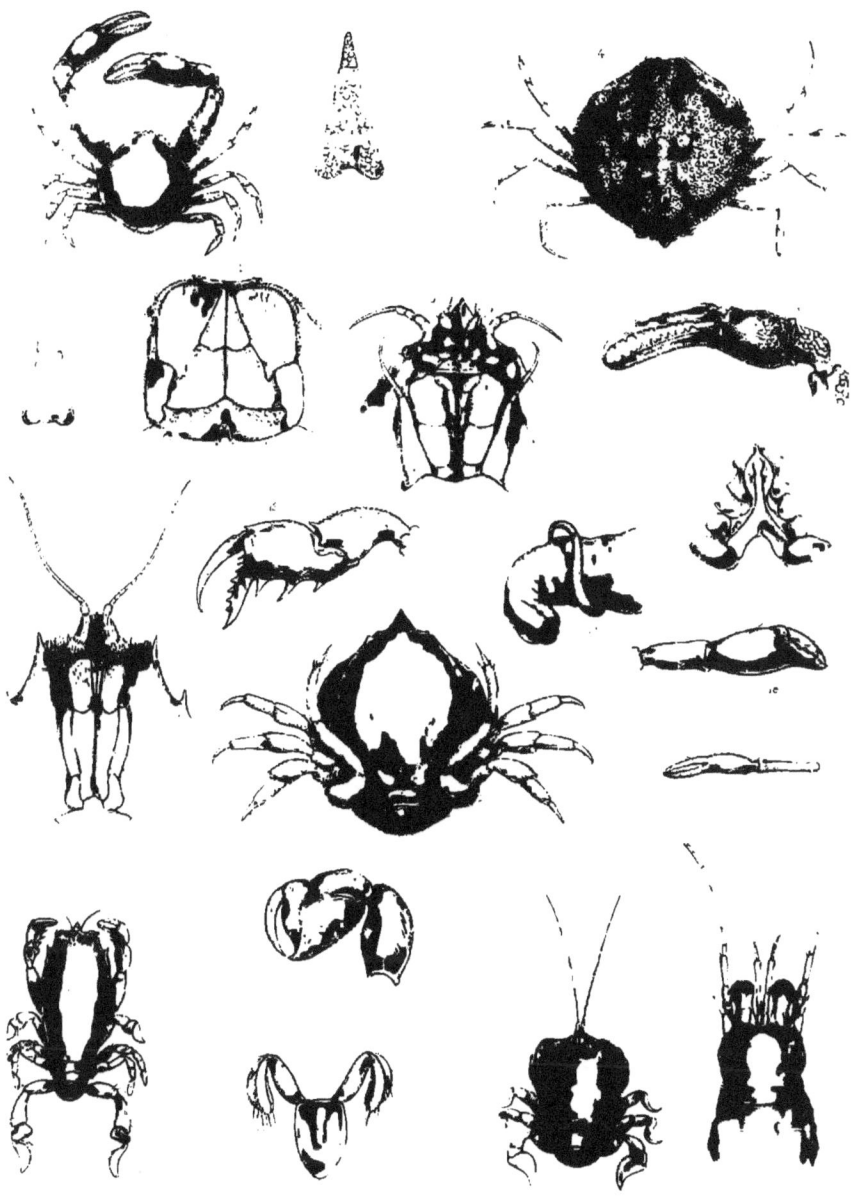

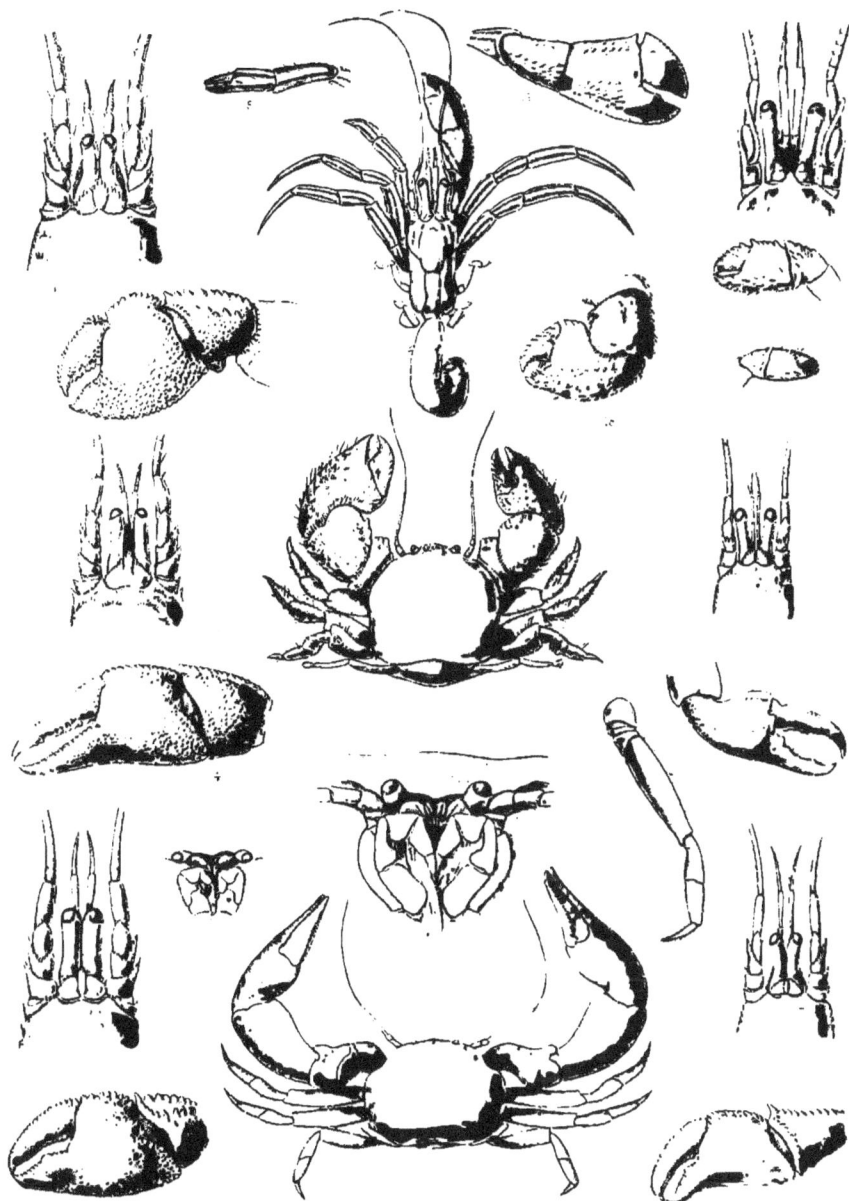

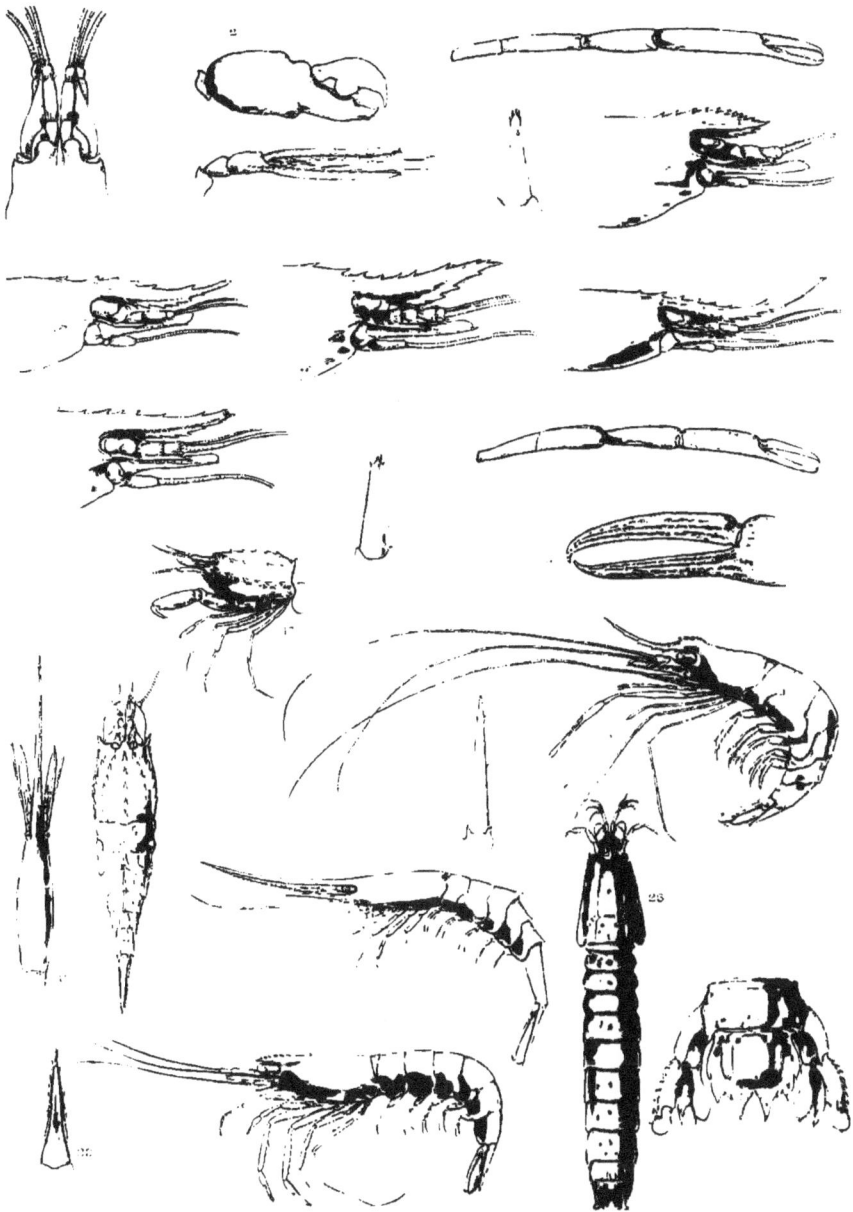

www.ingramcontent.com/pod-product-compliance
Lightning Source LLC
Chambersburg PA
CBHW030600270326
41927CB00007B/995